# Ethnicity and Cultural Assimilation at Crossroads
## With the Case of Kashmiri Pathans

Dr. Mudasir Ahmad Lone

ISBN: 1497403278
ISBN-13: 978-1497403277


**Published By**

CreateSpace Independent Publishing Platform

**To**

**Ammi, Abuji**

**&**

**My Wife Sheema**

# CONTENTS

*Dedication*

*Acknowledgement*

*Preface*

## List of Tables, Graphs and Figures

## Description

# ACKNOWLEDGMENTS

All thanks and praises be to ALLAH - The Creator, The Sustainer, The Cherisher and The Destroyer. He who kept me steadfast, opened up new ways for me and kept my journey going as if pre-planned when actually I thought several times to give up due to economic and psychological obstacles. Indeed He does what He plans and man is just a puppet in His hands.

First up all with all due respect I am indebted to Prof. Abha Chauhan an ardent teacher, a sincere guide, an all time inspiration and a scholarly mentor for me. I have learned reading, dedication and never to compromise which I have tried my best to incorporate here and ever. She is the person who helped me to incorporate quality and worthiness in this work so that it becomes a document worth consultation and material.

This small academic effort of mine is a tribute to my late grandfather Haji Abdul Aziz Lone, a dedicated policeman, an artistic singer and a committed caretaker for me who ever dreamed of my ultimate success for a lifetime. I must never forget what he did for me but can't do anything except pray for him.

Tons of sincere and obliged thanks, with high submissiveness to my parents Inspector Gulam Hassan Lone and Ameera Hassan. *"Abuji and Ammi please always leave space at your feet for me"*.

With lot of love to my wife Sheema Mudasir, I feel short of words to express my regards for her who was left alone as a newlywed bride when I started working for this manuscript. My words will never be enough to compensate or thank her for the emotional support and the tears she shed for these years all my way to the completion of this work.

Thanks are due to my friends in need – Dr. Aubid Parrey, Masroof Amin, Abid Lone and Mudasir Reshi for their technical help during the initial stages.

Similar thanks to Mr. Salfi Aijaz Ahmad Bhat for his valuable guidance in the later stages of writing, designing and publishing.

I am thankful to the Pakhtoons of Kashmir in general and of Wantrag, Satranj Maidan and Daddu villages of Anantnag in particular for their mutual understanding and cooperation.

Sincerely, thanks one and all!

**Dr. Mudasir Shaheen**

## PREFACE

The book is an attempt to understand the interface between ethnicity and cultural assimilation. The Pakhtoons or Pashtuns are the world's largest (patriarchal) segmentary lineage ethnic group. According to *Ethnologue*, the total population of the group is estimated to be around 50 million.

The [I] chapter on "ETHNICITY: A CONCEPTUAL FRAMEWORK" debates about the conceptual analysis, theory, perspectives and discussions about ethnicity in sociology and Social anthropology.

The [II] chapter entitled "CULTURAL ASSIMILATION" provides a thorough understanding and analysis of this grand narrative of social anthropology. Besides it looks into the cultural assimilation of Kashmiri Pakhtoons with main implications for their society.

Chapter [III] "PAKHTOONS: SOCIETY, TRADITIONS AND ASSIMILATION" deals with those cultural aspects of Pakhtoon society which are linked with their tradition and have met assimilation. The main focus of this chapter has been to bring into limelight the nature and degree of assimilation of the cultural elements of the Pakhtoon society and the overall impacts of the process on the ethnicity of Kashmiri Pakhtoons. The scope of this chapter is confined mainly to the micro structures and institutions of Pakhtoon culture and society.

Chapter [IV] "ASSIMILATION OF MACRO-SOCIAL INSTITUTIONS AMONG PAKHTOONS" discusses the impacts of assimilation on the macro social institutions like political and economic systems of the Pakhtoon society through a comparative analysis with the Pathans of India and Pakistan. It also deals with the changes and new cultural adoptions in crafts and sports among the Kashmiri Pakhtoons. Assimilation has been analyzed in relation to the education and economic institutions like the occupational structure of the Pakhtoon society in Kashmir.

**DR. MUDASIR SHAHEEN**

# CHAPTER I
## ETHNICITY: A CONCEPTUAL FRAMEWORK

# CHAPTER I
# ETHNICITY: A CONCEPTUAL FRAMEWORK

## Ethnic identity: Concept and Nature

The construct, ethnic identity, can best be understood through an examination of its etymological origins. The term *ethnic* has Latin and Greek origins – *ethnicus* and *ethnikas* both meaning nation. It can and has been used historically to refer to people. *Ethos*, in Greek, means custom, disposition or trait. *Ethnikas* and *ethos* taken together therefore can mean a band of people (nation) living together who share and acknowledge common customs. The second part of the construct, *identity*, has Latin origins and is derived from the word *identitas*; the word is formed from *idem* meaning *same*. Thus, the term is used to express the notion of sameness, likeness, and oneness. More precisely, identity means "the sameness of a person or thing at all times in all circumstances; the condition or fact that a person or thing is itself and not something else" (Simpson & Weiner 1989).

Combining the definitions and interpretations of identity and ethnicity it can be concluded that they mean, or at minimum imply, the sameness of a band or nation of people who share common customs, traditions, historical experiences, and in some instances geographical residence.

At one level of interpretation the combined definition is sufficient to capture the manner in which the identity is generally conceptualized and used to understand ethno-cultural influences on its formation and development.

At another level identity is almost synonymous with ethnicity prompting some sociologists like Herbert Gans (2003) to suggest that identity is no longer a useful term. Additionally, because of its increasing popularity identity is rapidly becoming a cliché and, therefore, more and more difficult to understand (Gleason, 1996).

Definitions of ethnic identity vary according to the underlying theory embraced by researchers' and scholars' intent on resolving its conceptual meanings. The fact that there is no widely agreed upon definition of ethnic identity is indicative of the confusion surrounding the topic. Typically, ethnic identity is an affiliative construct, where an individual is viewed by themselves and by others as belonging to a particular ethnic or cultural group. An individual can choose to associate with a group especially if other choices are available (i.e., the person is of mixed ethnic or racial heritage). Affiliation can be influenced by racial, natal, symbolic, and cultural factors (Cheung, 1993).

Racial factors involve the use of physiognomic and physical characteristics, natal factors refer to "homeland" (ancestral home) or origins of individuals, their parents and kin, and symbolic factors include those factors that typify or exemplify an ethnic group (e.g., holidays, foods, clothing, artifacts, etc.). Symbolic ethnic identity usually implies that individuals choose their identity, however to some extent the cultural elements of the ethnic or racial group have a modest influence on their behavior (Kivisto & Nefzger, 1993).

Yuet Cheung (1993) defines ethnic identification as "the psychological attachment to an ethnic group or heritage" and thus centers the construct in the domain of self-perception.

The Netherlands sociologist, Sawiti Saharso (1989), extends the definition to include social processes that involve one's choice of friends, selection of a future partner, perception of their life-chances, and the reactions of others in one's social environment. Both definitions involve boundaries where one makes a distinction between "self" and "other". Saharso's definition extends the "others" boundary to include an attribution component.

An individual may strongly identify psychologically with an ethnic group, however, the strength and authenticity of the identity is contingent on the acceptance and acknowledgment of "in group" and "out group" members. Saharso's definition is consistent with the writings of the sociologist, Fredrik Barth (1969), argued that ethnic identity was a means to create boundaries that enabled a group to distance themselves from one another. Barth was quite forceful about his position as he strongly maintained that ethnic boundaries define a group and not the "cultural stuff that encloses it" (Sollars, 1996).

The psychologist, Jean Phinney (1990), notes that there are "widely discrepant definitions and measures of ethnic identity, which makes generalizations and comparisons across studies difficult and ambiguous".

Currently, the most widely used definition of the construct in psychology is the one developed by Phinney (1990, 2000, 2003). She maintains, that, "ethnic identity is a dynamic, multidimensional construct that refers to one's identity, or sense of self as a member of an ethnic group" (2003). From her perspective one claims an identity within the context of a subgroup that claims a common ancestry and shares at least a similar culture, race, religion, language, kinship, or place of origin. She goes on to add that, "Ethnic identity is not a fixed categorization, but rather is a fluid and dynamic understanding of self and ethnic background. Ethnic identity is constructed and modified as individuals become aware of their ethnicity, with in the large (socio-cultural) setting" (2003).

Phinney (1990, 2000) views subjective identity as a starting point that eventually leads to the development of a social identity based on ethnic group membership.

The cross-cultural psychologist Peter Weinreich (1986) not only views self-identity as a starting point, he believes that identity formation and development refers to different identity states where different social contexts will influence the identity state and one's actions. He asserts that "one's identity as situated in a specific social context is defined as that part of the totality of one's self-construal in which how one construes oneself in the situated present expresses the continuity between how one construes oneself as one was in the past and how one construes oneself as one aspires to be in the future".

Moreover, Weinreich maintains that ethnic self-identity is not a static process but one that changes and varies according to particular social contexts. Individuals, for example, may avoid situations where their identity is challenged, threatened, humiliated, and castigated; and seek out and sustain whenever possible settings that favor the identity state. Self-expression, maintenance of ethnic identity, and situated identities offer promise for understanding the complexities and dynamics of ethnic orientations through Weinreich's theory of Identity Structure Analysis (Weinreich & Saunderson, 2003). Most definitions of ethnicity include two central elements: a shared culture and a real or putative common ancestry. E. K. Francis (1947) defined the ethnic group as a sub-type of Gemeinschaft groups, which was a secondary group with some of the features of a primary group. The term ethnicity was first used by W. Lloyd Warner in his community studies, particularly in the work on Yankee City (Sollors, 1981). The use of the term ethnic dates to a century earlier but was not widely employed prior to the publication of William Graham Sumner's *Folkways* (1906). Since mid century, both *ethnicity* and *ethnic* have been used widely to describe certain types of identity and group affiliation, although without consensus about what they mean.Some scholars have sought to define the ethnic group in the broadest terms possible. This can be seen in the case of the editors of the *Harvard Encyclopedia of American Ethnic Groups* (Thernstrom et al. 1980), when in seeking to define ethnic groups, they offered the following list of features that they contended tend to coexist in various and differing combinations: common geographic origin; migratory status; race; language or dialect; religious faith or faiths; ties that transcend kinship, neighborhood, and community boundaries; shared traditions, values, and symbols; literature, folklore, and music; food preferences; settlement and employment patterns; special interests in regard to politics; institutions that specifically serve and maintain the group; an internal sense of distinctiveness; and an external perception of distinctiveness.

The term 'ethnic' denotes race. But when we speak of ethnic community the emphasis is on the distinct cultural identity of the group. The members of an ethnic group, who constitute a segment of the larger society, are assumed by themselves or by others to have a culture which they share exclusively among themselves. (P.B. Kar, 1994).

With some reference to the context of ethnicity it is considered important to draw attention to the basic conceptual issues related to it. Ethnicity as a concept has a close attention to the following issues that appear to be associated with the delineation of the boundary of ethnicity seem important: (i) Ethnicity as the primordial system of categorization; (ii) Ethnicity as a problem of minorities; (iii) Differential manifestation of ethnicity depending by and large on the orientation of society; (iv) Role of perspectives in the determination of ethnicity.

Ethnicity traces its origin from the term ethnic that relates to community of physical and mental traits possessed by the members of a group as a product of their common heredity and cultural tradition, primarily referring to a group distinguishable by certain common cultural attributes.

To Barth, ethnicity was perpetually negotiated and renegotiated by both external ascription and internal self identification. Barth's view is that ethnic groups are not discontinuous cultural isolates, or logical a prioris to which people naturally belong. He wanted to part with anthropological notions of culture as bounded entities, and ethnicity as primordialist bonds, replacing it with a focus on the interface between groups. "Ethnic Groups and Boundaries", therefore is a focus on the interconnectedness of ethnic identities (Barth 1969).

Barth writes, "Categorical ethnic distinctions do not depend on an absence of mobility, contact and information, but do entail social processes of exclusion and incorporation whereby discrete categories are maintained despite changing participation and membership in the course of individual life histories".

Though the term ethnicity had often been used in lieu of older terms such as "cultural" or "tribal" when referring to smaller groups with shared cultural systems and shared heritage, but ethnicity has the added value of being able to describe the commonalities between systems of group identity in both tribal and modern societies.

## Ethnicity: Theorizing, Perspectives and Approaches

The term 'ethnicity' was first used in modern sense by W. Lloyd Warner during the 1940s. By 1980s, the term had gained wide currency in Social sciences. Ethnicity is generally viewed in terms of shared past, cultural traditions, religion, languages and identity. Put simply, ethnicity connotes the positive feelings of identification with a cultural group or community (Momin, 2009).

One of the earliest and well known perspectives of ethnicity was given by Max Weber. He viewed ethnicity as based on subjective belief in common descent by an ethnic group because of similarities of physical type or of customs or of both, or because of colonization or migration (Weber, 1968). Such a perspective is applicable to the Pakhtoon ethnic origin as understood by Pakhtoons themselves. They regard themselves to be the descendants of Baba Khalid; actually Khalid Bin Walid, the legendary warrior of Prophet Mohammad [Peace be upon Him].

The sociologists of the Chicago School, notably W.I.Thomas and Robert Ezra Park, were particularly interested in the question of assimilation of immigrants.

In Communist Manifesto, Marx and Engels viewed ethnicity as a false consciousness and asserted that it would disappear with the emergence of the proletariat united by a common condition and shared material interests. Marx argued that capitalism implies a rational social order in which masses would relate to each other free of the encumbrances of class and birth (Fenton, 1999); in other words the social hold of ethnicity will fade away with modernization.

Both liberals and orthodox Marxists share a similar "modernization expectancy," assuming that through industrialization and "progress" ethnic phenomena would vanish. The functionalist and conflict schools of sociology, which were the dominant views at the macro-structural level up to the so-called "paradigmatic crisis" in the social sciences, continue to be reductionistic in their approach to ethnic phenomena.

Ethnicity was nearly a forgotten dimension in functionalist analysis. Even when dealing with a related phenomenon such as migration, traditional *functionalist demographic* analysis emphasized the "function" or mutual advantage to both the sending and recipient countries (Bonacich and Cheng, 1984).

On the other hand, the dominant conflict model of ethnicity was also lacking. It shared with functionalism the belief that ethnicity would diminish with modernization.

The most unmistakable argument regarding the decline of ethnicity is to be found in liberal-universalist sociology of Emile Durkheim. He argumented that the *natal milieu*, the *locale* and social obligations, especially of family will decline in the modern social order (Triyakian, 1971). Durkheim's most telling remarks regarding ethnicity were with respect to Jews. He thought that the kind of ties represented by an ethnic community such as Jews would decline in the modern state.

One of the influential perspectives to the understanding of ethnicity was provided by Frederick Barth. In his widely read book, *Ethnic Groups and Boundaries* (1969), he argued from a structural-functional perspective, that ethnic groups are socially constructed and therefore, attention should be focused on the boundaries that distinguish ethnic groups from one another. He argued that the discussion on the content and structure of ethnicity should be replaced by a consideration of the boundaries that set limits to ethnic identity.

The various approaches put forward by different social scientists when trying to explain the nature of ethnicity include primordialism, essentialism, perennialism, constructivism, instrumentalism, and modernism.

***Primordialism;*** regards ethnicity as a biological entity in that it is based on biological ancestry; and to have a historical continuity into the far past. Clifford Geertz, a profounder of this perspective had a slight shift as he argued that, though ethnicity is a primordial entity but not in itself but humans perceive it as such because it is embedded in their experience of the world.

***Essentialist primordialism;*** further holds ethnicity as *a priori* fact of human existence, and it precedes any human interaction. This theory sees ethnic groups as natural, not just as historical (Anthony D. Smith, 1999).

***Kinship primordialism;*** on the other hand views that ethnic communities are extensions of kinship units, basically being derived by kinship or clan ties where the choices of cultural signs as language, religion, tradition are made exactly to show this biological affinity.

***Perennialism;*** holds that ethnicity is ever changing as new patterns of ethnic identity are continuously created and re-created. Such an interpretation is found in the interpretation of Barth and Seidner. The present study has also utilized this perspective while dealing with the pros and cons of ethnicity among Pakhtoons. Ethnicity is culture and tradition 'in the society' because it is expressed, felt and viewed; thus constructed and destroyed in the society. No doubt, ethnically an individual is what he is, but in reality he becomes what the society makes him, particularly in today's globalized and post-modern world.

***Contextualist;*** views maintain that ethnic motivation and behaviour are structurally determined and correspond to objective and adaptive socio-economic interests. Patterson (1975) illustrated this view with reference to black Jamaicans and black Puerto Ricans. These people, who commute periodically between their countries and the United States, he claimed, could consciously manipulate their ethnicity. They could be members of the elite in their home countries, and blacks and Puerto Ricans in the United States. His point was that while the colour attribute remained unchanged, ethnicity changed by changing the social context.

The ***Situational Perennial*** explanation establishes that ethnicity is a tool used by the state and political authority of a society to manipulate resources such as wealth, power, territory and status; thus ethnic groups emerge, change and vanish through the course of history. The *perpetual* view of perennialism holds ethnicity as ever existing.

Some authors distinguish between older and newer forms of ethnicity. For instance, Glazer and Moynihan (1975) contend that the two main features behind the development of contemporary ethnicity are:"...the evolution of the welfare state in the more advanced economies of the world and the advent of the socialist state in the underdeveloped economies."

In contrast to the conjectural view, Rex (1982, 1986), Melville (1983) and Wallerstein (1988), among other authors, propose instead a historical approach to ethnicity, underlining the colonial origins of current inter-ethnic arrangements in the world system. One way to evidence the historicity of ethnic phenomena is by reference to migratory phenomena, a necessary pre-condition of inter-ethnic contact and further ethnic relations.

*Instrumentalist perennialism;* explains ethnicity as a mechanism of social stratification, meaning that ethnicity is the basis for a hierarchical arrangement of individuals. Donald Noel (1968) argues that stratification involves certain elements of ethnicity as race, religion or nationality as major criterion for assigning social positions. It emerges when specific ethnic groups are brought into contact with one another under the influence of ethnocentrism, competition and differential power.

*Constructivism;* rejects both primordialist and perennialist explanations of ethnicity and instead views it as the product of social interaction, maintained only in so far they are maintained as valid social constructs in societies (Lawrence and Hutchings, 1996).

Constructivists like Jan Penrose categorically rejects the primordialist argument pointing out that ethnic identity is socially constructed; that it is the product of processes which are embedded in human actions and choices rather than biologically given ideas whose meaning is dictated by nature.

Max Weber, one of the earlier influential writers who stressed the social construction of ethnic identity and ethnic group, viewed ethnic groups as 'human groups' whose belief in a common ancestry, in spite of its largely fictitious origins, is so strong that it leads to the creation of a community. Weber thus regarded ethnicity as based more on a set of beliefs and not on any objective features of group membership and especially biological traits.

More recently the constructivist approach to ethnic identity is strongly evident in the work of Charles Keyes who argues that ethnicity is the cultural construction of social descent that forms ethnic identity by determining the cultural characteristics that are used to decide who does or does not belong to the group.

*Modernism;* correlates the emergence of ethnicity with the moment towards nation states beginning with the modern period. Proponents of this theory, such as Eric Hobsbawm, argue that ethnicity and notions of ethnic pride, such as nationalism, are purely modern inventions, appearing only in the modern period of world history (Anthony D. Smith, 1999).

## Macro, mezzo and micro approaches to ethnicity

De Vos (1983) postulates an integrated multi-level approach for the study of ethnic issues:"...I make a plea for a multi-level approach, in which the experiential level on which identity is understood has to be seen in interaction with structural levels governing behavior, but these structural levels are to be found in the direction of psychological structure, as well as in a concept of a social structure existing prior to the individual" (De Vos, 1983).

A similar view is expressed by Rex (1982), who suggests that the phenomenology of *micro* sociological associations (such as racial typing and labeling in interpersonal situations) and the formal aspects of intergroup ethnic processes (such as assimilation, absorption, integration, etc.) need to be related to their historical, political and economic structural contexts.

*Macro*-perspectives on ethnicity commonly deal with issues of socio economic, cultural and political structures, providing models on socio-cultural adaptation (assimilation; cultural pluralism) and models addressing ethnic inequality. At the opposite extreme, a large portion of "ethnic" psychology continues to deal with isolated ethnic individuals as its study units. Somewhere in between anthropological and social-psychological studies handle issues of ethnic socialization, acculturation, and identification, at the *mezzo* level of analysis.

## An integrated approach

Ethnicity implies both structural (material) and cultural (subjective) features. Structural ethnicity refers to the relative location of an ethnic group in relation to all other social groups in the stratification system, namely, as ethnic stratification. In its cultural, social-psychological and psychological sense, ethnicity refers to a feeling of belonging to a group whose members share some phenotypical, cultural, linguistic, religious, national features, or a combination of some of these features. This psychological state of being has been characterized in the literature as a "consciousness of kind" (Shibutani, 1965) and (Rex, 1986), which is closely related to the notion of ethnic identity. As a social phenomenon, ethnicity manifests itself as an expression of interethnic relations. These relations have developed historically, blending colonial, racial, cultural and class dimensions, under complex circumstances. Ethnicity, as a social condition, lies somewhere in between family or primary group experience and participating as citizens in society at large. Interethnic relations constitute the context for both external/ascriptive ethnic identification and also for the personal process of attaining an ethnic identity. Finally, the views of Melville (1983), associating identity changes with changes in social structure are endorsed here, considering that "a shift in ethnic identity can occasion a shift in the type of interethnic relations, as well as the reverse."

## *Paradigm turnovers in the Perspectives on Ethnicity*

Among anthropologists and social theorists the approaches to understand ethnicity has ever been inconsistent. There has been a change from the traditional anthropological "etic" or trait approach to the more psychological, subjective or "emic" perspective in understanding ethnicity. This shift is present in Barth's interactive work on "ethnic boundary-maintaining" mechanisms. There, Barth wrote that "the differences between cultures and historic boundaries have been given much attention, yet the constitution of ethnic groups and the nature of the boundaries between them have not correspondingly been investigated. Even when two groups share basically similar cultural traits, ethnicity remains of importance to classify people according to "origins and background," beyond the level of clan and kinship. De Vos (1983) relates the above linguistic shift to changes in the use of the concept of culture from one depending on the categorization of behavioral or material traits toward a concern with cultural 'identity' as a subjective continuity in the minds of men. The traditional method of appraising "acculturation" by the adoption of cultural traits belonging to the immigrant's new cultural environment (in the host country), or by measuring the retention of previous traits (from the sending country), is no longer considered a useful approach to get at the hearts and minds of ethnic group members. Instead, De Vos (1983) suggests a "psycho-cultural" approach to understanding social belonging, as a vantage point to study their (ethnic) social behavior. The transfer from the concern with cultural socialization in simpler societies to the examination of complex and multi-national societies (DeVos, 1983). The change from the discrete and categorical perspective, which characterize ethnographic work to a relational, dialectic and historical perspective, concerned with the dynamics of social inequality (Melville, 1983). A changing concern from symmetrical to asymmetrical or conflict perspectives in anthropology, as exemplified in the works of Kuper (1975), Huizer (1979), Melville (1983), Stavenhagen (1986) and Hettne (1987).

Contending views on the "goodness/badness" of ethnicity are also present in the debate on modernization and development. Apter (1965), in the liberal tradition, viewed ethnic identity as a romantic vestige from the past and as an obstacle to nation-building, progress and development. Contrariwise, Nerfin (1978) and Sachs (1980) asserted that ethnicity, state modernity and development could perfectly coexist and support each other (Stavenhagen, 1984).

## Ethnicity: Primordial or a Social Construct

12

Scholars are divided in their opinion regarding how ethnic identity is formed and why it persists. Generally, one may speak of two main schools of thought on this subject: the *primordialist* school and the *constructivist* school.

Primordial views emphasize the primacy of ethnicity, close to kinship, in its impact on the psychological make-up of individuals. This approach to ethnicity is associated with the views of Geertz (1963). Similarly, Gordon (1978) argues for the primordial ethnic perspective: "...because it (ethnicity) cannot be shed by social mobility, as for instance social class backgrounds can, since society insists on its inalienable ascription from cradle to grave, becomes incorporated into the self." From the perspective of the primordialist school, ethnic identity is a biologically given or natural phenomenon. Understood in this sense , ethnic groups constitute the kinship network into which human individuals are born and become members of, thereby coming to acquire with other group members , the group's territory and objective cultural attributes such as language, race, religion, customs, tradition, food, dress, and music (Phadnis and Ganguly, 2001). Along with objective cultural markers, some primordialists such as Glazer and Moynihan (1974) also stress the psychological aspect of self and group related feelings of identity distinctiveness and its recognition by others as crucial determinants of ethnic identity selection and its persistence. The exact nature of these psychological feelings is not very clear, however. Rex, for instance, argues that in psychological terms three factors are important for group creation: the emotional satisfaction of belonging to a group; a shared belief in the origin and history (factual as well as mythical) of the group; and the acceptance of the social relations within the group as 'sacred' and as including not merely the living but also the dead. Ethnic identity from the primordialist perspective, therefore, is a subjectively held sense of shared identity based on objective cultural or regional criteria. Anthony Smith exemplifies this approach best when referring to six 'bases' or foundations of ethnic identity: A distinct group name in order to be recognized as a distinct community by both group members and outsiders; a shared belief by group members in the myth of common ancestry and descent; the presence of historical memories among group members (as interpreted and diffused over generations, often verbally); a shared culture; an attachment to a specific territory or homeland; and a sense of common solidarity.

Constructivists like Jan Penrose categorically rejects the primordiast argument pointing out that ethnic identity is socially constructed; that it is the product of processes which are embedded in human actions and choices rather than biologically given ideas whose meaning is dictated by nature.

This view holds that Ethnicity is socially constructed, rather than genetically determined; it represents our link to the past and is important to the psychological sense of survival (Keyes, 1981, Matthews & Wilson, 1999). It is the embodiment of shared beliefs, norms, values, preferences, in-group memories, loyalties and consciousness of kind (Schermerhon, 1978). Family ethnicity is the sum total of our ancestry and cultural dimensions and it is becoming an increasingly important concept (McAdoo, 1993).

Max Weber, (1912) one of the earlier influential writers who stressed the social construction of ethnic identity and ethnic group, viewed ethnic groups as 'human groups' whose belief in a common ancestry , in spite of its largely fictitious origins , is so strong that it leads to the creation of a community. Weber thus regarded ethnicity as based more on a set of beliefs and not on any objective features of group membership and especially biological traits. More recently the constructivist approach to ethnic identity is strongly evident in the work of Charles Keyes who argues that ethnicity is the cultural construction of social descent that forms ethnic identity by determining the cultural characteristics that are used to decide who does or does not belong to the group. Barth instead has focused on the point that "ethnic groups are categories of ascription and identification by the actors themselves" (1969). This definition severed the necessary links among race, culture, language, and ethnicity. It also implied that ethnicity is a part of a dynamic social process and introduced the possibility of change in actor's group membership. He considered the formation and maintenance processes of ethnic boundaries, instead of focusing solely on the cultural traits enclosed by those boundaries. Yinger brings out certain elements of ethnicity that the ethnic group is seen by others as distinct and separate in terms of cultural elements. That the members of the ethnic group themselves see them as distinct or separate in terms of some cultural aspects from all others around them. He further notices that the members of the ethnic group, apart from participating in common activities with others, also engage exclusively in activities which they consider to be their very own in order to retain their cultural distinctions (Kar, 1994). In the case of Pakhtoons of Anantnag, though ethnicity comprises the Pashtu language, turban and Khan dress, a golden beard etc; being a Pathan has different meanings for those who belong to the Pakhtoon ethnic group and the local cultural group, mainly Kashmiris. The Pakhtoon ethnicity, therefore, needs a subjective as well as objective understanding. For the Pakhtoons themselves, being a Pathan implies belonging to an ethnic group having a history of bravery and hospitability, having the high turban and sword, a people who will die but keep their promise and the like. For the locals, Pakhtoons are a people who speak Pashtu, eat lot of ghee and meat and are strong, usually wear a golden beard and are hospitable.

Thus, the totality of Pakhtoon ethnicity is based on the primordial as well as the constructionist principles; as some elements of their ethnic identity

14

belong to their tradition and genealogy while others are a matter of social construct.

## Ethnogenesis

The earliest use of the word *'ethnogenesis'* in English is cited by the Oxford English Dictionary as having been by Lester Singer, who noted that: "following emancipation, the group-forming process moved with much greater speed and intensity than before. I propose that this formative process be referred to as 'ethnogenesis', meaning by this term the process whereby a people, that is an ethnic group, comes into existence" (Singer, 1962).

There are two principal strands to ethnogenesis. The first and by far the more recent theme lie in the province of psychology and refer to the creation of ethnicity and identity at the personal individual level. This includes the subsequent construction of ethnicity at the societal level based on commonalities between how these individual identities find their public expression. The second strand has a longer heritage and operates primarily at societal level. It refers to the process through which new ethnicities, as a means of grouping and identifying people, merge either from within society or as a result of new or changed contact with that society. This strand has spawned a separate paradigm among medieval European historians (Curta, 2005; Gillett, 2006). As new groups emerge, the naming of the ethnicity evolves, with either new terms being created, or old terms being co-opted, to describe the new group. The two strands are, of course, not independent of each other, though they work in opposing directions – the individual positioning themselves within society versus social forces outside of the group assigning people through an "othering" process. The tension this creates can be seen in the completion of questionnaires about ethnicity, when people perceive a discrepancy between their ethnic identity, that is how they see themselves, and their ethnic identification, that is what they say about their ethnicity (Kukutai, 2008; Liebler, 2004). This is the strand which the ethnicity of Pakhtoons has taken; there is on one hand the ethnicity which is real and represents the original tradition and encyclopedic culture of Pakhtoons; on the other hand, there is ethnicity which Pakhtoons of Anantnag actually possess, that is a ruptured and disfigured form of ethnicity. So in their case it is a matter of 'being something and presuming something else', as far as their ethos and ethnic identity is concerned. In both cases the processes involve a two-way feedback mechanism. In the individual case, people identify themselves in complex environmental ways. They are influenced by how they see themselves, how they imagine other people see them in contrast to or in degree of similarity with other people, and when they interact with discriminatory environments. Sense of identity remains context sensitive – identification may change as the context changes – but it also has history, and as such is influenced by memory. Memory plays a key role in the creation and maintenance of identity (Kandel, 2007; Kandel 2008).

In the case of emergent groups, the process involves aggregate outcomes of these individual processes communicated in such a way as to generate a sense of group solidarity and cohesion as well as a sense of difference from other groups. New groups are one outcome of an increasing awareness of difference from existing categories within the normative framework. An important element in both cases is the awareness by individuals of how other people see them and to what degree they perceive other people's recognition of them as different.

One important aspect of the process which needs to be acknowledged at the outset is that group creation is not generally deliberative. The experimental work of Kirby, Cornish and Smith (2008) on language demonstrates well that the social structure which manifests itself as an ethnicity is the outcome of cumulative adaptive evolution, with structure beginning to manifest itself after very few alterations.

## The Expression of Ethnic Identity

Identity and culture are two of the basic building blocks of ethnicity. Through the construction of identity and culture, individuals and groups attempt to address the problems of ethnic boundaries and their meaning. Ethnicity is best understood as a dynamic, constantly evolving property of both individual identity and group organization. The construction of ethnic identity and culture is the result of both structure and agency- a dialectic played out by ethnic groups and the larger society (Nagel, 1994).

Ethnicity is the product of actions undertaken by ethnic groups as they shape and reshape their self-definition and culture; however, ethnicity is also constructed by external social, economic, and political processes and actors as they shape and reshape ethnic categories and definitions. Particular attention should be paid to the processes of ethnic identity formation and transformation, and to the purposes served by the production of culture - namely, the creation of collective meaning, the construction of community through mythology and history, and the creation of symbolic bases for ethnic mobilization.

Social identity is conceptualized as a sense of we-ness, or attachment to a group that one is a member of, and by comparison to others (Turner, 1999). The sense of we-ness in case of a social identity, however, remains culturally empty. It is therefore necessary for a cultural group to have a cultural base to express their ethnicity.

Cultural identity refers, in contrast, to the content of values, to meaningful symbols, and to life styles that individuals share with others (ibid). It is thus the cultural attributes, traditions and way of living which provides not only the shape but also reflection to ethnicity of a cultural group. There has come about an un-precedented revival and reawakening of ethnic identities in many parts of the world in recent years. This revival has been strengthened by the process of globalization, the worldwide salience of cultural diversity, the accelerated pace of technological, social and cultural change, extensive international migrations and increasing contacts between different ethnic groups, and the growing visibility of transnational diasporas (Giddens, 1991).

One of the early formulations of identity was offered by Eric Erikson from a psychoanalytic perspective. He saw identity as an internal process by which one defines and integrates various aspects of the self. Erikson argued that it is difficult to define identity in a precise manner because it concerns a process located in the core of the individual and yet also in the core of his communal culture, a process which establishes, in fact, the identity of these two identities (Erikson, 1959). What Erikson says, in other words, is that identity is necessarily processual and it entails a close interaction between individual personality and participation in society.

G.W. Allport, in his influential *The Nature of Prejudice* (1954) used the term 'identification' and suggested that it conveyed "the sense of emotional merging of oneself with others". A quite different kind of conceptualization of identity was developed in the sociological and anthropological tradition. Reference group theory, role theory and symbolic interactionism viewed identity as embedded in the groups to which an individual belongs and in the different roles he plays in different situations.

Ralph Linton, in his *The Study of Man* (1936), introduced role theory and suggested that the concept of social role was intimately linked with that of social status. In the course of time, role theory emerged as a major theoretical perspective in sociology. The symbolic interactionist perspective emphasise that identity is mediated as negotiated in the context of social processes and encounters. Symbolic interactionism shows a keen interest in the way social interaction shapes the self-perception and self consciousness of the individual.

Erving Goffman's *Stigma* (1963) focuses on the centrality of identity in the consciousness of the individual. Goffman and Peter Berger played a very important role, through their influential writings, in popularizing the sociological significance of identity. Berger emphasizes that identities are not only "socially bestowed but must also be socially sustained and fairly steadily so".

Thus if the Pakhtoons want to sustain their ethnic identity, they have to not only to retain and sustain their traditional and cultural ethos but also have to be 'what they are' that is their ethnicity should get a social as well as a conscious consideration. They have to be 'total' or 'more' Pakhtoons than being Kashmiris in their culture and tradition; as depicted by A.R Momin (2009) *"I am a Bakkerwal-why should I call myself a Gujjar?"*. If that would not happen, then the case will be *"I am not a person, I am always somebody else"* (Gyomroi, 1963).

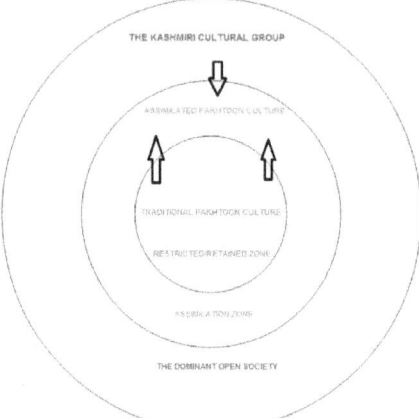

**The failure to retain the local culture results in the assimilation of it to the dominant culture.**

The question of identity has acquired an extraordinary salience in the contemporary social science literature. Recent researches has not only taken cognizance of the universal valorization of identity but have also focused on the role and functions of identity in different social, political and cultural contexts. There is general agreement that identity is complex, multilayered and multidimensional construct, which involves self identification as well as ascription by others. The process of identity formation has important cognitive, affective and vocational dimensions and is significantly influenced by changing situational contexts. Generally identities are not given once and for all, but are actively constituted and negotiated, and tend to evolve and shift. This suggests that identities are often multiple; (defined by gender, race, ethnicity, class), overlapping, hybridic and contested. Lola Romanucci-Ross, George De Vos and E. Roosens have provided interesting case studies and analysis of the ways in which the identities of a wide range of ethnic groups throughout the world have evolved and changed in response to social, political and economical opportunities and constraints afforded by particular contexts (Phinny, 2000). Identities may not always be clearly defined or perceived, but may also become blurred or confused, especially in contexts marked by hybridization or bi-culturation. This, for example, is the case with the young second generation Asian and African immigrants in Europe and North America, who are situated in a kind of cultural no man's land between the host society which does not accept them and the culture of their parents which restricts their freedom and with which they cannot fully identify.

As suggested in the foregoing, the process of identity formation is influenced by self- definition and self-identification as well as the perception, judgment and ascription of other people. Social recognition has a highly significant bearing on the individual's identity and self esteem and its absence or negation is likely to have negative, adverse consequences (Taylor, 1994). This is true of ethnic groups and cultural communities of individuals.

The integration of racially distant immigrants, including the descendents of immigrants born and brought up in western countries, in the larger societies has become more problematic because they carry, in addition to their own self defined identity, an ascribed identity or ethnic label, which is often negative, demeaning and stigmatizing.

The identity of Pakhtoons is also characterized by some stigmatization, however, not always negative yet considered culturally estranged by the local Kashmiris. The Pathans unlike Kashmiris have a colorful nature with respect to their dress pattern and costume and observe lot of music and dancing on their festive occasions like marriage and birth.

Though Pakhtoons have a live cultural expression historically and ancestrally as found in case of Pakhtoons of Afghanistan and Pakistan, but here their culture is lot assimilated. While there is drum and traditional folk dances of men on the other side, the Pakhtoons of Anantnag have D.J and rock music. Such examples reveal two things; one that Pakhtoons here express their identity mainly through cultural practices and second that they represent a new version of Pakhtoon identity.

The African-Americans (including the children of mixed white-black parents) are perceived and defined by the white majority not only in terms of their ethnic identity but also an ascribed identity, which stereotypes and stigmatizes them and marginalizes them for the American mainstream. It is extremely difficult, if not impossible, for most African-Americans to escape this ascribed identity (Kymlicka, 1998). Some researchers in social psychology indicate that ethnic consciousness and affirmation is likely to be more pronounced among groups which experience exclusion and discrimination. A significant theme is discussions of identity related to national identity. According to classical theory of the state, which was based on the assumption of a culturally homogeneous population, national identity was defined in terms of the ethos, cultural traditions and ethnic identity of the dominant national group. This view of national identity has become problematic in the context of multiethnic societies. If national identity is defined in ethnocentric homogenizing and exclusionary terms, which has been the case until recently in most countries of Asia, Africa and Europe, it can become a source of divisiveness, conflict and discord. It is likely to engender alienation and disaffection among ethnic and religious minorities (Parekh, 2000). Though ethnic identities appear to be conspicuously salient, they cannot be considered as fixed, bounded and static. Centuries of cultural interaction and exchange among different ethnic groups and religious communities have resulted in the overlapping, blurring and hybridization of identities. Ethnic affiliations and identities often cut across regional, religious and even national boundaries. The Kashmiri identity, for example, is shared in common by the people of Kashmiri descent on both sides of the Indo-Pakistan border as well as by the Kashmiri diaspora in Europe and North America. Similarly, the Sindhi identity is shared not only by the Sindhi Muslims and Hindus in Pakistan but also by the Sindhi Migrants and their descendents in India and the transnational Sindhi diaspora. Durkheim (1914) and Mauss (1938) suggested, in all societies sets of identities are chosen by or imposed upon individuals along their gender specific life spans. Such choices and impositions may be long-lasting or only short term. Identities often appear to be 'natural' – something man is born with. But the fact is that identifies are socially constructed through cultural practices like socialization. Take, for instance, what is often being regarded as innate/given, something rooted biology itself - one's gender identity. Thanks to cultural anthropologists and sociologists, we now know that gender is not sex, and the process of growing up as 'masculine' or 'feminine' is essentially a cultural construct. Yes, one is born as a male or a female. But this biological facticity is transformed into an attitude, a belief, an ideal through family socialization, school curriculum and religious beliefs, and eventually one acquires a 'masculine' or a 'feminine' identity.

Leela Dube's brilliant work focused on aspects of the process of socialization of Hindu girls through rituals and ceremonies, the use of language, and practices within and in relation to the family. She shows how women are produced as 'gendered subjects' (Dube, 2001) and how the cultural expectations concerning behavior, social norms and individual values are first indoctrinated after which they get a social recognition. This shows that ethnic identities acquire their significance through carefully evolved cultural practices.

A person may be born in a Brahmin family; but whether or not he acquires a Brahmin identity depends on the way he is socialized and trained to separate himself from non-Brahmins. Likewise, the potency of one's ethnic identity depends on the intensity of the cultural practices; for instance the specific festivals like *Durga puja,* Bengali New Year, and Tagore's birthday reinforce one's 'Bengali' identity.

Radical Feminists and Marxism often perceives alternative cultural practices through which one transcends socially imposed identities. Mead suggested that both aspects of the 'I' and 'me' are essential to the self in its full expression (Mead, 1934). Thus it is evident that identity of an individual in the society has two facets; one is provided by the society and the second is individual in nature, but in both the cases identity has a cultural expression.

## 'Ethnic Group': Concept, Nature and Composition

In anthropological literature ethnic group is used to designate a population which is a part of a plural society and yet is biologically self-perpetuating, shares a common cultural tradition and language, has an ascribed membership which identifies itself as being alike by virtue of a real or fictitious common ancestory, and is identified by others as constituting a distinct category in a plural society (Barth, 1969).

Barth's view is that ethnic groups are discontinuous cultural isolates, or logical *a prioris* to which people naturally belong. He wanted to part with anthropological notions of cultures as bounded entities, and ethnicity as primordialist bonds, replacing it with a focus on the interface between the groups.

*Ethnic Groups and Boundaries,* therefore, is a focus on the interconnectedness of ethnic identities. Barth writes: "categorical ethnic distinctions do not depend on an absence of mobility, contact and information, but do entail social processes of exclusion and incorporation whereby discrete categories are maintained despite changing participation and membership in the course of individual life histories.

In contemporary social science, an ethnic group is characterized in terms of a multiplicity of attributes _ religion, sect, caste, region, language, nationality descent, race, color and culture. These attributes singly or in different combinations, are used to define ethnic group. Anthony Smith has used the term 'ethnie' for ethnic group. Smith lists six characteristics of an ethnie as: collective name, a common myth, a shared history, a distinctive shared culture, association with a specific territory and a sense of solidarity (Smith, 1986). It is possible to identify at least five different senses in which ethnic group and ethnicity is conceptualized (Roosens 1989). First an ethnic group is conceptualized as a small social group tracing its origin to a common ancestor. Second, an ethnic group is viewed as a self defined group based on subjective factors chosen by the members from their past history or present existing conditions. Third ethnic groups are viewed as interest groups competing for benefits from the state (Glazer and Moynihan 1963). Forth ethnic group is considered as an identity- seeking instrument by the peoples of multi-cultural societies. Fifth it is conceptualized as a basis for seeking psychological unity, often based on common origin that is, sharing common blood, actual or fictitious (Devos and Ross, 1975).

Ethnic group is distinguished from nation and nationalism in that the latter two aim at political independence and constitutional rights and status (Conner, 1972). Ethnic group is also separated from clan as the latter is based on blood relationship. Similarly caste is a part of a larger collectivity with a hierarchical arrangement whereas ethnic group consists of horizontally aligned collectivities and indeed can exist in itself (Jackson, 1984).

Ethnic groups can be of two distinct types: *homelands societies* and *diaspora communities.* Ethnic groups are considered as homelands societies when they are the long-time occupants of a particular territory. Ethnic diaspora communities, on the other hand are found in foreign countries. They are caused by population migrations, induced mainly by oppression in their home state and/ or by the attraction of better economic prospects and opportunities.

The Pakhtoons also fit the characteristics of a diaspora as a distinct ethnic group in the Kashmiri community. The cause thereof is that the Pakhtoons are a migrant population who came to the valley about a hundred years before, marked by the push factors of political turmoil and lack of economic security as the record goes. However, as the perennialist approach provided by Barth proposes, this ethnic group also did not or more precisely could not remain continuous and underwent lot of modifications giving it the cultural and structural pattern of a transformed ethnic group.

## Migration and Ethnicity

Immigrants in the urban context tend to acquire an ethnic identity which is different from the older residents. Wirth called the new cultural settlements of immigrants as 'ghettos' and argued that such settlements attempt to reproduce their native cultural and social milieu (Wirth, 1938).

In the Indian context Mythily (1959) has brought to light the existence of a well-knit community life and neighborhood ties of immigrants with the host society. She noted the creation of a small cultural world of their own by the south Indian immigrant community in Mumbai, in their efforts to maintain their own identity in a culturally mixed neighborhood.

Initially, Pakhtoons by settling mainly in the geographically segmented areas like foothills, formed clusters to ensure cultural distinctiveness, kinship nearness and also socio-economic security of the villages. Such cultural distinctiveness however was a promising factor till the end of the first generation of the actual migrants i.e. the great-grands or grands of the present day Pakhtoons. During the course of fieldwork respondents with an age of above hundred years were interviewed. If the Pakhtoons today have some traditional cultural identity with them, it is due to such members of their ethnic group.

Most immigrants choose to leave their own culture. They have uprooted themselves and they know when they come, that their success depends on integrating into the institutions of the host society (Kymlicka, 1998).

This may have possibly been one of the reasons for Pakhtoons to assimilate into the Kashmiri culture. As the study reveals, initially Pakhtoons were denied the provision of permanent resident ship by the then rulers of the state before Bakshi Gulam Mohammad. The need was, therefore to attain the cultural structure of the community into which Pakhtoons were seeking membership.

Though the immigrants have a choice to keep their ethnicity but they are expected to assimilate into the mainstream host culture. Immigrant populations can keep their culture alive at the private level by cherishing their values and language thus keeping their ethnicity.

Kymlicka argues that equal treatment for immigrants implies equal opportunity to integrate into the mainstream culture. Some cultural rights may be needed, and given, to assist the realization of this goal of integration. The immigrant group can not claim the public recognition of their ethnicity, yet the host society as per Kymlicka also has certain obligations to protect the immigrant culture.

Pakhtoons after coming to Anantnag mainly started dwelling hilly settings away from the local Kashmiri villages, however, in the areas the former were just the migrant new comers, they did not find the Kashmiris waiting for them for a warm emotional welcome; there was at least from the beginning an environment of hospitality for these new people perhaps for the reason that they cherished the same religious belief.

Anthropological studies of international migration have contributed to an understanding of the ways in which local cultures and social institutions are reproduced by migrant communities (Gardener 1955). Gardener uses the term *'culture of migration'* for the reproduced culture by migrant communities in the Gulf States and Bangladesh under the impact of certain socio-economic changes. One important aspect of such retainment of ethnicity by the migrant population is the maintenance of kinship ties as found by scholars like Ballard (2001) and Lefebvre (1999) while studying migrant groups from Pakistan.

Migration, acculturation and assimilation are the main social processes responsible for modernizing the traditional ethnic groups. Scholars analyzing ethnicity in a migrant context are concerned with the pattern of immigrant adjustment to their new environment. In fact, migrants coming from another place or region tend to simulate their own culture and lifestyle and social environment. Such simulation of their ethnic culture leads to maintain the characteristics of that ethnic group.

Desai (1963) argued that Indian immigrants in Britain maintain cultural and moral values which they bring with them from India. Immigrants express solidarity of the community and reinforce the cultural patterns, values and norms. There is growth of regional and cultural pride besides the immigrants make every effort to keep alive the interest among its members in their beliefs, language, literature, music and historical tradition of the culture of their place of origin.

The above studies establish that either an ethnic group maintains its ethnicity after migrating to a new region, by clinging to their tradition, belief and values etc; or they have to lose their ethnic identity under the pressures of modernization process like assimilation. Pakhtoons' representation of a Kashmiri cultural orientation rather than their own justifies this fact, that failing to preserve or recollect their ethnicity since their migration they are hardly recognized as Pathans and that too when they speak their ethnic language.

Desai (ibid) and Schack (1973) have regarded the creation of ethnic associations by immigrants as an important element of ethnicity preservation in an 'other' social environment. Associations based on ethnic membership both express and reinforce ethnic solidarity. Immigrant associations might also act as symbols of unity and identity of the immigrant community (De Witt John, 1969).

Pakhtoons by founding *The All J&K Pakhtoon Jhirga Forum* have been highlighting the issues concerning the declining trend of Pashtu language since decades through T.V and radio. These measures have not yet brought the desirable results in this regard, however, we could not under estimate such measures as these are the possible ways to retain and maintain the Pakhtoon ethnicity.

## Ethnicity for Language or, Language for Ethnicity

*"Language is the vessel in which the thought of preceding generations, the culture of our ancestors, is stored. Language binds us to our fellows and connects us to our remote ancestors"*

*_Comte:(PositivePhilosophie, Vol-I)*

This saying of the father of Sociology clearly entitles language to constitute ethnicity contrary to the common thought of scholars, that language is a constituent of ethnicity. However, in both the cases in general and as per the above statement of Comte in particular, it is clear that ethnicity and language not only have a bearing on each other but a change or changes with one will imply certain changes with the other. Goethe regarded language as an important attribute for culture when he said *'those who know no foreign culture know nothing of their own'*. To him if we want to learn about ourselves, we have to understand other people and to know others, we must know their language. The association between the two is so close that if we know the language of a people, we can know their ethnicity to a large extent. Turner (1987) writes that language isn't speech or the writer's word; but rather it is a particular way of thinking, which, in true

Durkheimian fashion, de Saussure viewed as a product of the general patterns of social and cultural organization among people. To Stuart Hall, language lies at the heart of culture understood as shared meanings, and language constructs meanings through representation. By language he does not mean only spoken languages, but a range of ways of communicating and comprehending between people, including body language, visual images, dress, and so on (Hall, 1997) .

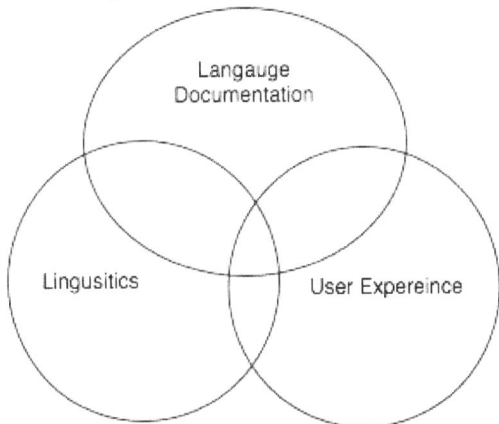

**In a new society language constitutes much of ethnicity and not merely script and texts.**

William Safran points out, that the characterizing relations between language and ethnic group are bidirectional; they constitute, and are constituted by each other (Safran, 1992). Glazer and Moynihan (1975), Inglehart and Woodward (1967), and Smith (1986) regard language as an important ethnicity marker.

It is true that an ethnic group is not necessarily coterminous with a linguistic or speech community. But, there is no gainsaying that in a multiethnic society characterized by cultural contentions, language could become an important element of ethnic identity (Gupta, ed. 2004). Thus, the efforts at revival of languages like Hindi and Urdu and their propagation, could be viewed as a conscious reaction against the loss of distinctive cultural heritage of the communities speaking them. Several organizations and individuals, religious and/or cultural in orientation, play a role in it.

The ethnic order in virtually every society is entwined with its language structure. Somewhere there may be a monolingual society with no accents or dialects that, nonetheless, has distinctive ethnic groups, based on different ancestries, religions or races.

Far more common, however, are societies where variation in language use and identification is highly correlated with, and casually interdependent with, ethnic variation. The sharper the language divide, other things being equal, the clearer are the ethnic lines of division. Since other things are seldom equal_ groups may vary by class, region, religion, race; but dialect or accent may be stronger markers of ethnicity (Yinger, 1997).

Linguistic symbols are potential bases for differentiating one ethnic group from another. There are in fact a number of ethnic groups in India which are recognized by way of the languages they speak. Gujarati, Bengali, Manipuri, Gojri etc. are a few examples to be mentioned.

In Sri Lanka where previously to be Sinhalese implied being Buddhist, now to be Buddhist implies being Sinhalese (Brass, 1991). This is how the religious tradition which is a component of ethnicity has a direct bearing on language or so to say ethnicity and language require and represent each other to form the cultural identity of a social group. For instance in case of Muslims of India, the attempt was made to promote the Urdu language as a symbol of Muslim identity but the effort has meaning only in the north and failed among Bengali Muslims (Brass, 1974) .

During the present study, all the respondents agreed with the fact that their language is an essential component of their culture. As per the views of the educated and employed people, the very first impact of modernization on their culture will come on to language itself. The laborers working within Kashmiri culture have a good speaking hold on Kashmiri dialect. The older men and particularly women who have lowest contact with other cultures hardly know a word other than Pashtu language. M. Haralambos (2006) wrote that the experiments done by William Lobov on cultural deprivation clearly reveals that one of the first cause as well as consequences of this is linguistic deprivation. In yet another experiment Lobov draws the results that cultural exposure leads to effective communication and interaction. Same could be applied to Pakhtoons as the population having more cultural exposure like students and employees have learned other languages, mainly Kashmiri. For house wives and young girls the cultural deprivation has gradually kept them linguistically deprived also and they could not communicate with the local cultural groups. The root cause of this cultural and consequently the linguistic deprivation in case of Pakhtoons is again low or negligible social contact. The relationship however, is indirect because the social contact depends on demographic location and the extent of urbanization. The villages falling near the main town like Wantrag in Mattan show more assimilative twist with respect to language. People here speak comparably clear Kashmiri than geographically isolated and less urbanized villages like Cherhad in Akingam and Manzmu in Qazigund. Urbanization in case of Pakhtoons has a local- regional perspective here because to be more urbanized means to be more close to assimilation into the Kashmiri people who represent the major and dominant cultural group in the urban areas as compared to the country side where the Pakhtoons dwell.

## Ethnicity - Religion Relationship

There is a close, fair to say, a natural affinity between religion and ethnicity. This affinity is strongest where the sense of a primordial attachment to an ancestral group and its traditions is most deeply felt. It is weakest where the ethnic boundaries have been only recently drawn, where those boundaries are temporary or situational or markers of a pan-ethnic cluster of related but diverse groups. Almost nowhere, however, can an ethnic order be described and analyzed without reference to a religious factor (Yinger, 1997).

Increasing globalization, ethnic religious conflict, and continuing and changing patterns of immigration have heightened scholarly interest in ethnic religious communities. Immigration and ethnicity scholars are no longer placing religion on the back burner. Most studies on ethnicity and or religion, however, speak to either ethnicity or religion theories and fail to see the interconnected nature of the two social forces. Putting the similar functions of ethnicity and religion together, groups that are both ethnic and religious can have a stronger basis for meaning-construction and cohesion.

Ethnic religious organizations enable individuals to find community and construct a religious as well as an ethnic identity. Separate ethnic congregations may thus be popular in part because ethnicity and religion perform similar desirable functions and provide a more significant source for meaning and group solidarity. The symbiosis between ethnicity and religion is perhaps most evident in Black Protestantism.

In the United States, 78 percent of Blacks affiliate as Protestants and the majority of black adults, 59 percent, are affiliated with historically black Protestant churches. Stronger ethnic identities also correlate with stronger religious affiliation. According to the Faith Matters 2006 Survey, those with a stronger ethnic identity are less likely to leave the religion of their parents; are more likely to marry with someone in his/her childhood religion; and report that it is important that their children marry someone of the family religion. Blacks and Latinos, who tend to have stronger ethnic/racial identities than whites, are also twice as more likely than whites to remain in their parent's religion.

Several theories of the origin and philosophy of religion square with the assertion of a close religion-ethnicity connection. The theories put forward by Simmel and Erik Erikson, Freud and Marx, and Gramsci connecting religion with family, clan and socialization respectively clearly suggest a religion-ethnicity association. Durkheim's *The Elementary Forms of Religious Life* (1912) *is* a much more instructive guide to the connection between ethnicity and religion.

Although political, military, and economic affairs receive most of the headlines, religious developments of the recent years have also been of major significance, particularly where an ethnic factor is involved. Religious movements particularly conservative and fundamentalist, often have an ethnic strand and attachment to an ethnic revival. In religiously pluralistic societies such as India and the United States, religious groups wanting to be secure from secular trends shift their allegiance to movements that promise to protect the threatened values and tradition which are among the vital constituents of ethnicity.

There are in fact certain religions where the ethnic identity in itself expresses the religious identity. Avijit Pathak (2006) argued that rituals like *Durga puja*, stress on moral values like chastity and feminity, faithfulness to the husband etc. frames not only the religious but the social identity of a Hindu girl. The Sikhs must keep beard, wear turban, and have a sword with them because these are the requirements on part of their religion as well as their ethnic identity. This has a clear implication that preserving one's ethnic identity will preserve the religious identity as well and vice-versa, particularly in a tradition bound society like India.

The Pakhtoons of Anantnag belong exclusively to the Muslim community. The relationship between their ethnicity and religion is, however complex to be understood. Though keeping beard, wearing turban, keeping women in the veil etc. are among the principles of Islam also, but the observance of such Islamic norms does not convey the religiosity of Pakhtoons. It may be termed as a cultural coincidence that the Pakhtoon tradition contains certain values which are Islamic in nature.

Thus the observance of their tradition and culture, which otherwise appears to be Islamic, would not mean that Pakhtoons are fundamental Muslims. However, if they tend to be more religious, seemingly they strictly follow the normative and value structure of Islam but actually they are rejuvenating their traditional values. It should not be misinterpret here that they will be religious for the sake of their ethnicity, neither will they be more ethnically conscious for their religious well being. Both Pakhtoon ethnicity and religion are firmly related yet have their own existence.

There being similarity of tradition and value operation between Islam and Pakhtoon culture, religiosity provides the benefit of ethnic maintenance and preservation to Pakhtoons. In other words, if Pakhtoons are religious, it is helping their ethnicity to prosper i.e. their religiosity is directly related to their ethnicity.

But this direct relationship is mainly confined to the sacred content of their tradition, representing belief. For instance keeping beard, modesty of women, keeping one's promise, being hospitable etc. If we study the relationship of their religion with the ritualistic part of Pakhtoon culture representing custom, the relationship is mainly inverse. Dancing and singing of women, *talwar-bazi*, throwing over of money notes on marriage ceremonies etc. are a few instances from their culture which their religion does not approve of. Conclusively, with a few exceptions, religion fosters ethnic rigidity among Pakhtoons.

## A Political Understanding of Ethnicity

Ethnicity in a political context has reference to certain issues viz; ethnicity as a problem of minorities, notion of ethnicity usually operating within the boundary of nation state, role of perspectives in the determination of whether a given process should be identified as ethnicity or nationalism (Danda, 1991).

Ethnicity is sometimes treated as a divisive, discriminatory and a device for exploitation. And at other times, it is seen as having positive functions of collective organizations in certain context that is, "both a vehicle for state building and for its limitations" (Enloe, 1978). To Cohen emergent ethnicity is mainly a defensive political protest, resulting from intensive competition at the political level (Cohen, 1974).

As per Phadnis and Ganguly (2001), it seems that ethnic group transforms itself into a *nation* when political and statist ideas develop within it. The state on the other hand is a legal concept describing a social group that occupies a defined territory. As long as an ethnic nation is coterminous with a state, it can be termed a *nation state*. Out of the approximately 180 states in the international system today, roughly 90 % (about 160 states) are ethnically heterogeneous. In other words, the majority of states in the world today are multi-national or multi-ethnic.

There are several types of ethno genetic processes associated with state formation and state control. Some states develop within a network of culturally similar polities, a grouping that may be called a "civilization" (Renfrew, 1986; Yoffee, 1993).

State sometimes preserve and at others, tend to suppresses the ethnicity of a group particularly immigrant groups. States may attempt to divide and control by forcing such groups to maintain their traditional cultural practices. On the other hand, states may attempt to suppress local identities to encourage a unified identity of the state itself (Gailey, 1985).

Consequently, ethnic groups, particularly their elite may react in different ways to incorporation within a state (Barth, 1969; Brass, 1985). They may resist state attempts to maintain their distinctiveness or resist attempts to suppress their identity.

The role of state in the creation and maintenance of ethnicity has been widely recognized. The creation of ethnically identified educated elites provides leadership both culturally and in bargaining for state recognition. Every South Asian, or for that matter every Third World ethnic group, has in some way gone through this process. The state even may be taken over by an emerging ethnic group, or accommodate the group within its patronage network, or simply suppress it altogether. South Asian states have achieved or attempted all these strategies. Of all South Asian states, India has been the most accommodative (Brass, 1991).

## Ethnification

The process through which some collectivities are defined and perceived is known as ethnification. It occurs in at least four contexts; first when the mainstream cultural community in a multinational or polyethnic state asserts that it constitutes the nation; Waspization in the United States, Russification in the former Soviet Union for example.

Second when a collectivity belonging to the same land may be perceived as an outside element, for instance the way Hindu militants view Muslims and Christians in India (Oommen, 1997); and Kashmiri militants view Hindus in the valley. The third context occurs when the descendants of a people may be defined as aliens and driven out, even after they have been in a country for several centuries. Fourth a people may be driven out of its ancestral homeland because their religion is different.

The reverse of ethnification is nationalization, which happens when an elective affinity is shown to people who are believed to be ancestral kin. Thus, if Germans who have lived outside Germany for several decades or centuries declare that their ancestors were Germans, they are instantly acknowledged as nationals and given the status of returnees or *Aussiedlers* (refugees). Thus, those who are in reality ethnies are instantly transformed into nationals and citizens (ibid).

There are no chances of the Pakhtoon ethnicity to turn to a nation as they represent a small cultural population which is only confined to a state region. Our country has not witnessed any ethnic movement by Pakhtoon people in spite of the existence of Pakhtoons in other states like Gujarat and U.P as well.

One of the significant political issues related to the Pakhtoon ethnicity since about last six decades with the central government in general and the state government of Jammu & Kashmir in particular, is the grant of scheduled tribe status to Pakhtoons. Though most of the Pakhtoons consider it desirable, it will have some implications to their ethnicity.

The scheduled tribe status politically, will consider the Pakhtoon community and their culture as a segmented one, needing social economic and educational upliftment and the government may have certain provisions for them in this regard.

The study however shows that the reservation policy will have negative consequences so far as the Pakhtoon culture is concerned. It will increase the employment chances and ensures socio-economic mobility of Pakhtoons, whereby the tradition and other cultural elements like the local costume, language, housing pattern, etiquette etc. are taken towards a modern twist and hence away from their ethnic boundedness. 67% of the educated respondents agree with the fact that the scheduled tribe status will tell upon their language and culture, besides socializing the new generation in a modern way.

As compared to other tribal or segmented ethnic groups like Gujjars, Bakkerwals and Pahadis residing in this district of the Valley, Pakhtoons seem to be politically more conscious. An average Pathan here can debate hours together pertaining to the political issues relating to their community.

Regarding it developmental for their people, 79% Pathans irrespective of their age and education actively participate in politics through voting, electing their representatives to highlight the issues relating to their reservation, language, regional disparity etc., and meeting Ministers and so on. There are a couple of active political figures from this community like Kabeer Pathan from Pahalgam.

Migration into a different area or region brings certain challenges to the survival of the ethnicity of the immigrant group. Migration and thereby the mixing of different cultural groups often leads to the reduction of the link between territory and culture. The possibility of a culture sustaining its ethnic integrity is put, therefore, into jeopardy.

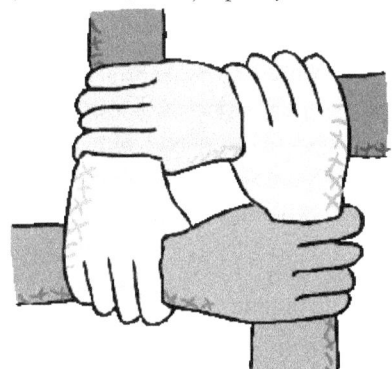

**Migration into a new society is often followed by cultural mixing.**

T.K Oommen (1997) argues that a nation may continue to be in its ancestral or adopted homeland and yet it may be ethnified by the native dominant collectivity. A second type is the denial of full-fledged participation to an immigrant collectivity which has adopted a new land as its homeland. A third is the tendency on the part of a settler collectivity to identify with its ancestral homeland even after several decades, sometimes even after centuries, of migration. Hertz (1944) wrote that immigrants may legally acquire the citizenship of a country where they have founded a new home. But they and their children must also assimilate it's the social outlook and national traditions. The Muslims of Bosnia, the Hindus of the Kashmir

31

valley and the Jews in Europe are a few examples of ethnification as a result of migration. People who migrate to alien lands are denied basic human and citizenship rights even when they become eligible for them; they are ethnified in that they are treated as strangers and outsiders. The immigrant workers in the Middle East from Asian countries, all belong to this category.

The ethnification of Pakhtoons after migrating to the Kashmir valley was multi-facet. The actual migrants of the community initially clinged to their tradition for a couple of decades. Later they were denied legal citizenship in the state, after which consequently or otherwise, these people started identifying themselves with Kashmiris.

Now for the last about twenty five years, realizing the fading away of their ethnic identity, Pakhtoons are again turning towards the reconstruction of their ethnicity, though slowly and un promisingly. Thus the overall shape and form of the ethnicity of Pakhtoons in the valley remains that of 'an ethnicity which cut across the regional border, was brought through migration, retained, and is assimilating and re constituted simultaneously'.

## Ethnicity and Urbanization

The relationship between ethnicity and urbanization or the question how they influence each other mainly concentrates over the debate of the homogenization of the former under the latter's impact. There is a great deal of qualitative and historical evidence from around the world about the effect of urbanization on ethnic homogenization. To start with Europe Weber, (1976) famously argued that France became culturally and linguistically homogenous in the late 19th century through urbanization, industrialization and education and the resultant was "spread of urban values. In particular urban migrants not only spread urban values back to the countryside and turned "peasants into Frenchmen," but also homogenized cities themselves by "shattering the hold of local speech and lore in the urban centers" (Weber, 1976).

Roshwald, (2001) similarly describes the rise of nationalism among the urban intelligentsia of the Austro-Hungarian, Russian and Ottoman Empires in the early 20th century. Finally, in the USSR urban migrants assimilated into Russian society despite Soviet efforts at promoting non-Russian languages and cultures (Harris, 1945). In Greece ethnic minorities such as the Sarakatsans "tend to drop their identity as Sarakatsans when they leave herding and migrate to urban areas" (Schein, 1975).

In the Asia-Pacific region evidence on the integrative effect of urbanization also dates back decades. In Thailand migrants to Bangkok from the northeast found that their local village ties and identities were unhelpful in making sense of the urban environment; in fact, local differences between the migrants and other North-Easterners became relatively insignificant in the city. (Keyes, 1966).

In China there is strong evidence that members of the Bai ethnic minority in Yunan province have retained their ethnic identity in the countryside but shed it in the cities (Wu, 1991). In Papua New Guinea Levine, (1999) similarly describes how migrants to urban areas abandon their local tribal identities in favor of regional identities or even a "highland" vs. "coastal" dichotomy. Chai, (1996) presents evidence of the role of the urban environment in consolidating pan-Malay identities in Malaysia.

In South and South-West Asia Khoury, (1983) and Özoğlu, (2001) describe the rise of Arab and Kurdish nationalism among the urban intelligentsia of the Middle East in the decades before World War I, respectively, with similar evidence for interwar period as well (Gershoni, 1997).

In India there is evidence that attempts by Hindu nationalists to emphasize larger communal identities over caste or ethno-linguistic identities have found much of their support in towns and cities, in particular through the urban-based Bharatiya Janata Party and the Rashtriya Swayamsevak Sangh (Hansen, 1999; Jaffrelot, 1996). Hyman (2002) argues that one of the reasons nationalism in Afghanistan has had such a minimal political impact is because of its inability to reach beyond the urban elite.

To turn to Africa, (Coleman, 1954) argues that urbanization in the mid-20th-century "loosened kinship ties, accelerated social communication between 'detribalized' ethnic groups, and, in general, contributed to 'national' integration." Indeed, as noted by Freund, (2007); Kasfir, (1979) and Wallerstein (1960), Africans have often assimilated into larger ethnic groups in order to find security and prestige in the difficult urban environment.

The Ibo of Nigeria, Jola of Senegal, Duala of Cameroon, Luyia and Mijikenda of Kenya and Bangala of the DRC can thus be seen as classic examples of previously different ethnic groups amalgamating into larger ethnic identities as urban migrants found commonalties among each other and transferred these new identities back to their rural brethren as well (Eckert, 1999; Nugent, 2008; Southall, 1970; Willis, 1993; Young, 1976).

The same logic applies to urban migrants who have assimilated into already-existing groups such as northern Nigerian migrants who became Hausa in the southern city of Ibadan or the ethnic minorities who became Batswana in late 20th century Botswana, the country with the highest rate of urbanization of any country in the world since 1950 (Cohen, 1969; Solway, 2004). Bryceson, (2010) argues that the cosmopolitan nature of Dar es Salaam promoted the development of a strong Tanzanian national identity in the postcolonial context.

In Latin America Blanksten, (1960) long ago noted that "the Indians who migrates to the big city becomes a *mestizo* almost in so doing; he has not lived there very long before he is counted as a creole or a 'white'. Indeed, urbanization "contributes to the development of common sets of political attitudes and experiences on the part of the people who live in the growing cities of Latin America...The overall effect of the movement to the cities is integrative" (Blanksten, 1960). Evidence for this integrative effect dates back to the colonial period, when ethnic differences by the Spanish upon the indigenous population of Mexico broke down over time in the city of Oaxaca (Chance, 1978).

More recently activism among urban intellectuals in Guatemala has led to an attempt to unite the speakers of all twenty-some Maya language groups under a pan-Mayan identity (Warren, 1998), while in Ecuador Indians continue to assimilate into *mestizo* or *cholo* communities in urban settings (Kyle, 2000).

Finally there are a few evidences to show that urbanization and ethnicity are directly proportional, for instance North America, where decades of contradictory evidence from the US seems to show that urbanization actually leads to the persistence of ethnic divisions rather than assimilation into larger identities (Dahl, 1961; Wolfinger, 1965).

Relating the above research to the Pakhtoon ethnicity in an urban set up, it was found during the present study that those populations which live in close proximity to the towns or urban centers like Pakhtoons of Mattan area; or those who have migrated further to more urban dwellings like those living in Srinagar or those in Gujjar Nagar and Talab Tillu in the Jammu city show more or in certain cases a total assimilation or homogenization to the cultural groups they are living with. The hypothesis that the ethnicity among Pakhtoons is inversely related to the extent of the urbanization of the area wherein they live, therefore seems justified.

# REFERENCES

Atal, Yogesh. (2006). *Changing Indian Society*. Jaipur: Rawat.

Ballard, R. (1997) Negotiating race and ethnicity: exploring the implications of the 1991 Census. *Patterns of Prejudice*. 30: 3-33.

Barth, Frederick. (1969). *Ethnic Groups and Boundaries*. London: George Allen and Unwin.

Bhurgava, Rajeev; Kumar, Amiya; Sudarshan, R. (1999). *Multiculturalism, Liberalism and Democracy*. India: Oxford University press.

Brass, Paul R. (1991). *Ethnicity and Nationalism: Theory and Comparison*. New Delhi: Sage.

Chacko, Pariyaram M. (2005). *Tribal Communities and Social Change*. London: Sage.

Chai, S.K. (1996). A Theory of Ethnic Group Boundaries. *Nations and Nationalism*. 2(2), 281-307.

Chandra, Bipan; Mahajan, Sucheta. (2007). *Composite Culture in a Multicultural Society*. New Delhi: Pearson Longman India.

Chaudhary, Buddhadeb. (1990). *Tribal Development in India: Problems and Prospects*. New Delhi: Inter India Publications.

Cheung, Y. W. (1993). Approaches to ethnicity: Clearing roadblocks in the study of ethnicity and substance abuse. *International Journal of Addictions*, 28(12), 1209-1226.

Clifford Geertz. (Ed.) (1963). *Old societies and new states: the quest for modernity in Asia and Africa*. New York: The Free Press of Glencoe & London.

Cohen, A. (1969). *Custom and Politics in Urban Africa: A Study of Hausa Migrants in Yoruba Towns*. London: Routledge.

Coleman, J. S. (1954). Nationalism in Tropical Africa. *American Political Science Review, 48* (2), 404-426.

Connor, W. (1994). *Ethnonationalism: The quest for understanding*. New Jersey and West Sussex: Princeton University.

Curta, F. (Ed.) (2005). *Borders, barriers, and ethnogenesis*. Brepols: Turnhout.

Danda, Ajit K. (1991). *Ethnicity in India*. New Delhi: Inter India Publications.

Das, Man Singh; Bardis, Panos D. (1978). *The Family in Asia*. Bangalore: Vikas Publishing House.

Dahl, R. (1961). *Who Governs? Democracy and Power in an American City*. New Haven, CT: Yale University Press.

Desai, Rashmi. (1963). *Indian Immigrants in Britain*. London: Oxford University press.

Devos, George A; Lola Romanucci-Ross. (1975). *Ethnic Identity: Cultural Continuity and Change*.

De Vos, George. (1983). *Ethnic Identity and Minority Status: Some Psycho-*

*Cultural Considerations.* In, Anita Jacobson, Widding. (Ed.). *Identity: Personal and Socio-Cultural, A Symposium.* Almqvist & Wiksell, Uppsala. 135-158.

DeWitt, John. (1969). Early *Globalization and the Economic Development of the United States and Brazil.* USA: British Library Cataloguing.

Doshi, S. L. (2008). *Postmodern Perspective on Indian Society.* Jaipur: Rawat.

Dube, Leela. (2001). Anthropological *explorations in gender: Intersecting fields.* New Delhi: Sage publications.

Dumont, Louis. (1980). *Homo Hierarchicus.* New York: Oxford University press.

Durkheim, E. (1914a). *The Dualism of Human Nature and its Social Conditions.* University of Mexico.

Emberling, Geoff. (1997). Ethnicity in Complex Societies: Archaeological Perspectives. *Journal of Archaeological Research,* (Vol. 5), 295-99. New York.

Epstein, A. L. (1978). *Ethos and Identity: Three Studies in Ethnicity.* London: Tavistock.

Erasov, Boris. (2006). *The Sociology of Culture.* Jaipur: Rawat.

Erik Erikson. (1959). *Whose work, Identity and the Life Cycle.* Vol. 1. New York.

Fenton, Steve. (1999). *Ethnicity: Racism, Class and Culture.* London: Macmillan Press.

Francis E. K. (1947). The Nature of the Ethnic Group," *American Journal of Sociology,* 52(1947):393-400.

Fried, Morton H. (1959). *Readings in Anthropology* (Vol-2). New York: Vail-Ballou Press.

Gans, H. (2003, March 7). Identity. *The Chronicle of Higher Education,* p. 84.

Gershoni, I. (1997). *Rethinking the Formation of Arab Nationalism in the Middle East, 1920-1945: Old and New Narratives.* In I. Gershoni & J. Jankowski (Eds.). *Rethinking Nationalism in the Arab Middle East,* (pp. 3-25). New York: Columbia University Press.

Giddens, Anthony. (1991). *Modernity and Self-Identity: Self and Society in the Late Modern Age.* Stanford University Press.

Gillett, A. (2006). Ethnogenesis: A contested model of early medieval Europe. *History Compass,* 4(2): 241-280.

Glazer, Nathan. (1987). *Affirmative Discrimination: Ethnic Inequality and Public Policy* (2nd ed.). Haward University Press.

Glazer, N & Moynihan D. P. (1970). *Beyond the melting pot: the Negroes, Puerto Ricans, Jews, Italians, and Irish of New York City.* Cambridge: MIT Press.

Gleason, P. (1996). *Identifying identity: A semantic history.* In W. Sollars. (1996). *Theories of ethnicity: A classical reader.* New York: New York University Press.

Gordon, M. (1964). *Assimilation in American Life.* New York: Oxford University Press.

Gupta, Surendra K. (2004). *Emerging Social Science Concerns.* New Delhi: Concept Publishing.

Gyomroi, E. L. (1963). The Analysis of a Young Concentration Camp victim. *Psychoanalytic Study of the Child*, 18:484-510.

Hasnain, Nadeem. (1994). *Tribal India*. Delhi: Palaka Prakashan.

Hall, Stuart. (Ed.). (1997). *Cultural Representations and Signifying Practices*. London: Sage.

Haralambos, M; Heald, R. M. (2006). *Sociology: Themes and Perspectives*. New Delhi: Oxford University Press.

Hertz, Frederick. (Ed.). (1944). *Cultural Representations and Signifying Practices*. London: Sage.

Hettne, Bjorn. (1988). *Europe Dimensions of Peace*. Zed Books.

Honigmann, John J. (1963). *Understanding Culture*. Calcutta: Oxford and IBH Publishing.

Huizer, Gerrit. (1979). *The Politics of anthropology: From colonialism and sexism toward a view from below*. Mouton.

Hyman, A. (2002). Nationalism in Afghanistan. *International Journal of Middle East Studies,* 34(2), 299-315.

J. H. Turner. (1999). Toward a General Sociological Theory of Emotions. *Journal for the Theory of Social Behaviour*, Volume 29, Issue 2, pages 133–161.

Kandel, E. (2007). *In search of memory: The emergence of a new science of mind*. New York: Norton.

Kandel, E. (2008). *Principles of neural science*. New York: McGraw-Hill Professional.

Kar, Parimal B. (1994). *Society: A Study of Social Interaction*. New Delhi: Jawahar Publishers.

Keyes, C. (1966). Ethnic Identity and Loyalty of Villagers in Northeastern Thailand. *Asian Survey,* 6(7), 362-369.

Kimball, Solon T. (1965). *Culture and Community*. U.S.A: Harcourt, Brace & World.

Kivisto, P., & Nefzger, B. (1993). Symbolic ethnicity and American Jews: The relationship of ethnic identity to behavior and group affiliation. *Social Science Journal,* 30, 1-12.

Kukutai, T. (2008). *Ethnic self-prioritisation of dual and multiethnic youth in New Zealand*. Wellington: Statistics New Zealand.

Kupiainen Jari; Sevanen, Erkki; Stotesbury John, A. (Eds.). (2004). *Cultural Identity in Transition: Contemporary Conditions, Practices and Politics of a Global Phenomenon*. New Delhi: Atlantic Publishers.

Kyle, D. (2000). *Transnational Peasants: Migrations, Networks and Ethnicity in Andean Ecuador*. Baltimore, MD: Johns Hopkins University Press.

Kymlica, W. (1998). *Finding our way: Rethinking ethno cultural relations in Canada*. Toronto: Oxford University.

Lawrence, Bobo; Hutchings, Vincent L. (1996). *Perception of Racial Group Competition*. American Sociological Review.

**Lefebvre**, Alain. (1999). *Kinship, Honour, & Money in Rural Pakistan:*

*Subsistence Economy & the Effects of International Migration.* Curzon.

Levine, H. B. (1999). Reconstructing Ethnicity. *Journal of the Royal Anthropological Institute,* 5(2), 165-180.

Lieberson, Stanley. (1963). *Ethnic Patterns in American Cities.* New York Free Press.

Liebler, C. (2004). Ties on the Fringes of Identity. *Social Science Research,* 33(4): 702-723.

Madan, T. N. (3rd ed. 2001). *Muslim Communities of South Asia: Culture, Society and Power,* New Delhi: Manohar.

Magray, Bashir Mohammed. (2003). *Tribal Geography of India: Jammu & Kashmir.* Jammu: Oberoi Book Service.

Mahajan, Gurpreet. (2002). *The Multicultural Path: Issues of Diversity and Discrimination in Democracy.* New Delhi: Sage.

Mallick, Ross. (1998). *Development Ethnicity and Human Rights in South Asia.* London: Sage.

Mandelbaum, David G. (1970). *Society in India.* Vol-1 *Continuity and Change.* Bombay: Popular Prakashan.

McAdoo, H. P and Ou, Y. (1993). *Socialization of Chinese American children.* In H.P. McAdoo (Ed.), *Family ethnicity: Strength in diversity (pp: 245-270).* Thousand Oaks, CA: Sage Publications.

Mehta, Lalit K. (1999). *Caste, Clan and Ethnicity: A Study of Mehtas in Rajasthan.* Jaipur: Rawat.

Mead, George, Herbert. (1934). *Mind, Self, and Society.* Chicago: University of Chicago Press.

Melville, Margarita, B. (1983). Ethnicity: An analysis of its dynamism and variability focusing on the Mexican/Anglo/Mexican American interface. *American Ethnologist,* vol.10, 272-89.

Mishra, Omprakash. (Ed.). (2004). *Forced Migration in the South Asian Region: Displacement, Human Rights and Conflict Resolution.* New Delhi: Manak Publications.

Momin A.R. (2009). *Diversity, Ethnicity and Identity in South Asia.* Jaipur: Rawat.

Moynihan, Daniel. (1965). *The Negro Family: the Case for National Action.* Washington, D.C: U.S. Dept. of Labor.

Nagel, J. (1994). *Constructing Ethnicity: Creating and Recreating Ethnic Identity and Culture.* Oxford University Press.

Nair, K.S. (1978). *Ethnicity and Urbanisation.* Delhi: Ajanta Publishers.

Noel, Donald L. (1968). *A Theory of Origin of Ethnic Stratification.* Oxford University Press.

Oomen, T.K. (1997). *Citizenship, Nationality and Ethnicity.* Cambridge: Blackwell.

Osella, Fillippo; Gardner, Katy (Eds.). (2004). *Migration, Modernity & Social Transformation in South Asia.* New Delhi: Sage.

Parekh, B. (2008). *A new politics of identity*. Basingstoke: Palgrave McMillan.

Park. R.E; Burgess, E.W. (1921). *Introduction to the Science of Society*. Chicago: University Press.

Parmu, R.K. (1969). *A History of Muslim Rule in Kashmir [1320-1819]*. New Delhi: Peoples Publishing House.

Pathak, Avijit. (2006). *Modernity, Globalisation and Identity: Towards a Reflexive Quest*. Delhi: Aakar books.

Pathy, Jaganath. (1988). *Ethnic Minorities in The Process of Development*. Jaipur: Rawat.

Patterson, Orlando. (1975). *Context and Choice in Ethnic Allegiance: a Theoretical Framework and Caribbean Case Study*. In Glazer and Moynihan (Eds.). op.cit. 305-349.

Phadnis, Urmila; Ganguly, Rajat. (2001). *Ethnicity and Nation Building in South Asia*. New Delhi: Sage.

Phinney, J. S. (1990). Ethnic identity in adolescents and adults: Review of research. *Psychological Bulletin, 108*, 499-514.

Phinney, J. (2000). Ethnic identity. In A. E. Kazdin (Ed.), *Encyclopedia of psychology, volume 3*, (pp. 254-259). New York: Oxford University Press.

Pratt, Jeff. (2003). *Class, Nation and Identity _The Anthropology of Political Movements*. London: Pluto Press.

Rao, Aparna. (1999). The many sources of identity: an example of changing affiliations in rural Jammu and Kashmir. *Ethnic and Racial Studies*, Volume 22, Issue 1.

Renfrew, Colin. (1986). *Peer Polity Interaction and Socio-Political Change*. Cambridge University Press.

Rex, John. (1982). *Theories of Race and Ethnic Relations*. Cambridge University Press.

Roosens, E. (1989). Creating ethnicity: The process of ethnogenesis. In H.R. Bernard (Ed.). *Frontiers of Anthropology*, Vol. 5, London: Sage.

Safran, Linda. (1992). *S. Pietro at Otranto: Byzantine art in South Italy*. Roma: Edizioni Rari Nantes.

Schack, W. A. (1973). *Urban Ethnicity and the Cultural Process of Urbanization in Ethiopia*, In Aidan Southhall, *Urban Anthropology*. New York: Oxford Press.

Schech, Susane; Haggis, Jane. (2000). *Culture and Development: A Critical Introduction*. U.K: Blackwell.

Schermerhorn, R. A. (1978). *Comparative Ethnic Relations*. New York: Random House.

Schein, M. D. (1975). When Is an Ethnic Group? Ecology and Class Structure in Northern Greece. *Ethnology, 14*(1), 83-97.

Simpson, J. A., & Weiner, E. S. (1989). *The Oxford English dictionary- Vol. VII*. (2nd ed.). Oxford: Clarendon Press.

Singer, L. (1962). Ethnogenesis and Negro-Americans today. *Social Research*, 29: 419- 432.

Singh, K.S. (Ed.). (2003). *People of India: Jammu & Kashmir* Vol xxv. In *Anthropological Survey of India.* New Delhi: Manohar Publishers.

Singh, Yogendra. (2000). *Culture Change in India: Identity and Glogalisation.* Jaipur: Rawat.

Singh, Yogendra. (1993). *Social Change in India: Crisis and Resilience.* Delhi: Har-anand Publications.

Singleton, Brian; Chaturvedi, Ravi. (Ed.). (2005*). Ethnicity and Identity: Global Performance.* Jaipur: Rawat.

Smith, D. Anthony. (1986). *The Ethnic Origins of Nations.* Basil Blackwell.

Smith, D. Anthony. (1999). *Myths and Memories of Nation.* Oxford University Press.

Sollors, W. (1981). Theories of Ethnicity. *American Quarterly,* 33, 257-283.

Sollors, W. (1996). *Theories of ethnicity: A classical reader.* New York: New York University Press.

Solway, J. (2004). *Reaching the Limits of Universal Citizenship: Minority Struggles in Botswana.* In B. Berman, D. Eyoh & W. Kymlicka (Eds.). *Ethnicity and Democracy in Africa.* Oxford: James Currey.

Stavenhagen, Rodolfo. (1983). *Amerindian Ethnic Movements and State Policies in Latin America.* In, William, Page (Ed.). *The Future of Politics.* London: Frances Pinter.

S. Thernstrom et al. (1980). *Harvard Encyclopedia of American Ethnic Groups.* Cambridge: Harvard Belknap Press.

Sumner, W. G. (1906). *Folkways.* Boston: Ginn.

Swift, Hugh. (1990). *Trekking in Pakistan and India.* London: Hodder and Stoughton.

Taylor, R. (1979). Black ethnicity and the persistence of ethnogenesis. *American Journal of* Sociology, 84(6): 1401-1423.

Thapan, Meenakshi. (Ed.). (2005). *Transnational Migration and the Politics of Identity.* New Delhi: Sage.

Turner, J.H. (2001). *The Structure of Sociological Theory.* Jaipur: Rawat.

Wallerstein, Immanuel. (1988). *The Modern World-System III (Studies in Social Discontinuity).* Academic Press.

Weber, E. J. (1976). *Peasants into Frenchmen: The Modernization of Rural France, 1870-1914.* Stanford, CA: Stanford University Press.

Webster, Merriam A. (1967). *Third New International Dictionary of Language.* London: G & C Merriam.

Weinreich, P; & Saunderson, W. (Eds.). (2003). *Analyzing identity: Cross-cultural, societal and clinical contexts.* New York: Routledge.

Wirth, Louis. (1938). Urbanism as a Way of Life. *The American Journal of Sociology,* Vol. 44, No. 1, pp. 1-24. The University of Chicago Press.

Wolfinger, R. E. (1965). The Development and Persistence of Ethnic Voting. *American Political Science Review,* 59(4), 896-908.

Wu, D. Y. (1991). The Construction of Chinese and Non-Chinese

Identities. *Daedalus,* 120 (2), 159-179.

Yinger, Milton J. (1997). *Ethnicity: Source of Strength? Source of Conflict?* Jaipur: Rawat.

Yoffee, Norman. (1993). Political Economy in Early Mesopotamian States. *Annual Review of* Anthropology, 24. 281-311.

Zimmer, B.G. (1970). *Participation of Migrants in Urban Structures.* In Jansen (Ed.), *Readings in Sociology of Migration.* London: Pergamon Press.

Retrieved Articles:

- Kirby, S; Cornish, H; and Smith, K. (2008). Cumulative cultural evolution in the laboratory: an experimental approach to the origins of structure in human language.
  Retrieved from: www.pnas.org/cgi/doi/10.1073/pnas.0707835105. Aug 8, 2010.
- Kukutai, Tahu. (October, 2008). Ethnic Self-prioritization of Dual and Multi-ethnic Youth in New Zealand.
- Liebler, A. Carolyn (April 30, 2004). American Indian Ethnic Identity: Tribal Non response in the 1990 Census.
- Matthews, L; Wilson, L.C. (1999). Ethnic tolerance in urban Guyana: A conceptual and empirical analysis.
- Marcel Mauss. (1938). A category of the human mind: the notion of person; the notion of self.
- Mythili, G. (1959). Accelerating growth through globalization of Indian agriculture.

# CHAPTER II

# CULTURAL ASSIMILATION

# CHAPTER II

# CULTURAL ASSIMILATION

## Assimilation: Concept, Debate and Theory

The concept of Assimilation was first used in American race relations research to describe the process by which immigrant groups were integrated into the dominant white culture. Thus in R. Park's (1950) 'race relations cycle', the interaction between the host society and new immigrants was conceptualized in terms of four stages – contacts, competition, accommodation and assimilation. In its original usage, assimilation was used as a uni-dimensional, one-way process by which outsiders relinquished their own culture in favor of the dominant society. Recent research regards assimilation as reciprocal, involving mutual adjustments between host and migrant communities. Assimilation is often used interchangeably with Acculturation (Nicholas, Hill and Turner 2000). The assimilated group looses parts or takes on characteristics of the dominant culture. Assimilation is also a process of socialization.

Barth (1969) also argued that assimilation is directed by agents of change within the minority group, who choose for themselves one of three basic strategies:

(i) They may attempt to pass and become incorporated in the pre-established industrial society and cultural group;

(ii) They may accept a "minority" status, accommodate to and seek to reduce their minority disabilities by encapsulating all cultural differentiae in sectors of non-articulation, while participating in the larger system of the industrialized group in the other sectors of activity;

(iii) They may choose to emphasize ethnic identity, using it to develop new positions and patterns to organize activities in those sectors formerly not found in their society.

Assimilation, sometimes known as integration or incorporation, is the process by which the characteristics of members of immigrant groups and host societies come to resemble one another. That process, which has both economic and socio-cultural dimensions, begins with the immigrant generation and continues through the second generation and beyond.

The concept of assimilation has been debated extensively in the social science of migration since the early 20th Century, but it is now broadly accepted as a way to describe the ways that immigrants and their off spring change as they come in contact with their host society. In its current usage the concept of assimilation does not imply any superiority in the host society's views or a particular value to the changes in attitudes and behavior among immigrants across generation. Rather, assimilation is now most useful as a means for describing a social dynamic.

## Some useful Definitions of the concept

1.  According to Young and Mack, Assimilation is the fusion or blending of two previously distinct groups into one.
2.  For Bogardus, Assimilation is the social process whereby attitudes of many persons are united and thus develop into a united group.
3.  Biesanz, describes Assimilation as the social process whereby individuals or groups come to share the same sentiments and goals.
4.  For Ogburn and Nimkoff, Assimilation is the process whereby individuals or groups once dissimilar become similar and identified in their interest and outlook.

Assimilation also refers to the integration of the members of a minority group into the broader society to which they belong. According to Milton M. Gordon (1964), it is a seven-stage process, in which "acculturation," or the adoption by newcomers of the language, dress, and other daily customs of the host society, is the first step. "Structural assimilation," the second, involves the large-scale entrance of minorities into the cliques, clubs, and institutions of the host society, in a manner that is personal, intimate, emotionally affective, and engaging the whole personality. Once a group has achieved structural assimilation, the remaining stages naturally follow. Those include "amalgamation" or frequent intermarriage, the development of a sense of people hood based solely on the host society, the disappearances of prejudiced attitudes and of discriminatory behavior toward the minority, and the absence of civic conflicts in which the competing interests of the majority and minority groups are an issue.

Thus Gordon (1964) broke the assimilation process into seven sub processes: acculturation, or behavioral assimilation; structural assimilation or access to societal institutions; amalgamation, or marital assimilation; Identificational assimilation; attitude receptional assimilation, or the absence of prejudice; behavior receptional assimilation, or the absence of discrimination; and civic assimilation, or the absence of value and power conflicts.

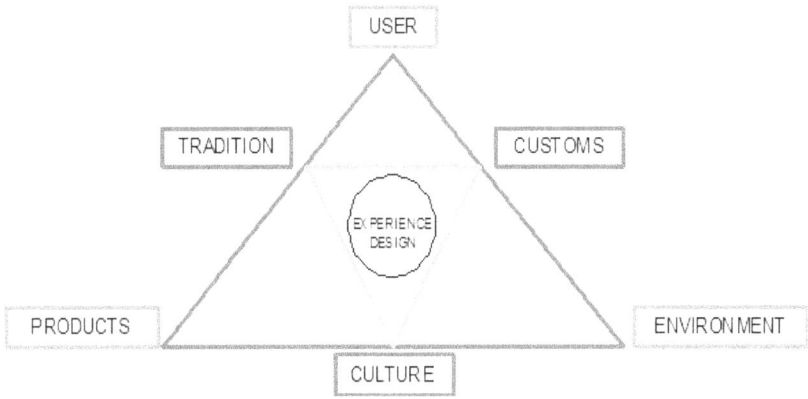

## In Assimilation, the new social experiences are directed away from the individual's culture.

Researchers have attempted to explain the assimilation rate for post 1965 immigrants in the United States with experiences of immigrants who entered the United States between 1880 and 1920. Many of the methods and theories that are used to assess immigrant assimilation today are derived from earlier immigrant studies. One of the leading theories in understanding immigrant assimilation came from William I Thomas and Florian Znaniecki whom published "The Polish Peasant in Europe and America". William I Thomas and Florian Znaniecki's study on Polish immigrants (1880–1910) assessed how these immigrants built an institutional community in the United States during the Napoleonic War.

Another influence on immigrant assimilation came from Robert Park, Ernest Burgess, and William I Thomas, in which they trained graduate students to study the experiences of immigrants in Chicago. Robert Park, Ernest Burgess, and William I Thomas provided these graduate students with theoretical tools such as Park's theory on collective behavior. The third theory on immigrant assimilation comes from Gordon's book, *Assimilation in American life*. Gordon highlighted the generational change in immigrant groups, it states that the first generation or foreign born were less assimilated and less exposed to American life than their American-born children (the second generation), and their grandchildren (third-generation) were more like the American mainstream than their parents.

Defining assimilation as a process of fusion and interpenetration, Park presents a deterministic social evolutionist view of immigrant incorporation. Influenced by Darwinian and humanistic philosophy, Park places assimilation as the end stage of a race relation cycle of "contact, competition, accommodation, and eventual assimilation". As immigrants come into contact with other groups in an urban setting, they compete and fight over scarce resources. Eventually, however, ethnic relations evolve past competition and toward accommodation and assimilation. Human cooperation and interpersonal intimacy replace impersonal competition and tendency for domination and move the cycle of race relations inevitably towards assimilation. The time frame in which immigrant groups assimilate into dominant society is unclear, but the process towards assimilation is "apparently progressive and irreversible". Like Park, other immigration scholars like Lloyd Warner and Leo Srole argue that assimilation of immigrants, namely white immigrants, is inevitable and simply a matter of time.

Assimilation may be distinguished from *accommodation*, a process of compromise characterized by toleration, and from *acculturation*, or cultural change that is initiated by the conjunction of two or more cultural systems or the transference of individuals from their original societies and cultural settings to new socio-cultural environments. Assimilation is to be distinguished also from amalgamation, or biological fusion.

Complete segregation and total assimilation of a group are opposite ends of a continuum along which may be located: varying degrees of limited desegregation; the substantial pluralism found in many communities in the United States, Canada, and Switzerland; a hypothetical integration which values structural and cultural differences, while insisting upon equal life opportunities for the members of all groups; partial assimilation; individual assimilation; and group assimilation (Williams 1964).

As a concept in American sociology, assimilation has had various meanings. Henry Pratt Fairchild (1925) equated assimilation with Americanization. For some scholars assimilation and acculturation are synonymous (Berry 1951; Bierstadt 1957, 1963). More often assimilation has included acculturation. According to a widely quoted point of view: "Assimilation is a process of interpenetration and fusion in which persons or groups acquire the memories, sentiments, and attitudes of other persons or groups, and, by sharing their experience and history, are incorporated with them in a common cultural life" (Park & Burgess 1921). Vander Zanden (1963) distinguishes *unilateral* assimilation, the process in which one group relinquishes its own beliefs and behavior patterns and takes over the culture of another, from *reciprocal* fusion, in which a third culture emerges from the blending of two or more cultures, and also from various intermediary levels of assimilation.

## *Multiculturalist view*

Multiculturalists claim that assimilation can hurt minority cultures by stripping away their distinctive features. They point to situations where institutions of the dominant culture initiate programs to assimilate or integrate minority cultures. Although some multiculturalists admit that assimilation may result in a relatively homogeneous society, with a strong sense of nationalism, they warn however, that where minorities are strongly urged to assimilate, there may arise groups which fiercely oppose integration. With assimilation, immigrants lose their original cultural (and often linguistic) identity and so do their children. Immigrants who fled persecution or a country devastated by war were historically resilient to abandoning their heritage once they had settled in a new country.

Multiculturalists note that assimilation, in practice, has often been forced, and has caused immigrants to have severed ties with family abroad. In the United States, the use of languages other than English in a classroom setting has traditionally been discouraged. Decades of this policy may have contributed to the fact, lamented by multiculturalists, that more than 80 percent of Americans speak only English at home. While an estimated 60 million U.S. citizens are of German descent, forming the largest ethnic group of American citizens, barely one million of them reported speaking German in their homes in the 2000 Census.

## Assimilationist view

Whereas multiculturalists tend to view the melting-pot theory as oppressive, assimilationists view it as advantageous to both a government and its people. Some tend to favor controlled levels of immigration, enough to benefit society economically, but not enough to profoundly alter it. Assimilationists tend to be opposed to programs that, in their view, give out special privileges to minorities at the expense of the majority.

Assimilationists believe that a nation has reached its present state of development because it has been able to forge one national identity. They argue that separating citizens by ethnicity or race and providing immigrant groups "special privileges" can harm the very groups they are intended to help. By calling attention to differences between these groups and the majority, the government may foster resentment towards them by the majority and, in turn, cause the immigrant group to turn inward and shun mainstream culture. Assimilationists suggest that if a society makes a full effort to incorporate immigrants into the mainstream, immigrants will then naturally work to reciprocate the gesture and adopt new customs. Through this process, it is argued, national unity is retained. The melting-pot theory works best, in their view, when the "ingredients" are added in modest increments, so that they can be properly absorbed into the whole.

### Assimilation, Diffusion and Acculturation

Cultural diffusion, as first conceptualized by Alfred L. Kroeber in his influential 1940 paper *Stimulus Diffusion*, or trans-cultural diffusion in later reformulations, is the spread of cultural items such as ideas, styles, religions, technologies, languages etc. between individuals, whether within a single culture or from one culture to another. The term 'diffusionist' was first used in 1893 to denote a scholar who believed that most folklore was borrowed from an Old World center of high culture, such as Egypt, Mesopotamia, or India (Oxford English Dictionary 1971). Diffusionism as an anthropological school of thought was an attempt to understand the nature of culture in terms of the origin of culture traits and their spread from one society to another. Versions of diffusionist thought included the conviction that all cultures originated from one culture center (heliocentric diffusion); the more reasonable view that cultures originated from a limited number of culture centers (culture circles); and finally the notion that each society is influenced by others but that the process of diffusion is both contingent and arbitrary (Winthrop 1991). Diffusionist research originated in the middle of the nineteenth century as a means of understanding the nature of the distribution of human culture across the world. By that time scholars had begun to study not only advanced cultures, but also cultures of non-literate people (Beals and Hoijer 1959). Studying these very diverse cultures created a major issue among scholars, which was how humans progressed from primeval conditions to superior states (Kuklick 1996). Among the major questions about this issue was whether human culture had evolved in a manner similar to biological evolution or whether culture spread from innovation centers by diffusion (Hugill 1996).

Two schools of thought emerged in response to these questions. The most extreme view was that there were a very limited number of locations, possibly only one, from which the most important culture traits diffused to the rest of the world. Evolutionism, on the other hand, proposed the "psychic unity of mankind", which argues that all human beings share psychological traits that make them equally likely to innovate. According to evolutionists, innovation in a culture was considered to be continuous or at least triggered by variables that are relatively exogenous. This set the foundation for the idea that many inventions occurred independently of each other and that diffusion had little effect on cultural development (Hugill 1996). The classical definition of acculturation was presented by Redfield, Linton, and Herskovits (1936): "acculturation comprehends those phenomena which result when groups of individuals having different cultures come into continuous first-hand contact with subsequent changes in the original culture patterns of either or both groups". Although acculturation is a neutral term in principle (that is, change may take place in either or both groups), in practice acculturation tends to induce more change in one of the groups than in the other (Berry, 1990). Acculturation is when a certain people of different cultures participate together but retains their own differences but assume some habits of the other. Assimilation is when people usually minorities assume the dominant culture habits usually over time. Assimilation can occur at lower levels, such as in a family unit. According to Gordon, acculturation (the first sub process of assimilation) occurs when an ethnic group's cultural patterns change to those of the host society.

Acculturation is the exchange of cultural features that results when groups come into continuous firsthand contact; the original cultural patterns of either or both groups may be altered, but the groups remain distinct (Kottak 2007). However, anthropologist Franz Boas (1888) argued that all people acculturate, not only "savages" and minorities: "It is not too much to say that there is no people whose customs have developed uninfluenced by foreign culture, that has not borrowed arts and ideas which it has developed in its own way", giving the example that "the steel harpoon used by American and Scotch whalers is a slightly modified imitation of the Eskimo harpoon".

Subsequently, anthropologists Redfield, Linton and Herskovits (1936) developed the often quoted definition: "Acculturation comprehends those phenomena which result when groups of individuals having different cultures come into continuous first-hand contact, with subsequent changes in the original culture patterns of either or both groups".

Despite definitions and evidence that acculturation entails two-way processes of change, research and theory have continued with a focus on the adjustments and changes experienced by aboriginal peoples, immigrants, sojourners, and other minorities in response to their contact with the dominant majority. Thus, acculturation can be conceived to be the processes of cultural learning imposed upon minorities by the fact of being minorities. If enculturation is first-culture learning, then acculturation is second-culture learning. This has often been conceived to be a unidimensional, zero-sum cultural conflict in which the minority's culture is displaced by the dominant group's culture in a process of assimilation.

According to the *Oxford English Dictionary*, the word *acculturation* was first used in English text in 1880 by J. W. Powell to describe changes in Native American languages: "The force of acculturation under the overwhelming presence of millions of Europeans has brought great changes". Another sociologist at the Bureau of American Ethnology, W. J. McGee (1898), defined acculturation to be a process by which "devices and ideas are interchanged and fertilized in the process of transfer" and emphasized that hostile groups often acculturate to one another. Powell (1900) agreed that dominant cultures could also acculturate to weaker ones: "Conquering tribes take the language of the conquered." Alexander Chamberlain, a linguist and anthropologist at Clark University, documented the acculturative adoption of aspects of Native and Afro-American cultures by the dominant White society (Rudmin, 1990, 1999a). Thurnwald

(1932) added the examples of the conquering Vikings adopting Russian language in Kiev, French in Normandy, and Italian in Sicily. In 1943, Devereux and Lock defined "antagonistic acculturation" to be the adoption of the technology of an alien culture but the rejection of its goals and values. The concept of acculturation has become widely used in cross-cultural psychology and has also been the subject of criticism because of the gradual erosion of the original meaning of the concept, so that it became synonymous with assimilation (Vasquez, 1984). Another of the obvious but dramatic findings of the history outlined here is that, within the arena of the social sciences, there is a long established and strong tradition of conceiving that many types of acculturation other than assimilation are possible for minorities. It is a mistake to argue that early theories attempted to limit the concept of acculturation to just processes of assimilation (Berry, 1997) or to just a choice between traditional lifestyles and modernization (Berry et al., 1989). It is, and has been, a weak argument to give merit to a new acculturation theory merely because it opposes the purported myth of "melting pot" assimilation.

The melting pot concept has been misunderstood and misused. As presented in Berkson's 1920 review of acculturation theory, the melting pot metaphor came from the pen of a Jewish playwright, Zangwill (1909), although possibly following the suggestion of St. John de Crèvecoeur (1792). The melting pot was conceived not as assimilation but as the mechanism for creating a new Nietzschean "superman." According to Berkson (1920; 1969), the amalgamation of immigrant cultures should take place without damaging morale or self-respect, but it would cause the "disappearance of divergent ethnic strains and cultures.

However, the melting pot was only one metaphor for cultural integration. Berkson himself favored the metaphor of "community" in which minorities live interspersed with others, engaging in the economic, political, and social life of the society and yet maintaining their minority heritage through deliberate family and school educational endeavors. Such double allegiance is greater than twice a single allegiance since knowledge of an additional language and culture results in a richer personality and prevents ethnocentrism (Berkson, 1920; 1969). Subsequent theories of acculturative integration have not advanced Berkson's early work but only reinvented it.

## Behavioral and Structural assimilation

Among the most famous conceptions of assimilation is the distinction between behavioral assimilation (otherwise known as "acculturation") and structural or socioeconomic assimilation. Behavioral assimilation/acculturation occurs when a newcomer absorbs the cultural norms, values, beliefs, and behavior patterns of the "host" society. This may also involve learning the host language and/or becoming a citizen. Within this process, the new comers may choose to retain much of their traditional culture, norms, and behaviors while still acquiring those of mainstream society, or to discard his/her traditional forms of culture entirely in favor of complete immersion and identification with mainstream society.

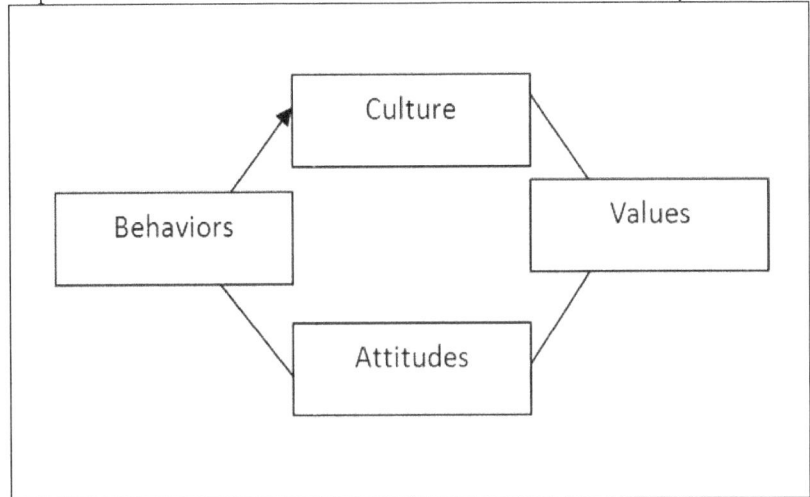

**At the individual level, assimilation starts with the blending of values and attitudes towards the host culture.**

The second major type of assimilation, structural or socioeconomic assimilation, refers to when a cultural group enters and become integrated into the formal social, political, economic, and cultural institutions of the host country i.e. when they begin to participate as full members of the host society. Alternatively, it can also refer to when they attain socioeconomic mobility and status (usually in the form of income, occupation, residential integration, etc.) equal to other members of mainstream society. The process of undergoing either behavioral or structural/socioeconomic assimilation can occur in a linear or "straight-line" manner in which the passage of time and the succession of generations lead to increasing economic, cultural, political, and residential integration into the dominant society. Or it can happen in a non-linear, circular, or "bumpy" manner in which the migrating group revive or retain old cultural traditions, norms, and behaviors and choose to remain somewhat isolated from mainstream society (the "ethnic resilience" model) or alternatively, to combine elements of both traditional and mainstream culture (sometimes referred to as "segmented-assimilation".

## Ideology and Assimilation

Psychological variables play an important role in the process of assimilation.

For example, Banton emphasizes that much of British conduct toward colored people and Jews is a form of avoidance of strangers that is found in nearly all societies, adding that if groups are to be respected they must to some extent be exclusive (Banton 1959). Asians constitute an accommodating group trying to live alongside the local community, while West Africans and West Indians seek acceptance within the community (Ibid). Attention should be called to attitudinal factors that have retarded assimilation in specific historical situations, particularly the belief that the members of one or another racial or ethnic group are un-assimilable. Practices and policies of segregation, mass expulsion, and even genocide have been rationalized on the ground that some groups are un-assimilable because of their innate inferiority. For example, the Nazi "racial" policies were based on the doctrine of the un-assimilability of the Jews. South Africa's policy of apartheid derives from the belief that differences between Europeans and Africans require social, political, and economic separation to permit each group to attain its fullest development. In the United States, a recrudescence of the belief in the innate inferiority of the Negro and, consequently, the necessity of opposing steps toward integration characterized the "race and reason" movement in the early 1960s (Comas 1961). The French colonial policy of "assimilationism" during the first half of the twentieth century was supported, like the continuing colonial policy of the Portuguese (Herskovits 1962), by the belief that for a long time only a select few among a non-Western people are capable of being absorbed into the metropolitan system. In contrast to the policy of forced separation of racial and cultural minorities, antipathy toward minority groups has also taken the form of forced assimilation. In 1917 the communists promised freedom for the customs and institutions of Russia's numerous cultural and national minorities. Stalin was instrumental in formulating the policy of separating statehood from nationality, and cultural autonomy was permitted within the framework of Soviet economics and politics. However, since 1940 the reinstitution of some aspects of the tzarist policy of Russification has dispersed some minorities. Jews have been labeled "cosmopolitans," and since 1957 a campaign against the remaining aspects of Jewish communal life has been carried on. The goal of this program appears to be the "total assimilation" of Jews (Goldhagen 1960). Opposition to assimilation also may be shown by members of a minority group. In the United States the Old Order Amish and numerous other religio-ethnic groupings have sought to preserve their separateness and distinctiveness (Williams 1964). Among Negro Americans a small but militant group known as the Black Muslims is virtually alone in not seeking complete assimilation. Black nationalists perceive white society as united in rejecting Negroes as full citizens. Thus, feelings of alienation and powerlessness cause these persons to reject American society and culture, and the leaders of the movement strive to develop an awareness of group identity among the urban masses of Negroes (Essien-Udom 1962; Lincoln 1961). Among the group's objectives are the establishment of a Negro homeland and a Black Nation. The history of these and many other minorities in the New World is discussed by Wagley and Harris (1958), who analyze the different strategies for working toward the opposite goals of assimilation and pluralism.

## Assimilation: An Individual or Social Process

Immigrant assimilation is viewed as individualistic rather than community-based. Not surprisingly, other social scientists took it rather as a narrow view taken by economists of the assimilation experience. Meanwhile, a large literature (mainly by non economists) has developed which sees immigrants as communities, not merely as individuals. This implies that the assimilation experience of particular ethnic origin groups must be viewed as just that: the assimilation of groups, rather than of individuals who happen to be part of such groups. In recent years, economists have paid more attention to the role of the ethnic communities in conditioning patterns of assimilation among individuals within that group.

Studies have examined the effects of ethnic concentration and immigrant ghettos on the economic outcomes of immigrants through processes such as the acquisition of language skills and mobility across occupations and localities. A better approach is to regard the assimilation process as a two way street. Assimilation depends not only on how immigrants fit into the host country's society and its wider culture but also on the degree to which the non-immigrant community accepts, accommodates and adapts to particular immigrant groups. If we adopt this view, then history matters: the more established is the tradition of immigration from a particular source, the more integrated that ethnic community will be, and the more easily new immigrants from that source will assimilate into the host society (Lieberson and Waters 1990).

Recent research on ethnic identity analyses the degree to which an immigrant is committed to the culture of the origin and the host country. Constant and Zimmermann (2008) classify those who identify strongly with the host country culture as assimilated and those who identify strongly with both origin country and host country cultures as integrated. Using data on immigrants to Germany, Constant et al. (2009) find that migrants who are culturally assimilated have higher employment probabilities and higher earnings than those who are not. Interestingly, they also find that those who are integrated do equally well in employment and have higher earnings than those who are assimilated. This suggests that retaining a degree of identification with the origin country may not lead to disadvantage in the labor market, and it may confer positive economic benefits for immigrants who also adapt to the host country culture.

There are significant advances that take the study of immigrant assimilation beyond the simple individualistic approach. But they still fail to capture the *interaction* between immigrant communities or ethnic groups and the host society. Such notions have been taken more seriously in the recent sociological literature on immigration which has moved beyond the so-called assimilationist approach, focusing more on "the process of interaction between host society institutions and structures and the characteristics of newcomers. While the assimilation perspective portrayed American society as a rather amorphous, homogenous entity, an absorbent sponge, the newer theories gave shape to this amorphous entity. They pointed out that the sponge is structured and that structure itself is subject to change (Schmitter Heisler 2000).

Since the pioneering work of Glazer and Moynihan (1963) and Gordon (1964), sociological research has focused on how immigrants from different origin countries and regions have evolved into distinct ethnic groups. These studies have increasingly brought the host society into the picture, focusing on the degree of receptivity towards immigrants at a number of levels. These include government policy, civil society and individual attitudes, all of which are seen as culturally conditioned.

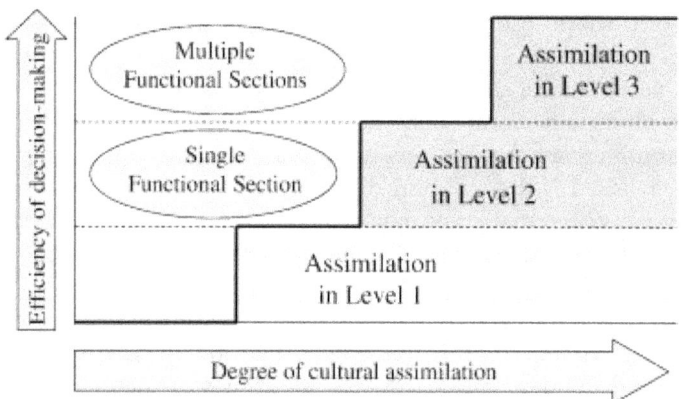

**Initially assimilation starts with the individual level and gradually involving multiple social sections and thus becoming a community process.**
**Source: assimilation.net**

Immigrants assimilate as communities, not just as individuals. New immigrants depend largely on the degree of integration of the community as a whole and not just on the skills and motivation of the individual immigrant and the connections of his or her immediate friends and relatives. Much of the emphasis in the sociological literature has been placed on the strategies of ethnic communities, stretching back to opportunities they faced when they first arrived (Portes and Rumbaut 1996). The early arrivals from a given source tend to be highly concentrated in certain occupational niches or in specific lines of small business—often related to particular ethnic goods.

Thus in New York, Chinese immigrants were initially concentrated in laundries, restaurants and the garment sector. Over time, the second-generation immigrants and their newly arrived co-ethnics diversified into a wider range of occupations, partly through the extension of ethnic networks, partly through the adaptation of the communities themselves to the norms of the host society and partly because they became less exceptional in the eyes of the host population (ibid).

## Cultural Assimilation: Induced or Spontaneous

Many scholars of ethnicity and cultural change take assimilation as a socio-political response to demographic multi-ethnicity that supports or promotes the assimilation of ethnic minorities into the dominant culture. The term assimilation is often used with regard to immigrants and various ethnic groups who have settled in a new land. New customs and attitudes are acquired through contact and communication. The transfer of customs is not simply a one-way process. Each group of immigrants contributes some of its own cultural traits to its new society. Assimilation usually involves a gradual change and takes place in varying degrees; full assimilation occurs when new members of a society become indistinguishable from older members.

A group (a state or an ethnicity) can spontaneously adopt a different culture due to its political relevance, or to its perceived superiority. The first is the case of the Latin language and culture that were gradually adopted by most of the subjugated people. The second is the case of subjugated, but older and richer culture, which sees it imitated by the new masters, e.g. the victorious Roman Republic adopted more from the Hellenistic cultures than it imposed in most domains, except such Roman specialties as law and the military. In this regard Social scientists mainly rely on four primary benchmarks to assess immigrant assimilation: socioeconomic status, geographic distribution, second language attainment, and intermarriage.

While arguing about the shift from *transitive* to *intransitive* understandings of assimilation, Rogers (2001) writes that the former see populations of immigrant origin as moldable, meltable, *objects*; the latter see persons comprising such populations as active *subjects*. As such, to be sure, they are not busy consciously 'assimilating'. Assimilating can, of course, be a deliberate, self-conscious activity; and the poignant – and sometimes tragic – ambiguities and ambivalences bound up with it have been movingly explored by novelists, memoirists, essayists, historians, and even a few sociologists (Bauman 1988; Laitin 1995). Yet for most historians and social scientists, assimilation is an emergent tendential property of social processes at an aggregate level, rather than something that happens (consciously or unconsciously) at the level of individual persons. As an emergent tendency at the aggregate level, assimilation is largely unintended and often invisible; and when it is made visible, it may be lamented. Yet even when it is lamented, the processual tendency we call 'assimilation' is not something done *to* persons, but rather something accomplished *by* them, not intentionally, but as an unintended consequence of myriad individual actions and choices in particular social, cultural, economic and political contexts (Alba 1995).

**Assimilation is not necessarily a forced phenomena but it always has a pressure associated with it for the migrant culture to assimilate. Cartoon Source: assimilation.net**

Cultural assimilation can happen either way; spontaneously or forcedly. A culture can spontaneously adopt a different culture or the case of subjugated, meaning that older and richer cultures forcedly integrate other weak cultures. The term assimilation is often used with regard to immigrants and various ethnic groups who have settled in a new land. New culture and attitudes toward the origin culture are obtained through contact and communication. Cultural changing is not simply a one-way process. Assimilation assume that a relatively tenuous culture get to be united to mighty culture. This process is going through contact with each cultures and accommodation.

Current definition of assimilation is usually used in the immigrants, but in multiculturalism, cultural assimilation can happened all over the world, not just be limited in specific area. For example, the united language gives people chance to study and work internationally, not just being limited to the same culture group. People from different countries make diversity and compose the "global culture" which means the culture combined by the elements from different countries. This "global culture" can be seen as a part of assimilation that causes cultures from different areas affect each other.

## Assimilation, Language and Family

Most research on the language situation of immigrant children and children of immigrants draws upon the assimilation model (Gordon, 1964). In this case, the linguistic assimilation of an ethnic group is considered a necessary step in acculturation and overall assimilation (Stevens and Swicegood, 1987). This approach predicts that over time ethnic and racial minorities will blend into mainstream culture, learning English and losing their native tongues. In fact, most argue that knowledge of a non-English language will rarely last past the third generation (Veltman, 1983). This process of linguistic assimilation is considered to take place because across generations and over time individuals have a greater length and degree of exposure to the host language, which increases opportunities and pressures to speak the dominant language. Increased knowledge and use of non-ethnic language often results in decreased fluency but not necessarily a complete loss of the native tongue. Research in the assimilation tradition has revealed the importance of several individual characteristics. For example, in the English societies children's knowledge of their parents' native languages varies by generation. Foreign-born individuals are much more likely than those who are native born, to speak non-English languages at home (Waggoner, 1988). Stevens (1985, 1992) also found that children of two foreign-born parents are more likely than those with just one immigrant parent to learn the parents' non-English language. Furthermore, the longer the foreign-born parents have resided in the United States, the less likely their children are to use the non-English (native) language. Fishman (1972) and Alba et al. (2002) argue that as the host language becomes more accepted as the dominant language in public spheres, the native language becomes confined to the most intimate social spheres, such as the home. As a result, the home language and family context are important domains to consider when attempting understanding patterns of minority language use. In this case, the home use of a native language and the social relations within the family are part of the setting where native language can be passed from generation to generation (Lopez, 1999). The transactional nature of assimilation is particularly notable in the evolution of languages. In some instances, assimilation results in the adoption of another country's language, which is then modified over time to become a new, distinct, language. For example, *Hanzi*, the written language of Chinese language, has been adapted and modified by other nearby cultures, including: Japan (as Kanji), Korea (as Hanja), and Vietnam (as Chữ-nôm). Another common effect of acculturation on language is the formation of *Pidgin* languages. Pidgin is a mixed language that has developed to help communication between members of different cultures in contact, usually occurring in situations of trade or colonialism. For example, Pidgin English is a simplified form of English mixed with some of the other language of the other culture. It blends English grammar with that of a native language. This was first used in Chinese ports and similar have developed in Papua New Guinea and West Africa.

Empirical evidence suggests that larger household size can help explain the language situation of migrant children as it influences their opportunities to speak and use the native language within the family (Garcı́aand Otheguy, 1988). At the same time, large families are associated with higher ethnic language speaking ability (Espenshade and Fu, 1997). Furthermore, the presence of grandparents and other adult relatives who speak the mother tongue may serve as a vital link for the children to learn the language, norms, and values of the homeland.

One of the most important predictors of language use is family socioeconomic status. Studies find that parents with more education and higher incomes are less likely to be fluent in a non-English language (Stevens, 1985), and their children experience a rapid loss of knowledge of their parents' native tongues (Portes and Hao, 1998; Portes and Schauffler, 1994). This is likely because these parents see English language proficiency as a mechanism for children to enter mainstream culture and succeed, thus they may discourage the use of a native tongue.

Two final predictors that have been found to affect patterns of language use are the size and geographic location of an ethnic group (Alba et al., 2002; Stevens, 1992). According to Stevens (1992), for those groups that are more highly segregated, the opportunities to maintain a native tongue are greater. Other research suggests that proximity to residential enclaves increases the probability that third-generation children will speak the ethnic language (Alba et al., 2002).

## Assimilation and Intermarriage

There is an inclination in the literature to attribute a relatively higher degree of assimilation to an immigrant who marries a spouse of a different ethnic or cultural origin than to one who remains ethnically connected to his own group through marriage (Richard, 1991). Sociological research on intermarriage has had three main areas of focus: causal factors, patterns of incidence and mate selection, and consequences of intermarriage for couples and their children (Richard, 1988). Historically, intermarriage has been considered an indicator of assimilation since Drachsler's study (1921) on intermarriage in New York City. Since then, Carpenter (1927) has argued that inter-marriage provides the most direct outlet by which the present and future generations may be joined together. For Bossard (1939), the intimate nature of marriage made intermarriage a realistic index of social distance between distinct groups and, therefore, an index of the process of assimilation. According to Hurd (1929), intermarriage is both an index and a method of assimilation while Nelson (1943) called intermarriage the "final test of assimilation". Jiobu (1988) states that it was the "litmus test of assimilation" and Hirschman (1983) has called it "the final outcome of assimilation".

Gordon (1964) argues that if large scale intermarriage takes place the minority group melts, as it were, into the host society. 'Identificational assimilation', which is when the immigrant identifies themselves as a member of the host society, takes place, and the remaining stages, the absence of prejudice, discrimination, value and power conflict, will naturally follow. This being the case, it is assumed that those who intermarry will have greater social, political and economic mobility because they portray characteristics that are similar to those of the host society (Richard, 1991). Lieberman and Waters (1988) state that intermarriage has been a long standing topic of interest for sociologists because it can be understood as an indicator of the degree of assimilation of ethnic and racial groups as well as an agent itself of further assimilation for the couples who intermarry and for the next generation. They assert that high rates of intermarriage are a necessary condition for assimilation. They further argue that intermarriage can have consequences for the individuals involved, as well as for the future viability of the ethnic groups, as it creates more ethnic heterogeneity and may possibly lead to a dilution of ethnic identity. Given the fact that the family is such a central force in the socialization process, Lieberman and Waters (1988) also claim that through intermarriage, the maintenance of an ethnic group is more difficult because a "homogeneous nuclear family, is more able and likely to pass on to offspring the ethnic feelings, identification, and cultural values that will help perpetuate the group". Ultimately, they conclude that after a few generations, the offspring of those who have intermarried become indistinguishable from the host society or in other words, assimilated (Lieberman and Waters, 1988). Despite the general connection between intermarriage and assimilation, not all scholars agree that intermarriage is the ultimate index of assimilation. Marcson (1950), for example, argues that groups may become assimilated without showing a high rate of intermarriage. Price and Zubrzycki (1962) point out that Marcson's theory confuses the notion of integration, which is defined as the process whereby two or more ethnic groups adapt themselves so well that they accept and value each other's contribution to their common political and social life, with assimilation, which they define as "not only integration, but economic absorption, social acculturation, and physical amalgamation", where the immigrant becomes completely impossible to differentiate from the dominant society.

More recently, Qian and Lichter (2001) have argued that "intermarriage is sometimes regarded as the final stage of assimilation among immigrant racial and ethnic minorities". These scholars suggest that intermarriage provides a measure of social distance in groups and of the strength of ethnic boundaries and solidarity as well as creating "an erosion of ethnic distinctiveness" but that it is often a neglected aspect of contemporary patterns of assimilation (Qian and Lichter, 2001).

## Miscegenation

Intermarriage between old stock Americans and white immigrant a group was acceptable as part of the melting pot narrative. Native Americans in the United States on reservations gained US citizenship with the Indian Citizenship Act of 1924, and were encouraged to become integrated in the society through educational programs. The country welcomes celebrities of Native American background, such as Will Rogers and Jim Thorpe, and elected a Native American as vice president in 1928.

The mixing of whites and blacks, resulting in multiracial children, for whom the term "miscegenation" was coined in 1863, was a taboo, and most whites opposed marriages between whites and blacks. In many states, marriage between whites and non-whites was even prohibited by state law through anti-miscegenation laws. By the early 20th century, many white Americans accepted that American culture was heavily influenced by African-American culture, but although they increasingly accepted and even celebrated this acculturation, most whites did not accept marriages between white Americans and African-Americans.

Today in the age of modernity and globalization most of the countries particularly the developed ones have an outlook as normal towards inter racial marriages as to the intra racial. In India today lot of incidences through the length of the country are witnessed of marriages between people of different ethnic origins like between Gujratis and Bengalis or between North Indians and the South Indians. In the valley as the present research has shown marriages between Pakhtoons and Kashmiris have been witnessed with clear implications of racial mixing and consequently misgenation. It was further found that the children so born are more likely to become Kashmiris rather than Pakhtoons because of the cultural dominance of the former people in both the cases whether a girl is taken by them in marriage or given away to Pakhtoons for that matter.

## Assimilation of Religion

Assimilation of religion not only includes shifting to a new form of religious belief or practice but also the erosion of the traditional religious structure. When religion doesn't remain in its fundamental or classic structure, it is said to be assimilated because every change is a new form of it which represents a new version of religion. From the classic works like Emile Durkheim's *Elementary Forms of Religious Life (1912)*, Weber's *Protestant Ethic and Spirit of Capitalism* to more contemporary studies on religion in the modern social world, the fact remained that secularization of religion is an outcome of modernization. Likewise what secularization has for religion, modernization has the same. Thus both become the agents for assimilation of religion as it involves the erosion of belief and ritual, paves the way for shifting to new religious forms like cultism and atheism. There is change from superstition to rationality. Both assimilation and secularization theories underestimate the resilience of ethnicity and religion. Ethnic and racial group identities and affiliations may have changed, but they certainly remain. Like ethnicity, religion too lives on. The secularization model also presents a social evolutionary perspective. In the face of increasing urbanization, rationalization, and dominance of science, characteristic of modernity, the decline and eventual disappearance of traditional religions become unavoidable. Religious belief systems were considered inevitable and irreversible. Religion was considered to be part of the "childhood" of the human race, "merely a survival from man's primitive past" that is destined to "disappear in the era of science and general enlightenment" (Ibid).

Bryan Wilson makes one of the strongest cases for secularization. Defining secularization as the "process whereby religious thinking, practice, and institutions lose social significance", Wilson views secularization as a non-ideological fact of modernity. In the past, the community was the primary locus of human life and within the community religion was the source of social knowledge and order. Eventually, however, a rational societal system superseded the patterns of communal order. "…whereas religion once entered into the very texture of community life, in modern society it operates only in interstitial places in the system". Living in a scientifically advanced modern world, humans develop a pervasive rational orientation to the world, which draws them away from religion. In this situation, religion has little hope; it will irreversibly decline in the process of rationalization_shifting from community to society based systems.

## Core measurements to immigrant assimilation

Researchers have assessed that assimilation exists among immigrants because we can measure assimilation on four primary benchmarks. These core measurable aspects of immigrant assimilation that were formulated to study European immigrants to the United States are still the starting points for understanding current immigrant assimilation. These measurable aspects of assimilation are socioeconomic status, spatial concentration, language attainment, and intermarriage.

1. *Socioeconomic Status* is defined by educational attainment, occupation, and income. By measuring socioeconomic status researchers want to find out if immigrants eventually catch up to native-born people in terms of human capital characteristics.

2. *Spatial Concentration* is defined by geography or residential patterns. The spatial residential model (based on theories of Park) proposed by Massey states that increasing socio-economic attainment, longer residence in the U.S, and higher generational status lead to decreasing residential concentration for a particular ethnic group.

3. *Language Attainment* is defined as the ability to speak English (here the host language) and the loss of the individual's mother tongue. The three-generation model of language assimilation states that the first generation makes some progress in language assimilation but remains dominant in their native tongue, the second generation is bilingual, and the third-generation only speaks English (the host language).

4. *Intermarriage* is defined by race or ethnicity and occasionally by generation. High rates of intermarriage are considered to be an indication of social integration because it reveals intimate and profound relations between people of different groups, intermarriage reduces the ability of families to pass on to their children a consistent ethnic culture and thus is an agent of assimilation. Although intermarriage was viewed as a firm base from which to begin an argument for assimilation, it was also seen as a way to gradually ease the transition into their new culture.

## Factors for Faster Assimilation

Research on assimilation has focused on why certain racial/ethnic groups assimilate faster than others. One factor is racial differences. White immigrants who came to the U.S. back in the 1800s did experience prejudice and discrimination. But because they were White, they were eventually able to integrate into American society more quickly and easily than non-White immigrants and minorities.

The second factor is the structure of the economy. During times of economic prosperity, there are plenty of economic opportunities to go around for everyone. But in times of economic difficulties, there is more economic competition and therefore, more hostility toward minorities and immigrants who are frequently seen as economic threats. In this situation, groups who are in similar economic situations are likely to be antagonistic toward each other because they're competing for the same jobs and social/economic resources.

The final reason why some immigrants assimilate faster than others is because of class differences. Some ethnic and immigrant groups on the whole have higher levels of education, job skills, and English proficiency than others. This in turn gives them specific advantages in achieving socioeconomic success faster than others by allowing them to get jobs that are higher-paying, more stable, and that offer higher status. As a result, they are able to achieve socioeconomic mobility and success faster than other groups.

Sociological research has also found that the strength of the child's relationship with his/her parents, along with the level of his/her attachment to the ethnic community also play important roles in determining ethnic identity among second generation Asian Americans. For example, if child-parent relationship is strong and healthy, the child is more likely to take on the parent's identity, whatever that may be (i.e. national origin, hyphenated American, pan-Asian, or just Asian). However, if the child has conflicts with his/her parents, the more likely the child will identify differently from the parent.

Studies also show that the strength of a child's ethnic community strongly affects his/her identity. Those who live within a cohesive ethnic community and who regularly participate in co-ethnic organizations and activities (i.e., peer groups, churches, etc.) are more likely to identify with a national origin or hyphenated-American identity, even if the ethnic group tends to be low-income or working class. In other words, socioeconomic success is not as important in determining ethnic identity as the level of social solidarity within the co-ethnic community. Perceptions of racism and discrimination can also have influences, like on the Asian American second generation ethnic identity. According to the situational/constructionist/instrumentalist perspective, for an Asian American to have a strong attachment to traditional forms of ethnic identity, it is not enough to just perceive or experience high levels of ethnic competition, prejudice, or discrimination. It is the person's reaction to these perceptions and experiences that will determine how s/he identifies.

That is, if s/he internalizes these experiences of competition and discrimination and his/her self-esteem is negatively affected as a result, s/he is more likely to be embarrassed to be identified as Asian American.

On the other hand, these experiences of competition and discrimination can also lead to a greater sense of unity and solidarity and as a result, greater identification with his/her Asian ethnicity.

## Assimilation Aftermath

One of the most famous theories of assimilation comes from sociologist Milton Gordon. He theorized that there are three possible outcomes of assimilation. The first is Anglo conformity, which is when the minority or immigrant is taught that the norms, values, and institutions of the majority group are superior and that they should adopt them in order to be accepted. This is symbolized as A+B+C=A.

The second outcome can be the melting pot, a term that almost all assimilating cultures have heard about. That's when different racial/ethnic groups come together and out of this interaction comes a new culture that incorporates elements from all groups into one. This can be represented as A+B+C=D.

The third possible outcome is cultural pluralism, which others have also called the *salad bowl*. This is when the different racial/ethnic groups keep their unique cultural norms, traditions, and behaviors, while still sharing common national values, goals, and institutions i.e. A+B+C=A+B+C. Gordon giving the example of American society, argues that Anglo conformity has best represented the history of assimilation in America. Research suggests that there can be notably institutional patterns to this seemingly individual process. These identities can also overlap, change over time, and even be one of many simultaneous identities in effect at the same time.

## Globalization: An Assimilationist View

*"I do not want my house to be walled in on
all sides and my windows to be stuffed. I
want the cultures of all lands to be blown
about my house as freely as possible. But I
refuse to be blown off my feet by any."*

_ *Mahatma Gandhi*

Globalization has been the more contentious, because it has effects both good and bad, and democracy has opened space for people to protest the bad effects. So, controversies rage over the environmental, economic and social consequences of globalization. But there is another domain of globalization, that of culture and identity, which is just as controversial and even more divisive because it engages ordinary people, not just economists, government officials and political activists. Globalization has increased contacts between people and their values, ideas and ways of life in unprecedented ways. People are migrating more frequently and more widely. Television now reaches families in the deepest rural areas of China. From Brazilian music in Tokyo to African films in Bangkok, to Shakespeare in Croatia, to books on the history of the Arab world in Moscow, to the CNN world news in Amman, people revel in the diversity of the age of globalization. For many people this new diversity is exciting, even empowering, but for some it is disquieting and dis-empowering. They fear that their country is becoming fragmented, their values lost as growing numbers of immigrants bring new customs and international trade and modern communications media invade every corner of the world, displacing local culture. Some even foresee a nightmarish scenario of cultural homogenization _ with diverse national cultures giving way to a world dominated by Western values and symbols. What all the cultures have in common is the fear of losing their cultural identity. Cross-border flows of investment and knowledge, films and other cultural goods, and people are not new phenomena. Indigenous people have struggled for centuries to maintain their identity and way of life against the tide of globalization.

## *The Melting Pot*

The melting pot theory, also referred to as cultural assimilation, revolves around the analogy that the ingredients in the pot (people of different cultures and religions) are combined so as to lose their discrete identities and yield a final product of uniform consistency and flavor, which is quite different from the original inputs. This idea differs from other analogies, particularly the *salad bowl* analogy where the ingredients are encouraged to retain their cultural identities, thus retaining their "integrity and flavor". Yet another food analogy is that of the *ethnic stew*, where there is a level of compromise between integration and cultural distinctiveness.

**The Melting Pot is a global representation of assimilation.**

The history of the "melting pot" theory can be traced from J. Hector St. John Crèvecoeur's 1782 volume, *Letters From an American Farmer,* through Frederick Jackson Turner's thesis of 1893 concerning the fusion of immigrants in the crucible of the Western frontier into a composite American people, and Israel Zangwill's *The Melting Pot* of 1909, to R. R. Kennedy's "Single or Triple Melting-pot" studies of 1944 and 1952 (Gordon 1964).

In the 1780s, Hector Jean offered one of the earliest descriptions of the formation of the American population as the physical melding of diverse European peoples into a new, single people. Although melting pot implies mutual change leading to the creation of a new alloy, most who adopted the phrase described a process, which Milton Gordon later called "Anglo-conformity," through which newcomers adapted to norms derived from an Anglo-American heritage. Alternative visions arose almost immediately. In the 1800 and the early 1900, some people gave America the name, the melting pot. People imagined this because thousands and thousands of immigrants coming from around the world were coming into the United States in hope of a better life.

The new nation welcomed virtually all immigrants from Europe in the belief that the United States would become, at least for whites, the "melting pot" of the world. This idea was adopted by the historian Frederick Jackson Turner (1893) who updated it with the frontier thesis. Turner believed that the challenge of frontier life was the country's most crucial force, allowing Europeans to be "Americanised" by the wilderness (Takaki, 1993).

A major influx of immigrants occurred mainly after the 1830s, when large numbers of British, Irish, and Germans began entering, to be joined after the Civil War by streams of Scandinavians and then groups from eastern and southern Europe as well as small numbers from the Middle East, China, and Japan. Before the outbreak of World War I in 1914, the American public generally took it for granted that the constant flow of newcomers from abroad, mainly Europe, brought strength and prosperity to the country. The metaphor of the "melting pot" symbolized the mystical potency of the great democracy, whereby people from every corner of the earth were fused into a harmonious and admirable blend. Although the term melting pot may be applied to many countries in the world, such as Brazil, Bangladesh or even France, mostly referring to increased level of mixed race and culture, it is predominantly used with reference to USA and creation of the American nation, as a distinct "new breed of people" amalgamated from many various groups of immigrants. As such it is closely linked to the process of *Americanisation*. The theory of melting pot has been criticised both as unrealistic and racist, because it focused on the Western heritage and excluded non-European immigrants. Also, despite its proclaimed "melting" character its results have been assimilationist. This criticism that the melting pot produces a society that primarily reflects the dominant culture instead of fusing into a completely new entity is reiterated by other sociologists, anthropologists, and cultural geographers as "Anglo-conformity" (Kivisto 2004). This type of assimilation was seen as working like a one-way street and it was viewed as something that depended primarily on the cooperativeness of immigrants to be reoriented towards the dominant culture.

## Theorizing on Immigrant Assimilation

Theoretical interest in assimilation focuses on the descendants of immigrants and the rate of their convergence towards native norms. Two theories dominate the literature: linear assimilation theory and the more recently articulated segmented assimilation theory. Under linear assimilation theory we expect sharp differences between native and immigrant groups in family structure in the initial era of immigration and expect these differences to diminish across time. In the ethnicity model, ethnicity should have significant but diminishing effects; in the generational model, generation should have pronounced effects in the first generation, and weaker ones in the second. The interaction model should reveal little difference among ethnic groups in ethnic/generation interactions, revealing the same linear process.

Under segmented assimilation theory we expect differences between native and immigrant groups in family structure; such differences should diminish across time for some groups but increase for others. In the ethnicity model, ethnicity effects should diminish for some groups across time but not for others. In the generational model, differences between generations should not be pronounced.

Although a product of the early 20th century and subject to criticism in recent scholarship, linear assimilation (often simply assimilation theory) retains considerable appeal for many who see it as still the most useful way to understand how the integration of ethnic groups occurs (Morawska, 1994; Barkan, 1995; Alba & Nee, 1997, 2003). Linear assimilation predicts a steady, generational transition in which immigrant-origin groups take on the demographic, economic and cultural characteristics of natives. In family forms, distinct ethno cultural characteristics fade in strength over time and ethnic families become indistinguishable from native ones (Gordon, 1964; Goldscheider & Goldscheider, 1989; Alba, 1995; Wilmoth et al., 1997; Abbasi-Shavazi & McDonald, 2000; Arias, 2001). The assimilation model implies pronounced generational effects; first-generation families are expected to be patently distinct, second-generation ones less so, and so forth. The chief alternative to linear assimilation models emerged from the apparent failure of assimilation theory to explain contemporary assimilation patterns. Segmented assimilation theory responds to unexpected trends since 1960 in family structure, socioeconomic status, and educational achievement among descendants of certain immigrant groups (Waters, 1990; Gans, 1992; Skop, 2001). Hernandez (2004), for example, notes that 47% of children of Mexican immigrant origin live in non-nuclear settings, versus 18% for their native white counterparts. Only 5% of native children have a grandparent in the home as compared with 13% of the Mexican children. Increases in marital instability, greater incidence of female-headed families, and educational and economic deficiencies among second- and third-generation groups are all at variance with standard assimilation's predictions (Portes & Zhou, 1993; Portes, 1995).

Based on these unexpected trends, segmented assimilation theory posits two distinct assimilation trajectories for the descendants of recent immigrants (Portes & Rumbaut, 1996; Zhou, 1997). One, upward assimilation, leads towards the socioeconomic status, family structure, fertility and marital features common to the majority of native-born persons. The other trajectory is downward assimilation, towards the socio-economic status and family structures among native-born groups marginalized by racial or ethnic prejudice. Thus, some immigrant groups move 'straight in the opposite direction to permanent poverty and assimilation to the underclass' (Portes & Zhou, 1994).

The divergent trajectories of segmented assimilation are linked to the characteristics immigrants bring with them (education, skills and culture) and to the modes of incorporation offered them by the host society (economic opportunity, immigration policy and discrimination). One critical feature in the mode of incorporation offered by the host society is economic opportunity; segmented assimilation theory focuses on the lack of labour markets for the relatively unskilled and undereducated, opportunities said to be readily available to immigrants in the US economy at the turn of the century (Portes *et al.*, 2005; but see Waldinger, 2007).

Although the loss of employment opportunities has potent effects, ethnic and racial characteristics also shape assimilatory paths in the segmented model (Portes, 1995; Zhou, 1997). Here, segmented assimilation postulates two cultural explanations for divergent assimilation paths. The first finds that the stubborn cultural values of certain groups (primarily Asian in origin) lead to resistance through enclave strategies, the formation of resilient families, and an emphasis on educational success among descendants, all features of upward assimilation. A concomitant explanation contends that some ethnic groups – largely of Latino and Afro-Caribbean origin – appear to have weak cultural ties and may follow a downward assimilation path towards the norms of the marginalized populations of inner cities (Portes & Rumbaut, 2001). This path is largely a consequence of prejudice in the host population. Portes *et al.* 2005 submit that 'Children of Asian, black, mulatto, and mestizo immigrants cannot escape their ethnicity and race, as defined by the mainstream because the strong effects of discrimination throws a barrier in the path of occupational and social acceptance' (ibid). Likewise, Hernandez & Darke (1999) argue that the primary reason for a lack of economic improvement across generations among Mexican, Haitian and Dominican immigrants is that 'racial and ethnic stratification greatly limits their opportunities' (ibid). The impact of discrimination against persons whose ethnicity or race is the same as that of disadvantaged groups in the US is usually found among the children of immigrants (rather than the first generation) who turn towards the seductions of ghetto cultures, which become a primary reference for socialization (Portes & Zhou, 1993; Rumbaut, 1994; Portes & Rumbaut, 2001). Thus, from the perspective of segmented assimilation theory, while cultural values might shelter some groups from the corrosive impact of American conditions, ethnicity is for others a marker for discrimination by the majority white population that leads to negative outcomes.

The negative effects of discrimination can reputedly be seen in family structure. Rumbaut reports 'striking increases in the prevalence of marital disruption over time in the United States and particularly in succeeding generations' (Rumbaut, 1996 ; Gil & Vega, 1996). Rapid increases in marital instability among Dominicans, Puerto Ricans and Haitians 'mirror' those among impoverished African Americans and native Hispanics and constitute a form of assimilation towards US norms, albeit a negative one (Fernández-Kelly & Schauffler, 1994; Portes & Zhou, 1994; Landale & Ogena, 1995; Portes, 1995; Waters, 1996).

The children and grandchildren of immigrants mimic the dominant culture traits rather than those of their culture of origin or of white natives (Matute-Bianchi, 1991; Suárez-Orozco, 1991; Portes, 1995, 1997). Landale & Oropesa (1995) found third-generation Latino children in 1990 much more likely than first-generation children to live in single-parent families, and substantially more likely than non-Latino white children. Hernandez & Darke (1999) located similar sharp increases in risk of single-parent families for third-generation children in 1990.

Brandon (2002) notes that 'Mexican, black, and other Hispanic children increasingly live in single-mother families, which by all measures indicates downward assimilation'. Although scholars have recently raised objections to the broad claims of decline in segmented assimilation theory (Perlmann & Waldinger, 1997; Farley & Alba, 2002; Alba & Nee, 2003; Smith, 2003; Waldinger & Feliciano, 2004), the argument continues to receive substantial scholarly attention (see Portes & Rumbaut 2005a) and strident defence by its most prominent proponents (Portes *et al.*, 2005). Recent tests of assimilation have focused on children (Portes & Rumbaut 2001), as they provide the generational sequence necessary for examining convergence, or the lack of it.

## Factors affecting Assimilation

The process of assimilation is affected by the interaction of several classes of variables: demographic, ecological, racial, structural, psychological, and cultural. There is at present no systematic comparative analysis of the variables that are most significant in different types of situations. The importance of group size can be seen in the case of Hawaii, where there is a stronger tendency for members of the smaller ethnic and racial groups to marry outside their own groups than for those of larger groups; also, women from groups with a more balanced sex ratio out marry to a greater extent than women from groups with a less balanced sex ratio (Cheng & Yamamura 1957). Ecological factors have been important where "cultural islands" created by immigrant groups often provide security but also isolate newcomers from the mainstream culture. Likewise, demographic and ecological factors for example apparently affected the likelihood of Negro assimilation in Great Britain (Collins 1955). Park (1930) held that assimilation might, in some senses and to a certain degree, be described as a function of visibility, and he attributed the Negro's lack of assimilation in the United States, during three hundred years, to physical rather than cultural traits. This oversimplified explanation has been replaced by one that stresses the interaction of racial, ecological, historical, structural, and other variables. Other variables of importance in "passing" are age and socioeconomic status; people who are well established in the Negro community and older people seldom pass socially and completely. However, color continues to be an important factor; for example, a study of Chicago's Negro community shows that color affects choice of marriage partners, recruitment into the professions, social relations, and other aspects of life (Wilson 1960).

Recent studies have shown that color and social class are not the only variables affecting the differential assimilation of Negroes. In a study of New Orleans Negroes, primary role identifications occasioned by conditioning in one of four "social worlds" (the middle class, the matriarchy, the male gang, the isolated family, and a residual group of the culturally marginal) were found to play a larger part in the self conceptions and the experiences of individuals than any identification with the Negro race in general (Rohrer & Edmonson 1960). For overseas students in London, finding a room depends largely on color: approximately 70 per cent of the landladies were unwilling to accept colored students and, in the case of very dark Africans or West Indians, the figure was 85 per cent. By virtue of sharing halls of residence and dining rooms, as well as having more opportunities for participation in university societies, the social life of colored students is fuller in Oxford and Cambridge than in London (Senior 1957).

## A Report on Global Assimilation Index

Immigrants from India and China are quick to assimilate into the economic fabric of the United States, but are not as quick when it comes to assimilating culturally and in civic matters, a study by Jacob Vigdor, Associate Professor of Public Policy Studies and Economics at Duke University, has found.

Billed as the first annual Index of Immigrant Assimilation, the study measured three types of assimilation: economic (employment, education, home ownership); cultural (intermarriage, English proficiency, family size); and civic (citizenship rates, military service, voting). It then compared the assimilation rates of recent immigrants by country of origin, and found that immigrants from Vietnam, Cuba and the Philippines have the high ratings across the board.

The overall assimilation index for all countries averages out to 28 on a scale of 100, but the index for India is under 20, and China only barely tops the 20 mark. Mexico rates 13 points, while Canada scores a high 53. In terms of overall assimilation, immigrants from Mexico and Central America have index values below those of Indians; the index value for India is below that of China.

Immigrants born in Canada, Cuba, the Dominican Republic, Korea, the

Philippines, and Vietnam have assimilation-index values higher than the national average of 28. 'This report introduces a quantitative index that measures the degree of similarity between native and foreign-born adults. It is the ability to distinguish the latter group from the former that we mean when we use the term assimilation, ' the report said. In terms of economic assimilation, immigrants from Canada, Cuba, the Philippines and Korea are indistinguishable from mainstream Americans; these four countries are followed by Vietnam and India. Immigrants from Mexico are the least economically assimilated of any group, with those from El Salvador a close second. Individuals born in the Dominican Republic and China also display economic assimilation levels at or below the national average.

When it comes to culture, Canadians are almost indistinguishable from native-born Americans. "Immigrants born in the Philippines and the Dominican Republic also show relatively high levels of cultural assimilation. At the other end of the spectrum, immigrants born in China and India show the greatest degree of cultural distinction from the native-born," the report said. In terms of cultural assimilation, India's index value of 39 is the lowest among major origin countries for immigrants in the United States. When considering a wider array of origin countries, immigrants from Bangladesh have a slightly lower score, 38.

In civic assimilation also, Indian immigrants do not perform as well as they ought to, the study found. Civic assimilation is a measure of immigrants' formal participation in American society, primarily through naturalization. To some extent, civic assimilation is an even stronger indicator of immigrants' intentions than is cultural assimilation. The choice to become a naturalized citizen, or to serve in the United States military, shows a tangible dedication to this country, the report said. In terms of such civic assimilation, Vietnam tops the list with Philippines, Korea and Cuba following in that order; India is well down the list, bettering only countries like Mexico and El Salvador.

On the question of why immigrants from some nations show faster assimilation than others, Bridget pointed out that "Cultural factors, including language and intermarriage, are the most important governing factors. Immigrants from both India and China are well integrated into the American economy, and have civic assimilation scores at or above the overall average. Cultural assimilation for both groups is below the average for all immigrants," she said. Religion was not included directly in the study. "Indirectly, though, pressure to marry within one's own religious group, coupled with the fact that Hindus form a small share of the native-born population, could explain the low intermarriage rates that lead to the low cultural assimilation index value.

"In general, cultural assimilation takes longer than either civic or economic assimilation. Those who immigrate as adults may have the greatest difficulty in learning a new language, and may already be married when they arrive in the United States. The children of these immigrants, however, will likely bear a much stronger resemblance to the native-born. Throughout the twentieth century, the children of immigrants to the US have been very difficult to distinguish from the native-born," she said."This report neither proposes nor endorses any policy responses. Its sole purpose is to present information in a manner useful to concerned citizen and policy makers who hope to make informed decisions," Professor Vigdor wrote. Fig. 5

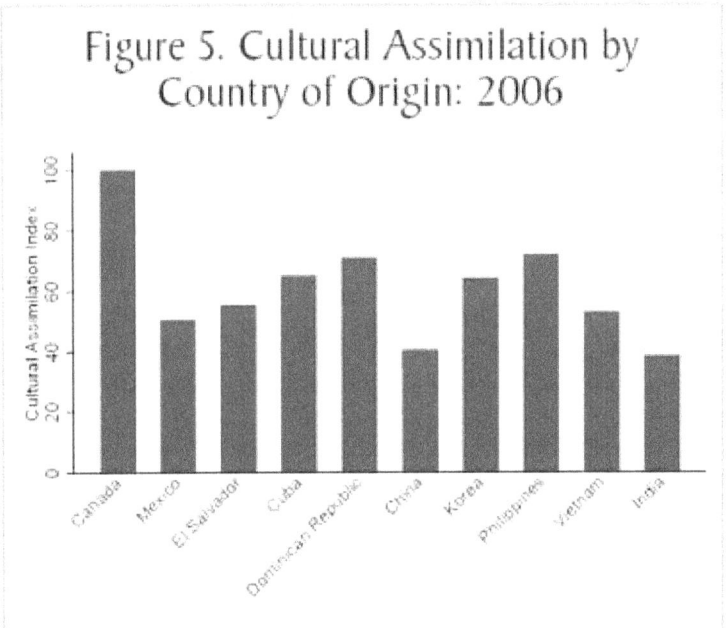

Figure 5. Cultural Assimilation by Country of Origin: 2006

Source: A Report on Global Assimilation

**Theoretical Models of Assimilation**

Assessing present levels of assimilation among today's immigrant groups requires considering the possibility that the process itself may be changing. To ascertain this, we must first understand three major theories of immigrant and ethnic-group integration. The theories are the classic and new assimilation models, the racial/ethnic disadvantage model, and the segmented assimilation model.

*Classic and new assimilation models*

The notion of the United States as a melting pot has been part of public consciousness for a century or more. In 1908, Israel Zangwill's play of that name captivated Broadway. The sociological paradigm that has constituted the most prominent perspective on immigrant group mobility is classic assimilation theory, which dates to the Chicago School in the 1920s. More recently it has been represented in the work of sociologists like Milton Gordon, Richard Alba, and Victor Nee.

In general, classic assimilation theory sees immigrant/ethnic and majority groups following a "straight-line" convergence, becoming more similar over time in norms, values, behaviors, and characteristics. This theory expects those immigrants residing the longest in the host society, as well as the members of later generations, to show greater similarities with the majority group than immigrants who have spent less time in the host society.

Early versions of the theory have been criticized as "Anglo-conformist" because immigrant groups were depicted as conforming to unchanging, middle-class, white Protestant values.

In 1964, Gordon postulated several stages that follow the acquisition of culture and language. First comes structural assimilation (close social relations with the host society), followed by large-scale intermarriage; ethnic identification with the host society; and the ending of prejudice, discrimination, and value conflict.

In what they call "new assimilation theory," Alba and Nee refined Gordon's account by arguing that certain institutions, including those bolstered by civil rights law, play important roles in achieving assimilation. They give the example of Jewish organizations that persuaded the New York City Council in 1946 to threaten the tax-exempt status of colleges or universities that discriminated on the basis of race or religion.

More so than in earlier versions of this theory, Alba and Nee stress that the incorporation of immigrant groups also involves change and acceptance by the mainstream population. Classic assimilation theory as a whole works best, however, when the mainstream is easily defined. While Alba and Nee acknowledge that assimilation takes place within racially and economically heterogeneous contexts, this has led to the criticism that they are trying to define assimilation so broadly that the concept loses meaning.

## *The racial/ethnic disadvantage model*

Other scholars argue that the assimilation of many immigrant groups often remains blocked. This stream of thought, called the racial/ethnic disadvantage point of view, is reflected in the writings of Nathan Glazer, Patrick Moynihan, and Alejandro Portes and his colleagues.

To be sure, some of these writers emphasize racial and ethnic pluralism as much or more than they do ethnic disadvantage. For example, Glazer and Moynihan's *Beyond the Melting Pot*, published in 1963 before the most recent wave of immigration, argues that ethnicity can constitute a resource as well as a burden for achieving economic mobility.

But in general, this literature, especially its more recent versions, argues that language and cultural familiarity may often not lead to increased assimilation. Lingering discrimination and institutional barriers to employment and other opportunities block complete assimilation.

Because immigrants compare socioeconomic opportunities in the host country to those in their countries of origin, they may not perceive these barriers. However, by the second or third generations, they may realize that the goal of full assimilation may be more difficult and take longer than originally presumed.

This realization can have social and cultural consequences, including sometimes the re-emergence (or simply emergence) of racial/ethnic consciousness.

Critiques of this model suggest that it overstresses racial/ethnic barriers and fails to adequately explain evidence of socioeconomic mobility.

## The segmented assimilation model

Yet assimilation does appear to elude some immigrants' descendants, even as late as the third generation. However, uneven patterns of convergence do not necessarily indicate lack of assimilation, but rather may reflect a "bumpy" rather than "straight-line" course, as sociologist Herbert J. Gans described the process in 1992.

Others have noted that just as some members of immigrant groups become cut off from economic mobility, others find multiple pathways to assimilation depending on their national origins, socioeconomic status, contexts of reception, and family resources, both social and financial (ibid).

As a result, the assimilation experiences of recent immigrants are more variegated and diverse than the scenarios provided by the classic assimilation and the ethnic disadvantage models. In 1993, Portes and Min Zhou combined elements of both the straight-line assimilation and the ethnic disadvantage perspectives into a framework they call segmented assimilation.

They theorize that structural barriers, such as poor urban schools, cut off access to employment and other opportunities _ obstacles that often are particularly severe in the case of the most disadvantaged members of immigrant groups. Such impediments can lead to stagnant or downward mobility, even as the children of other immigrants follow divergent paths toward classic straight-line assimilation.

Heavily disadvantaged children of immigrants may even reject assimilation altogether and embrace attitudes, orientations, and behaviors considered "oppositional" in nature, such as joining a street gang. More advantaged groups may sometimes embrace traditional home-country attitudes and use them to inspire their children to achieve, a process Portes and Zhou call selective acculturation.

Consequently, segmented assimilation focuses on identifying the contextual, structural, and cultural factors that separate successful assimilation from unsuccessful or even "negative" assimilation.

Portes, Zhou, and their colleagues argue it is particularly important to identify such factors in the case of the second generation, because obstacles facing the children of immigrants can thwart assimilation at perhaps its most critical juncture.

Thus, while many children of immigrants will find pathways to mainstream status, others will find such pathways blocked, particularly as a consequence of racialization. Portes, Patricia Fernández-Kelly, and William Haller argue: Children of Asian, black, mulatto, and mestizo immigrants cannot escape their ethnicity and race, as defined by the mainstream. Their enduring physical differences from whites and the equally persistent strong effects of discrimination based on those differences, throw a barrier in the path of occupational mobility and social acceptance. Immigrant children's identities, their aspirations, and their academic performance are affected accordingly.

Critics of this model argue that the perspective may erroneously attribute poor economic outcomes primarily to racialization when they may actually stem from other constraints like family financial obligations or factors such as lackluster job growth that slow the rate of mobility.

They also point out that since the model has not been empirically tested beyond the current second generation (the members of which are still very young), segmented assimilation may misinterpret oppositional attitudes historically found among the young and misconstruct the pace of assimilation.

## A Model of Contingent Identificational Assimilation

As Bean, Stevens, and Wierzbicki note, this interaction suggests that the relationship between socio-cultural and economic aspects of incorporation is changing from the sequential for implied in the classic assimilation model toward a form involving multiple contingencies and dynamic interplays. Racial and ethnic identification occurs at several levels: reactive (becoming more racially/ethnic as a result of experiencing discrimination); symbolic (becoming more prominently but superficially racially/ethnic as a result of achieving success); or selective (becoming more strongly racially/ethnic in some ways more than others to facilitate economic achievement).

Among those of lower social class, reactive identification is most likely to arise from the repeated experience of discrimination and may also contribute to the hardening of oppositional attitudes and the incurrence of downward assimilation. This interaction of social class and identification suggests that racial/ethnic identification is most intense among those in the lowest social classes. Selective assimilation tends to develop among those with better resources and socio-economic prospects. Their frequent higher levels of education make them more opportunistic than oppositional with respect to economic incorporation, and they usually belong to ethnic networks and institutions with enough resources to offer support unavailable outside the ethnic community. In their case, dense ethnic social ties trump weaker interethnic ties, with the result that they often tend to choose ethnic identities more than a majority group identity.

## REFERENCES

Alba, Richard. (1988). *Cohorts and the Dynamics of Ethnic Change.* In M. W. Riley; B. Huber and B. Hess (Eds.), *Social Structures and Human Lives.* Newbury Park, CA: Sage.

Alba, Richard D. (1990). *Ethnic Identity: The Transformation of White America.* New Haven, CT: Yale University Press.

Alba, Richard. (1995). Assimilation's quiet tide. *Public Interest,* No. 119, pp. 3–18.

Alba, R. & Nee, Victor. (2000). Rethinking assimilation theory for a new era of immigration. *International Migration Review*, 31, 826-874.

Alba, Richard D. and Victor, Nee. (2003). *Remaking the American Mainstream: Assimilation and the New Immigration.* Cambridge, MA: Harvard University Press.

Alba Richard. (2005). Bright vs. blurred boundaries: Second generation assimilation and exclusion in France, Germany, and the United States. *Ethnic and Racial Studies*, Volume 28, Issue 1.

Alba, Richard; Roxane, Silberman & Irène, Fournier. (2007). Segmented assimilation in France? Discrimination in the labour market against the second generation. *Ethnic and Racial Studies*, Vol 30, Issue 1.

Abercrombie, Nicholas; Hill, Stephen and Turner, S. Bryan. (2000). *The Penguin Dictionary of Sociology.* London: Penguin.

Arias, E. (1998). *The Demography of Assimilation: The Care of Cubans in the United States.* Doctoral Dissertation. Department of Sociology, University of Wisconsin-Madison.

Banton, Michael. (1959). *White and Coloured: The Behaviour of British People toward Coloured Immigrants.* New Brunswick, N.J: Rutgers Univ. Press.

Barkan, Elliot, R. (1995). Race, religion and nationality in American society: A model of ethnicity – from contact to assimilation. *Journal of American Ethnic History,* Vol.14, no. 2, pp. 38–101.

Bauman, Zygmunt. (1988). Entry tickets and exit visas: paradoxes of Jewish assimilation. *Telos,* Vol. 77, pp. 45–77.

Beals, Ralph, L. and Harry, Hoijer. (1953). *An Introduction to Anthropology.* New York: Macmillan.

Bean, Frank, D; and Gillian, Stevens. (2003). *America's Newcomers: Immigrant*

*Incorporation and the Dynamics of Diversity*. New York: Russell Sage Foundation.

Berkson, Isaac. (1920). *Theories of Americanization: A Critical Study with Special Reference to the Jewish Group*. New York.

Berry, Brewton. (1951). *Race Relations*. Boston: Houghton Mifflin.

Berry, J. W; Kim, U; Minde, T; & Mok, D. (1987). Comparative studies of acculturative stress. *International Migration Review*, 21. 491-51.

Berry, John, W. (1997). Immigration, Acculturation, and Adaptation. *Applied Psychology*, Vol. 46, Issue 1, pages 5–34, January 1997.

Berry, John, W. (2005). *Acculturation: Living successfully in two cultures*. Canada: Queen's University.

Bierstadt, Edward, Hale. (1922). *Aspects of Americanization*. Cincinnati: Stewart Kidd.

Boas, Franz. (1888). *The Aims of Ethnology*. London: Allen and Unwin.

Boas, Franz (1948). *Race, Language and Culture*. New York: Macmillan.

Bossard, James, H. S. (1939). Nationality and Nativity as Factors in Marriage. *American Sociological Review*, Vol. 4, No. 6 (Dec., 1939), pp. 792-798.

Brandon, Peter, D. (2004). The Child Care Arrangements of Preschool-Age Children. In, Immigrant Families in the United States. *International Migration*, Vol. 42 (1).

Briggs, X. (1998). Brown kids in white suburbs: Housing mobility and the many faces of social capital. *Housing Policy Debate*, Vol. 9, pp. 177-221.

Carpenter, Niles. (1927). Immigrants and Their Children: A Study Based on Census Statistics Relative to the Foreign-Born and the Native White of Foreign or Mixed Parentage. *Census Monography*, Vol. VI. Washington.

Cheong, Yong, Hun. (Ed.). (1992). *Asian Tradition and Modernization: Singapore*. Times Academic Press, for the Center for Advanced Studies, National University of Singapore.

Cheung, Gordon, C. K. (2004). Chinese Diaspora as Virtual Nation: Interactive Roles between Economic and Social Capital. *Political Studies*, 52(4), pp. 664–684.

Collins, Randall. (1968). *A comparative approach to political sociology*. In, Reinhard Bendix et al. (Eds.). *State and Society*. Boston: Little Brown.

Collins, Sydney. (1955). The British-born Coloured. *Sociological Review*. New Series 3: 777.

Comas, J. (1961). "Scientific" racism again? *Current Anthropology*, 2 (4): 3010-3340.

Constant, A.F; Zimmermann K.F. (2008) Measuring ethnic identity and its impact on economic behavior. *Journal of European Economic Association*, 6(2–3):424–433.

Constant, Amelie, F; Klaus, F. Zimmermann. (2008). Measuring ethnic identity and its impact on economic behavior. *Journal of the European*

*Economic Association*, Vol 6, Issue 2-3, pages 424–433, April-May 2008.

Crèvecoeur, Hector, St. John, de. (1782). *Letters From an American Farmer.* Dent: Everyman's Library.

Devereux and Lock. (1943). In, Rudmin, Floyd W. Critical history of the acculturation psychology of assimilation, separation, integration, and marginalization. *Review of General Psychology*, Vol 7(1), Mar 2003, 3-37.

Drachsler, Julius. (1921). *Intermarriage in New York City.* New York: Colombia University Press.

Espenshade, T. and Fu, H. (1997). An Analysis of English-Language Proficiency among U.S. Immigrants. *American Sociological Review.* 62:288-305.

Essien-Udom, E. U. (1962). *Black Nationalism: A Search for an Identity in America.* University of Chicago Press.

Fairchild, H. P. (1925). *Immigration: A World Movement and its American Significance.* New York: Macmillan.

Farley, Reynolds and Alba, Richard. (2002). The new second generation in the United States. *International Migration Review*, Vol. 36, pp. 669_701.

Fishman, J. A. (Ed.). (1972). *Readings in the sociology of language.* New York: Mouton Publishers.

Furnham, A. & Bochner, S. (1986). *Culture shock: Psychological reactions to unfamiliar environment.* London: Methuen.

Gans, J. Herbert. (1992). Ethnic Invention and Acculturation: A Bumpy-Line Approach. *Journal of American Ethnic History,* 11:42-52.

Glazer, N; Moynihan. (1963). *Beyond the melting pot: the Negroes, Puerto Ricans, Jews, Italians and Irish of New York City.* Cambridge: MIT.

Glazer, N. (1993). Is Assimilation Dead? *The Annals of the American Academy of Social and Political Sciences*, 530:122-136.

Goldhagen, Erich. (1960) The glorious future – Realities and Chimeras. *Problems of Communism,* 90, No. 6, p. 7.

Gordon, Milton, M. (1964). *Assimilation in American Life: The Role of Race, Religion, and National Origins.* New York: Oxford University Press.

Hector, St. Jeans. (1904). *Letters from an American Farmer.* New York.

Hernandez, D.J and Drake, K. (1999). *Socioeconomic and demographic risk factors and resources among children in immigrant and native-born families: 1910, 1960, and 1990.* In Hernandez, D.J. (Ed.). *Children of Immigrants: Health, Adjustment, and Public Assistance.* Washington, DC: National Academy Press.

Herskovits, Melville, J. (1962). *The Human Factor in Changing Africa.* New York: Knopf.

Hirschman, Charles. (1983). America's melting pot reconsidered. *Annual Review of Sociology,* Vol. 9, pp. 397–423.

Hugill, Peter, J. & Kenneth, E. Foote. (1994). *Re-reading cultural geography.* Austin: University of Texas.

Hurd, Burton, W. (1929). *Origin, Birthplace, Nationality and Language of the Canadian People.* 1921 Census Monography, Dominion Bureau of Statistics.

Ottawa: King's Printer.

Jiobu, Robert, M. (1988). *Ethnicity and Assimilation*. Albany: State University of New York Press.

Kim, Young, Yun. (1979). *Toward an interactive theory of communication-acculturation*. In B. Ruben. (Ed.). *Communication Yearbook*. 3, 435-453.

Kivisto, Peter. (2004). What is the Canonical Theory of Assimilation? *Journal of the History of the Behavioral Sciences*, 149-163.

Kottak, Conrad, Phillip. (2007). *Windows on Humanity*. McGraw Hill: New York.

Kroeber, Alfred L. (1940). Stimulus diffusion. *American Anthropologist*, 42 (1).

Kuklick, H. (19960. Functionalism. In A. Barnard and J. Spencer (Eds.). *Encyclopedia of Social and Cultural Anthropology*, pp. 246-51. London: Routledge.

Laitin, David. (1995). Marginality: a micro perspective. *Rationality and Society*, Vol. 7, no. 1, pp. 31–57.

Lieberson S.; Waters M.C. (1990). *From many strands: ethnic and racial groups in contemporary America*. New York: Russell Sage Foundation.

Lincoln, Charles Eric (1961). *The Black Muslims in America*. Boston: Beacon.

Lopez, David, E. (1996). *Language: Diversity and Assimilation*. In, R. Waldinger and M. Bozorgmehr, (Eds.). *Ethnic Los Angeles*. New York: Russell Sage Foundation.

Marcson, Simon. (1950). A Theory of Intermarriage and Assimilation. *Social Forces*, 29:75-8.

Matute, Bianchi, M. E. (1991). *Situational Ethnicity and Patterns of School Performance Among Immigrant and Non-Immigrant Mexican-Descent Students*. In M. Gibson, and J. U. Ogbu (Eds.), *Minority Status and Schooling: A Comparative Study of Immigrant and Involuntary Minorities*. New York: Garland.

McGee, W. J. (1898). Practical acculturation. *American Anthropologist*, 11, 243–249.

Morawska, E. (1994). In Defense of the Assimilation Model. *Journal of American Ethnic History*, 13(2):76-87.

Nee, Victor and Ingram, Paul. (1998). *Embeddedness and beyond: Institutions, exchange, and social structure*. In, Mary Brinton and Victor, Nee (Eds.). *The New Institutionalism in Sociology*. New York: Russell Sage Foundation.

Nelson, Lowry. (1943). Intermarriage among Nationality Groups in a Rural Area of Minnesota. *American Journal of Sociology, 48*:585-92.

Nicholas, Abercrombie; Stephen Hill; Bryan S. Turner. (2000). *The Penguin dictionary of Sociology*. Penguin Books.

Park, R. E. (1926/1950). *Race and Culture*. The Free Press: USA.

Park, Robert, E. (1930). *Assimilation, Social*. Encyclopedia of the Social Sciences. New York: Macmillan.

Park, R. E. (1928). Human Migration and the Marginal Man. *American Journal of Sociology*, 33(6):881-893.

Perlmann, J. and R. Waldinger. (1997). Second Generation Decline? Children of Immigrants, Past and Present - A Reconsideration. *International Migration Review*, 31(4).

Phinney, Jean, S. (1990). Ethnic Identity in Adolescents and Adults: Review of Research. *Psychological Bulletin*, 108 (November): 499-514.

Portes, Alejandro and Hao, Lingxin (1998). E Pluribus Unum: Bilingualism and Loss of Language in the Second Generation. *Sociology of Education*, 71: 269-294.

Portes, Alejandro and Min, Zhou. (1993). The New Second Generation: Segmented Assimilation and Its Variants. *The Annals of the American Academy of Political and Social Science*, 530: 74-80.

Portes, A. and R. G. Rumbaut. (1996). *Immigrant America: A Portrait*. (2nd ed.). Berkeley and Los Angeles: University of California Press.

Portes, Alejandro, and Rubén, Rumbaut. (2001). *Legacies: The Story of the Immigrant Second Generation*. Berkeley: University of California Press.

Portes, Alejandro and Schauffler, Richard. (1994). Language and the second generation: Bilingualism yesterday and today. *International Migration Review*, Vol. 28, no. 4, pp. 640–61.

Price, C. A. and J. Zubrzycki. (1962). The Use of Inter-Marriage Statistics as an Index of Assimilation. *Population Studies*, 16(1): 58-69.

Qian, Zhenchao and Daniel, Lichter. (2001). Measuring Marital Assimilation: Intermarriage Among Natives and Immigrants. *Social Science Research*, 30: 289-312.

John H. Rohrer and Munro, Edmonson. (Eds.) (1960). *The Eighth Generation: Cultures and Personalities of New Orleans Negroes*. New York: Harper & Brothers.

Redfield, Robert; Linton, Ralph; Herskovits, Melville, J. (1936). Memorandum for the study of Acculturation. *American Anthropologist*, Vol. 38, Issue 1, pages 149–152, January-March 1936.

Rogers, Brubaker. (2001). *The Return of Assimilation? Changing Perspectives on Immigration and its Sequels in France, Germany, and the United States*. Los Angeles: University of California.

Rudmin, Floyd. (1990). Constructs, measurements and models of acculturation and acculturative stress. *Critical Acculturation Psychology*, Volume 33, Issue 2, March 2009, Pages 106–123.

Rumbaut, R. G. (1997). *Ties that bind: immigration and immigrant families in the United States*. In, A. Booth et al. (Eds.). *Immigration and the Family: Research and Policy on US Immigrants*. New Jersey: Lawrence Erlbaum Associates, Inc.

Rumbaut, R.G and Portes, A. (Eds.). *Ethnicities: Children of Immigrants in America*. Berkeley: University of California Press.

Schmittet, Heisler, B. (2000). *The Sociology of Immigration*. In C. Brettel and J. Hollifield (Eds.). *Migration Theory: Talking across Disciplines*. New York: Routledge.

Senior, Clarence and Reuben, Hill. (1957). Research on the Puerto Rican Family in the United States. *Marriage and Family Living*, Vol. 19, No. 1.

Stevens, G. (1985). Nativity, Intermarriage, and Mother-tongue Shift. *American Sociological Review*, 50:74-83.

Stevens, G. & Swicewood. (1987). The linguistic context of endogamy. *American Sociological Review*, Vol 52, No. 1, Feb; 1987.

Stevens, G. (1992). The Social and Demographic Context of Language Use in the United States. *American Sociological Review*, 57:171-185.

Suarez-Orozco, C. (1991). *Transformations: Migration, Family life, and Achievement Motivation among latino Adolescents*. Stanford, CA: Stanford University Press.

Takaki, Ronald. (1993). *A Different Mirror: A history of Multicultural America*. London: Little Brown and Company.

Thomas, William, Isaac; Znaniecki, Florian; Zaretsky, Eli. (1996). *The Polish peasant in Europe and America: a classic work in immigration history*. University of Illinois Press.

Thurnwald, R. (1932). The psychology of acculturation. *American Anthropologist*, 34, 557–569.

Tipple, G. (1991). *Self help transformations of low cost housing: an introductory study*. Newcastle: Cardo.

Vasquez, A. (1984). Les implications ideologiques du concept d'acculturation. *Cahiers de Sociologie Economique et Culturelle*, I. 83-121.

Veltman, C. (1988). Modelling the Language Shift Process of Hispanic Immigrants. *International Migration Review*, 22 (4): 545-562.

Warner, L; Srole, L. (1945). *The Social Systems of American Ethnic Groups*. Yale University Press: New Haven USA.

Waters, M. and Lieberson, S. (1988). *From Many Strands: Ethnic and Racial Groups in Contemporary America*. New York: Russell Sage Foundation.

Waters, Mary. (1999). *Black Identities: West Indian Immigrant Dreams and American Realities*. Cambridge, MA: Harvard University Press.

Yinger, J. Milton. (1981). Toward a theory of assimilation and dissimilation. *Ethnic and Racial Studies*, Vol. 4, no. 3, pp. 249–64.

Waggoner, D. (1988). *The under-education of American youth*. San Antonio, TX: Intercultural Development Research Association.

Waggoner, Dorothy. (1991). *Under-education in America: The Demography of High School Dropouts*. Westport, CT: Auburn House.

Wagley and Harris. (1958). *Minorities in the new world*. New York University press.

Williams, Robin, M. Jr. (1964). *Strangers Next Door: Ethnic Relations in American Communities*. Englewood Cliffs: Prentice-Hall.

Wilson, Byron. (2008). *Heritage and Legacy*. New York: Palgrave Macmillan.

Wilson, James, Q. (1960). *Negro Politics: The Search for Leadership. New* York:

Free Press.

Wilson, Kelda, M. and Byron, Loosle. (2000). In Dutch John, Excavations: Seasonal Occupations on the North Slope of the Uinta Mountains. *Heritage Report*, 1-01/2000. 16, 2.

Winthrop, R. H. (1991). *Dictionary of Concepts in Cultural Anthropology*. New York: Greenwood.

Wu, David, Yen-ho. (1991). The Construction of Chinese and Non-Chinese. *Identities Daedalus*, vol.120, No.2, Spring 1991, pp.159-179.

Yu, E. E; Phillips, E. & Yang, E. (Eds.). (1981). *Koreans in Los Angeles*. Los Angeles: Koryo Research Institute.

Zangwill, I. (1909). *The Melting Pot*. New York: MacMillan.

Zangwill, Israel. (1925). *The Melting Pot. (Vol-XII): The Works of Israel Zangwill*. London: The Globe Publishing Co.

Zubrzycki, J. (1962). *Settlers of the Latrobe Valley*. The Australian National University: Canberra.

# CHAPTER-III

# PAKHTOONS: SOCIETY, TRADITIONS AND ASSIMILATION

# CHAPTER-III

# PAKHTOONS: SOCIETY, TRADITIONS AND ASSIMILATION

This chapter deals with those cultural aspects of Pakhtoon society which are linked with their tradition and have met assimilation. The main focus of this chapter has been to bring into limelight the nature and degree of assimilation of the cultural elements of the Pakhtoon society and the overall impacts of the process on the ethnicity of Pakhtoons in Kashmir. The scope of this chapter is confined mainly to the micro structures and institutions of Pakhtoon culture and society. The micro-individual structures of society are everyday customs and types of lifestyles which sustain the core of ethnic identity. They are renegotiated daily and are strongly influenced by the interpersonal interactions across boundaries which reinforce ethnic identity. At the micro level the food people eat, an individual's dress, language, familial hierarchy, age, sex and many other factors become central markers of identity (Barth, 1969; Fenton, 1999). At the micro-scale people modify their identity in relationship to the histories, geographies and social interactions of their everyday life. One implication of this is that ethnic mobility and ethno genesis have intrinsic connections. Identity creation for the individual is a continuous process, so ethno genesis at the individual psychological level can never be complete. As these identities evolve with changing environmental stimuli, an individual may choose to adopt a different set of existing descriptors to better encapsulate what is seen as the core set of identities, resulting in ethnic mobility.

In case of Pakhtoons of Kashmir Valley, that set of descriptors comprise almost all the elements of Kashmiri culture which were immediately available to the former ethnic group for adoption and absorption to their ethnic identity. During this blending process of the internal local culture of Pakhtoons and the external dominant Kashmiri culture, there was no obstacle left for the assimilation of Pakhtoon ethnicity. In some cases, these changes of identity may require adoption of a new descriptor as none of the existing descriptors sit comfortably with the individual. Should a significant number of people find resonance in the same or a similar descriptor; this can lead to the creation of a new ethnicity with general social acceptance as a valid ethnic group (Wimmer, 2008a; 2008b). At the macro-scale, this process links directly with questions of otherness, power and authority, and how these relate to the legitimation of identity.

The social process of creating ethnicity draws on contextual information from the historical, social and political environment. People when thinking about their identity may invoke spiritual beliefs and ancestral connections over material symbols, for instance, or when labeling others consider dress over food (Bonilla, 2005). The scale at which these influences operate differs and offers one way of systematizing thinking about ethnicity.

## The People

Let us first discuss the origin of the names Pathan and Afghan and their link with the terms Pashtun and Pakhtoon. The term Pakhtun or Pashtun, according to Raverty (1878), is derived from the Persian word 'Pusht' meaning 'back'. Since the tribes lived on the back of the mountains, Persians called them Pashtun which is also pronounced Pakhtoon. Some scholars think that the word Pashtun or Pakhtoon comes from the Old Iranian word *parsava*, parsa meaning robust men or knights. In Indian languages it was spelt as *Pakhtana* or Pathan. Herodotus and several other Greek and Roman historians have mentioned a people called *'Paktye'* living on the eastern frontier of Iran. By the word *Paktye* they meant the people of the frontier. According to the Encyclopaedia of Islam the word *Pathan* is from the Sanskrit word *Pratisthana* (Ghani, 2008). Pashtun (also spelled Pushtun, Pakhtoon, Pashtoon, Pathan) are a people who live predominantly in southeastern Afghanistan and the northwestern province of Pakistan. They are one of the largest ethnic groups in the world. There is no true written history of the Pakhtoons in their own land. Pashtun are traditionally pastoral nomads (herders who move frequently to find grazing land) with a strong tribal organization. Each tribe is divided into clans, sub clans, and patriarchal families. The Pakhtoons are typically characterized by their usage of the *Pashto* language and practice of *Pashtunwali*, which is a traditional set of ethics guiding individual and communal conduct. Their origins are unclear but historians have come across references to various ancient peoples called *Paktha* (*Pactyans*) between the 2nd and the 1st millennia who inhabited the region between the Hindu Kush and Indus River and may be the early ancestors of Pashtuns (Nath, 2002).

The Pashtuns are the world's largest (patriarchal) segmentary lineage ethnic group. According to *Ethnologue*, the total population of the group is estimated to be around 50 million but an accurate count remains elusive due to the lack of an official census in Afghanistan since 1979. Estimates of the number of Pashtun tribes and clans range from about 350 to over 400. The vast majority of Pashtuns are found in the traditional Pashtun homeland, located in an area south of the Oxus River in Afghanistan and west of the Indus River in Pakistan, which includes Khyber-Pakhtunkhwa, Federally Administered Tribal Areas (FATA) and part of Balochistan. Additional Pashtun communities are located in western and northern Afghanistan, the Gilgit–Baltistan and Kashmir regions and northern Punjab province of Pakistan, as well as in the Khorasan province of Iran. There are also sizeable Muslim communities in India, which are of largely Pashtun ancestry. Throughout the Indian subcontinent, excluding Pashtun-dominated regions, they are often referred to as *Pathans*. Smaller Pakhtoon communities are found in the countries of the Arabian Peninsula, Europe, London and the Americas, particularly in North America (Smith, 2003).

In spite of being a minority ethnic group here, Pakhtoons of Anantnag are one the largest tribal groups. Other tribal groups include Gujjars, Bakkerwals and *Bemi* who dwell in some particular areas of the district like Andu and Gopalpora, and are migrants from Pakistan and speak Pahadi and Punjabi languages. The main difference, however, is that Pakhtoons unlike the other ethnic groups have assimilated faster and have ever since the last 100 years shown increasing accommodation trends with the local dominant cultural group, the Kashmiris.

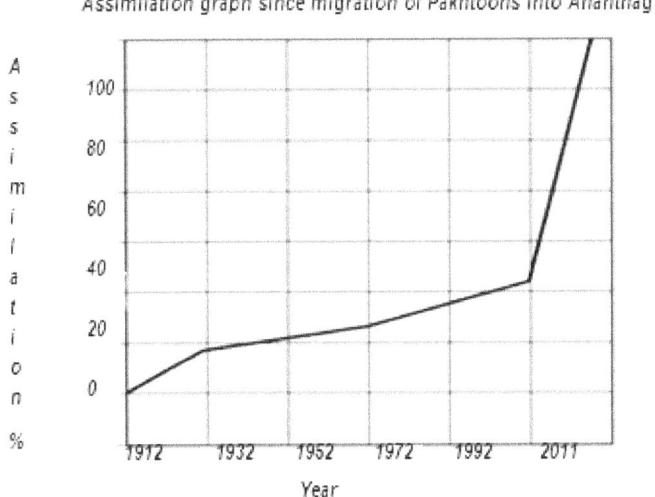

Assimilation graph since migration of Pakhtoons into Anantnag.

**Source: Field based data.**

As mentioned in the earlier chapters Pakhtoons migrated about a century before and that is about in 1912 which has been taken as the time period where there was negligible cultural assimilation. Gradually their assimilation kept on increasing and has reached to its apex by 2012 with there being almost no difference between Pakhtoons and Kashmiris in Anantnag. As shown in the graph above, the assimilation has intensified since the last two decades under the impacts of modernization paving way to education, frequent communication and mixing of cultures.

## Ethnic Definition

The ethno-linguistic definition is the most prominent and accepted view as to who is and is not a Pakhtoon. Generally, this most common view holds that Pakhtoons are defined within the parameters of having mainly eastern

Iranian ethnic origins, sharing a common language, culture and history, living in relatively close geographic proximity to each other, and acknowledging each other as kinsmen. Thus, tribes that speak disparate yet mutually intelligible dialects of *Pashto* acknowledge each other as ethnic Pakhtoons and even subscribe to certain dialects as "proper", such as the *Pukhto* spoken by the Yousafzai in Peshawar and the *Pashto* spoken by the Durrani in Kandahar. These criteria tend to be used by most Pakhtoons in Pakistan and Afghanistan[2] (Ali, 1995).

## Tribes

The famous Pakhtoon tribes, to mention a few, are Yousafzais of Bajaur and Malakand Agencies, Afridis of Khyber Agency, Kohat and Peshawar, Mohmands of Mohmand Agency, Orakzais of Orakzai Agency, Turis and Bangash of Kurram Agency, Waziris of North Waziristan Agency, Mahsuds and Urmars of South Waziristan Agency, and Bhittanis and Sheranis attached to Tank and D.I. Khan Districts. The Khattak tribe of the well known warrior-poet Khushal Khan Khattak is also one of the well known tribes of Peshawar and Kohat border. There are other smaller tribe such as Shinwaris, Mullagoris, Shilmanis, Safis, Zaimukht, Muqbil, Mangal, Zadran, Para Chamkani, Kharoti, Jadoon and Daur etc. (ibid).

The diagram below shows the ancestral links as well as the overall tribal divisions and sub-divisions of the Pakhtoon society residing not only in Afghanistan but have spread to almost all countries of the world particularly London, Britain, USA, India, UAE and France.

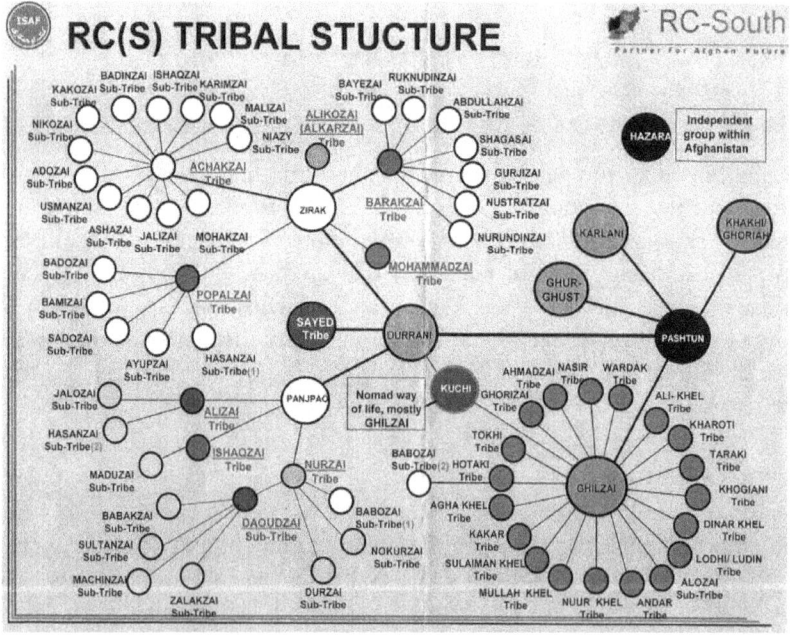

Clearly such tribal divisions of the Pakhtoons in Afghanistan and Pakistan are a clue that they are retaining their cultural-traditional status in these countries. The absence of such differentiation among the Pakhtoons of the valley in particular and in Anantnag in general is a matter of concern in that majority of them simply ascribe themselves to be a Pathan with no such clear demarcation as belonging to any particular tribe. Majority of the Pakhtoons of Anantnag are not sure about their ethnic/tribal origin. Most of them 80 % who could say something about their ancestral lineage told that they belong to the *Khankhel* sub-tribe. Clear tribal divisions are, however, prevalent among Pakhtoons of Gutlibagh in Srinagar.

## Ancestral definition

The patrilineal definition as believed by Pakhtoons almost in every part of the world is based on an important orthodox law of *Pakhtunwali* which mainly requires that only those who have a Pashtun father are Pashtun. This law has maintained the tradition of exclusively patriarchal tribal lineage. This definition places less emphasis on what language one speaks, such as Pashto, Persian, Hindko, Urdu or English. There are various communities who claim Pashtun origin but are largely found among other ethnic groups in the south and central Asian region who generally do not speak the Pashto language. These communities are often considered overlapping groups or are simply assigned to the ethno-linguistic group that corresponds to their geographic location and mother tongue. They include some who usually speak Dari (Persian), Urdu, Hindi and English rather than Pashto. Claimants of Pashtun heritage in South Asia have mixed with local Muslim populations and are referred to as Pathan, the Hindi-Urdu variant of *Pashtun*. These communities are usually partial Pashtun, to varying degrees, and often trace their Pashtun ancestry through a paternal lineage. The Pathans in India have lost both the language and presumably many of the ways of their ancestors, but trace their fathers' ethnic heritage to the Pashtun tribes (Tyagi, 2009).

### Theories on Pakhtoon Ethnology

Different hypotheses have been suggested about the origin of the Pakhtoons. Khawaja Niamatullah describes them as descendants of Jews, connecting them with the lost ten tribes of Israel. This theory of the Semitic origin of the Pakhtoons has been supported by some Pakhtoon writers, including Hafiz Rahmat Khan, Afzal Khan Khattak and Qazi Attaullah Khan.

A number of orientalists like H.W. Bellew, Sir William Jones and Major

Raverty have also subscribed to this view on the basis of Pukhtoon physiognomy, and the striking resemblance of facial features between Pakhtoons and Jews. They believe that the prevalence of biblical names, certain customs and superstitions, especially smearing of the door post and walls of the house with blood of sacrificial animals, further substantiates this theory. But these presumptions do not hold good in view of the fact that resemblance in features and certain characteristics do not provide a scientific criterion for the ethnology of a race or a section of people.

This can equally be said about the Kashmiris and certain other tribes who can hardly be distinguished from Pakhtoons in physique, color and complexion. Similarly a scrutiny of the social institutions of the Arabs of the middle ages and present day Pakhtoons would lead one to believe that Pakhtoons are not different from them in their social organization (Burns, 1835).

Syed Bahadur Shah Zafar Kaka Khel in his well written book *Pukhtana* (1981) and Sir Olaf Caroe in his book *The Pathans* (1958) place little reliance on Niamatullah's theory of the Semitic origin of the Pakhtoons and say that his account of the Pakhtoons suffers from historical inaccuracies. To disprove the assertion that the Pakhtoon tribes had embraced Islam after the return of Qais Abdul Rashid from Medina, the accounts of Al-Beruni and Al-Utbi, the contemporary historians of Mahmud of Ghazna, establish "that four centuries later than the time of Qais the Province of Kabul had not been Islamized and this was achieved under the Ghaznavies.

The Hindu Shahiya Kingdom extended almost to Kabul. Mahmud had to fight against infidel Afghans of the Sulaiman mountains. Even Prithvi Raj had a cavalry of Afghans in the battle of *Tarian* against Mohammad Ghori in 1191. Other writers, after a careful examination of the physical anthropology of the Pukhtoons say that difference in features of the various Pukhtoons point to the fact that they must have "mingled with races that passed through their territory to conquer Hindustan" (ibid).

Sir Alexander Burnes in his *Travels into Bokhara*, which he published in 1835, speaking of the Afghans said: "The Afghans call themselves Bani Israel, or the children of Israel, but consider the term *Yahoodi*, or Jew, to be one of reproach. The Afghans look like Jews and the younger brother marries the widow of the elder. The Afghans entertain strong prejudices against the Jewish nation, which would at least show that they have no desire to claim – without just cause a descent from them.

William Moorcroft traveled during 1819 to 1825 through various countries adjoining India, including Afghanistan. "The *Khaibarees*, he says, "are tall and have a singularly Jewish cast of features." According to their own tradition they believe themselves to be descendants from the Hebrew. They preserved the purity of their religion until they met with Islam (Frazer, 1843).

Joseph-Pierre Ferrier wrote his History of the Afghans in 1858. It was translated by Capt. W. M. Jesse. He too was disposed to believe that the Afghans represented the Ten Tribes of Israel. In support of his view he recorded, among others, a very significant fact: "When Nadir Shah marching to the conquest of India arrived at Peshawar, the chief of the tribe of *Yoosoof Zyes* (Sons of Joseph) presented him with a Bible written in Hebrew and several other articles that had been used in their ancient worship and which they had preserved. These articles were at once recognized by the Jews who followed the camp. So the presence of Bibles among Afghans shows their Jewish origin."

This is not to assert that the ethnic or linguistic stock can be necessarily traced through to tribes of similar names today. The case would be rather that these were sub-stratum agglomerations of people who, through contact with later-comers, modified their language and were assimilated to later cultures, but retained in the more inaccessible places sufficient of their older selves to boast their original names. The theory does at least give a starting-point to Pathan history and the stock belief in the *Bani Israel* (Caroe, 1958).

We find that the very natural character of Israel reappear in all its life and reality in countries where people call themselves Bani Israel and universally claim to be the descendants of the Lost Tribes. The nomenclature of their tribes and districts, both in ancient Geography, and at the present day, confirms this universal natural tradition.

Lastly, we have the route of the Israelites to Afghanistan and India marked by a series of intermediate stations bearing the names of several of the tribes and clearly indicating the stages of their long and arduous journey. Sir William Jones, Sir John Malcolm and the missing Chamberlain, after full investigation, were of the opinion that the Ten Tribes migrated to India, Tibet, and Cashemire [Kashmir] through Afghanistan (Moore, 1861).

Among more contemporary writers Dr. Alfred Edersheim believed that modern investigations have pointed the Afghans as descendants from the Lost Tribes. There is one important people (of whom there is much more to be said) who call themselves Bani Israel, who claim a descent from Cush and Ham, who have adopted a strange mixture of mosaic law in ordinances in their moral code, who (some sections at least) keep a feast which strongly accords with the Passover; and for whom no one has yet been able to suggest any other origin than the one they claim, and claim with determined force, and these people are the Pakhtoons. Dr. Navras Aafreedi, an Indian historian who did a genetic study on the Afridi clan of Pashtuns in Malihabad Uttar Pradesh, India, said that 650 out of the 1,500 members possess genetic material similar to genetic material found in Jews (Moore, 1861).

On the basis of the proof of the Jewish origin of Pakhtoons as provided by scholars discussed above the ancestral lineage of Pakhtoons is shown below which joins with the present day tribal divisions as found among them.

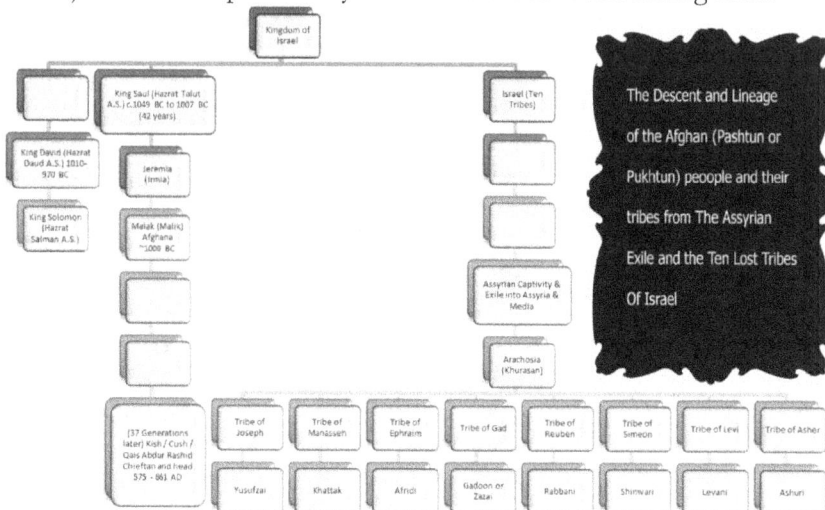

Source: Pakhtoon.org

## Pakhtoons: Clue to Lost Tribes of Israel

Israel is to fund a rare genetic study to determine whether there is a link between the lost tribes of Israel and the Pakhtoons of Afghanistan and northern Pakistan. Historical and anecdotal evidence strongly suggests a connection, but definitive scientific proof has never been found. Some leading Israeli anthropologists believe that, of all the many groups in the world who claim a connection to the 10 lost tribes, the Pakhtoons, or Pathans, have the most compelling case. Pashtuns themselves sometimes talk of their Israelite connection, but show few signs of sympathy with, or any wish to migrate to, the modern Israeli state (McCarthy, 2010).

Now an Indian researcher has collected blood samples from members of the Afridi tribe of Pashtuns who today live in Malihabad, near Lucknow, in northern India. Shahnaz Ali, from the National Institute of Immuno Haematology in Mumbai, is to spend several months studying her findings at Technion, the Israel Institute of Technology, in Haifa. A previous genetic study in the same area did not provide proof one way or the other. The Assyrians conquered the kingdom of Israel some 2,730 years ago, scattering 10 of the 12 tribes into exile, supposedly beyond the mythical Sambation river. The two remaining tribes, Benjamin and Judah, became the modern-day Jewish people, according to Jewish history, and the search for the lost tribes has continued ever since. Some have claimed to have found traces of them in modern day China, Burma, Nigeria, Central Asia, Ethiopia and even in the West. But it is believed that the tribes were dispersed in an area around modern-day northern Iraq and Afghanistan, which makes the Pashtun connection the strongest (ibid). Their tribal groupings have similar names, including Yusufzai, which means sons of Joseph thought to be the most fair looking tribe of the Pakhtoons; and Afridi, thought by some to come from *Ephraim*. Some customs and practices are said to be similar to Jewish traditions: lighting candles on the Sabbath, refraining from eating certain foods, using a canopy during a wedding ceremony and some similarities in garments. Weil cautioned, however, that this is not proof of any genetic connection. DNA might be able to determine which area of the world the Pakhtoons originated from, but it is not at all certain that it could identify a specific genetic link to the Jewish people.

"Pathans, or Pashtuns, are the only people in the world whose probable descent from the lost tribes of Israel finds mention in a number of texts from the 10th century to the present day, written by Jewish, Christian and Muslim scholars alike, both religious as well as secularists," (Aafreedi 2005). The implications of any find are uncertain. Other groups that claim Israelite descent, including those known as the Bnei Menashe in India and some in Ethiopia, have migrated to Israel. That is unlikely with the Pashtuns. But Weil said the work was absorbing, well beyond questions of immigration "I find a myth that has been so persistent for so long, for 2,000 years, really been fascinating" she wrote (ibid).

**Social Life and Other Issues: Myths & Realities**

At the first site, Pakhtoons seem to be less social and a segmented type of people, but after a couple of meetings, they become as social that they will not forget to invite you on the marriage of their youngest son. There are, however, some pre-conceptions and myths about these people, some good and some bad which have proven out to be wrong during the course of the present study. Table 1.1 below shows the actual status of some of such facts attributed to Pakhtoons against their actual status as observed during field work.

| Attributed Fact/ Myth | Factual observation* |
|---|---|
| Pakhtoons will die for their promise. | False/ They seldom keep their promises. |
| Pakhtoons are brutal and fearless. | False/ They usually make decisions on emotional basis. |
| Pakhtoons are hospitable. | True/ They prefer to invite than being invited. |
| Pakhtoons are fundamentally religious. | False/ They keep religion as the local Kashmiris do, with no fundamental twist. |
| Pakhtoons have smart physique and are fairer. | True/ They can be clearly distinguished in public gatherings |

| | like in gardens by their fair complexion. |
|---|---|
| Pakhtoons are less social. | False/ They don't trust strangers at first hand like Kashmiris but are easier to mix with. |
| Pakhtoons are shy and prefer being segmented. | False/ It may be true for Pakhtoons of Afghanistan and Pakistan; actually they love to express themselves. [In Anantnag they are known for their colorful costume, make-up, dance and drums and rich food they eat.] |

**Table 1.1: *These facts have been found in Anantnag and may not be generalized for the Pakhtoons of the Kashmir Valley.**

In Pakhtoon culture, it is often considered preferable to establish interpersonal relationship with someone from the same ethnicity, but not necessarily from the same tribe. Dating, such as boyfriend and girlfriend, is rarer in Pakhtoon culture than in neighboring cultures but is spreading now among the elite urbanite Pakhtoon due to the rapid increase of internet and mobile phone usage.

There are some cultural practices which seem to be unchanged and one among them is marital age. It has been noticed here that irrespective of the nature of social setting, Pakhtoons marry at a young age but there is no consciousness of ethnicity preservation in it like other cultural practices. For instance using the traditional hearth for making *Roti*, marrying at a young age has simply become a tradition among them and it has been found that once something becomes a tradition among Pakhtoons, they stick to it perhaps because it depicts a change in itself in their previous cultural status. Pakhtoons' love for modernization may be one reason for the various cultural changes as the present study reveals that historically Pakhtoons have been living a life of secludedness with segmented life and strict social set up and may have now become absolute and tired while living that way. The new generations have been found to welcome the modernizing changes in their traditional culture and there is a clear difference evident in ideology, costume and way of life of the older and new generations here.

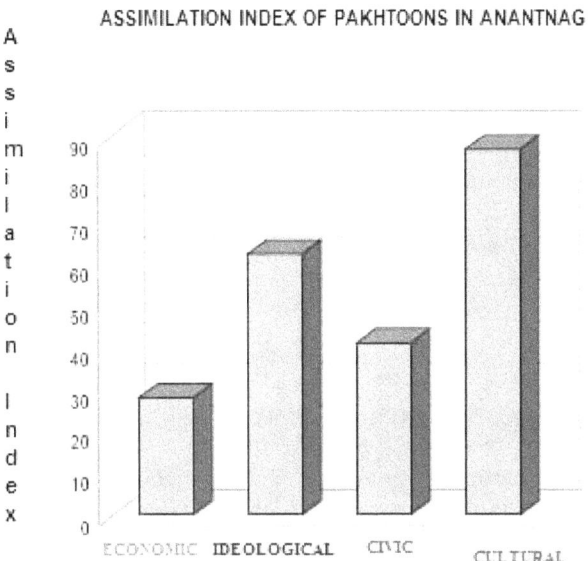

**Source: Field based data.**

In the above diagram assimilation has been taken both as assimilation with Kashmiris and as an outcome of the modernization of Pakhtoon society in order to derive an average assimilation index. The ideological assimilation is a clear indication that the other variables will witness further assimilative changes with more development and modernization of the Pakhtoon social settings in the district. It encapsulates the shift in the attitude, belief and thinking marked from traditionalism to modernism; from fundamental to liberal outlook and from a local to global way of life. Further the change in ideology has been and presently is one important factor for their assimilation since they migrated into a state and country with comparably liberal social traditions from their previous homeland and social organization.

## Social Organization today

Despite administrative divisions Pakhtoons maintain a conception of their cultural and ethnic unity. This idea stems from the segmentary tribal structure and the associated notion of descent from a common ancestor. A. S. Ahmed (1976) has identified two principles of social Organization among the Pathan, *nang* (honor) and *qalang* (taxes or rent). In areas where *nang* prevails traditional values are practiced, there is little social stratification, and there is no Central political authority. In qalang landownership, not lineage membership, gives status and social stratification is prevalent, along with political centralization in the hands of an aristocracy. In both contexts mullahs, Sayyids and occupation groups play their special roles in Pathan society but stand outside Pathan genealogy. As in case of the Pakhtoons of Anantnag no such traditional principles exist, though they talk about honor in cases of women and keeping promises etc.

## Conflict

As noted, the rivalry with father's brother's son for property, power, and wives is a constant source of conflict, as is Pakhtunwali itself, since even petty quarrels can escalate to a point where honor is involved. Efforts to encapsulate the Pathan into political systems seen as alien are also a source of conflict. It is frequently at such times of external threat that religious leaders assume political importance since resistance takes the form of a holy struggle or jihad. Conflict resolution is done through the *Jirga* or through the intervention of Religious figures (Lindholm, 1982).

Having met modernization and an ideological shift, Pakhtoons now not only have forgotten such anomic social traditions but as a matter of fact don't want to be a part of such a social set up again.

### Assimilation in Social Etiquette, Customs and Protocol
### Dress pattern

Traditional male dress is *qmis,* a loose-fitting shirt that reaches to the knees, and *shalwar,* full trousers tied at the waist with a string. A vest is usually worn over the shirt. Footwear consists of *chaplay,* thick leather shoes. Most Pakhtoon adult males wear *pagray,* turbans. Long strips of cotton cloth are wound around the head, leaving the forehead exposed because it is touched during prayer. The turban is fastened so that one end dangles. The loose end is used as a type of washcloth for wiping the face. Usually men also wear a long, wide piece of cloth called a *chadar* on their shoulders. The turban and vasket are considered important for the traditional Pakhtoon costume.

Like other traditional costume, the Pathan sandals and Pathan cap are also not used today in Anantnag; however, some of the tradition loving Pakhtoons still manage to import this attire from their relatives on the other side as there are periodical visits from both sides among them.

**Forgotten tradition *pakol* (Pathan cap). Courtesy: Wantrag Anantnag.**

Rural women wear baggy black or colored trousers, a long shirt belted with a sash, and a length of cotton over the head. City women wear the same type of trousers, a qmis (long shirt), and a cotton cloth to cover their heads. Over their clothing, they also usually wear a *burqa* —a veil that covers them from the head to below the knees (Ali, 1995).

The impacts of assimilation on the cultural structure are quite evident on the dress and costume of Pakhtoons here. While as in the rural sector of Anantnag like in the villages Wantrag, Cherpura and Rinhi the dress pattern of Pakhtoons is not differentiable from the locals. In the areas of more urban effect or located in or around a town like Pingwan and Satranj Maidan, the pattern of dress and costume is more urbanized than the local Kashmiris.

One finds the Pakhtoon youth conspicuous wearing a colorful combination of jeans with half T-shirt or bright *kurta pajamas* more importantly with groomed golden dyed hair and sometimes with black eyes wearing predominant *surma*. As far as the traditional costume is concerned it is only used on social and cultural occasions like marriages and informal meetings like mourning etc. Table 1.2 shows the present status of various cultural traits assimilated in the three major Pakhtoon villages of Anantnag.

**The "new" Pakhtoons. Courtesy: Wantrag Anantnag.**

The dress pattern of Pakhtoons has not only been assimilated but modernized to an extent where there is no resemblance of the present dress code particularly in vogue among the young generations and that known as the Afghan dress. This researcher was not able to trace a single family among the chosen sample of villages where the traditional dress of Pakhtoons could be found.

Traditionally the rules were that men should wear conservative suits and shoes. If working in the country in a non-commercial capacity then wearing the traditional Afghan dress (long shirt and trousers) is best. Women must always dress modestly and conservatively. The general rule is to show as little flesh from the neck downwards. If working in business, women should wear knee-length, loose fitting business skirts with loose fitting professional trousers underneath. Wearing headscarf is advisable.

| Village | TRAITS ASSIMILATED FROM KASHMIRIS | | | | | | | |
|---|---|---|---|---|---|---|---|---|
| | Language | Dress pattern | Housing pattern | Marital customs | Food habits | Religious faith & festivals* | Occupational structure | Ideology& belief |
| Wantrag | ✓ | ✓ | ✓ | ✓ | ✓ | ✓ | ✓ | ✓ |
| Satranj Maidan | ✓ | ✓ | ✓ | ✓ | ✓ | ✓ | ✓ | ✓ |
| Daddu | ✓ | ✓ | ✓ | ✓ | partially | ✓ | ✓ | ✓ |

**Table 1.2.*There is more shrine worship among Pakhtoons of Anantnag than among the Pakhtoons of Afghanistan and Pakistan.**

There have been four main factors responsible for the dress pattern assimilation in Pakhtoons of Anantnag as shown in the diagram below. When a cultural group migrates to a new society, they have to incorporate the compelling changes of the social, topographical, religious and personal conditions from the host society into their own. The personal factors are directly linked with the social individual and thus have remained most responsible for the assimilative changes of the traditional dress code of Pakhtoons. Wearing of *Pheran* (long woolen outer garment worn by Kashmiris) is an example for the climatic factor, yet another one responsible for the aforesaid. The social and religious factors being linked with the identity of the host culture were with due course of time realized by Pakhtoons to be necessarily incorporated into their culture so as to get a fairly un-differentiable mix up with the host culture.

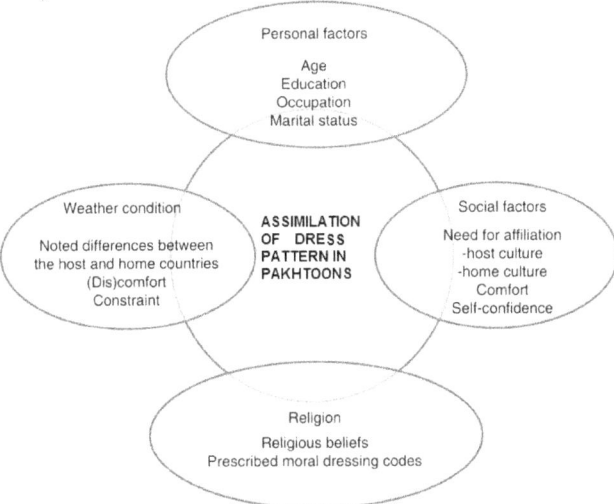

## Etiquette: How They Should Be and How They Are

### *Meeting and Greeting*

When meeting someone the handshake is the most common form of greeting. Pakhtoons occasionally place their hands over their hearts and nod slightly. One should always enquire about things like a person's health, business, family, etc. Women and men will never shake hands let alone speak directly to one another. Eye contact should also be avoided between men and women. Between men eye contact is acceptable as long as it is not prolonged - it is best to only occasionally look someone in the eyes.[55]

This is how actually the so called Pakhtunness operates among the Pakhtoons of Anantnag. In the Chapter on Ethnicity it was argued that they are retaining a few aspects of their ethnic identity, some cultural and yet others psychological.

## *Mixing Between Genders*

Free mixing between genders only takes places within families. In professional situations such as at businesses or universities, males and females may be co-workers, but are nevertheless cautious to maintain each other's honor. Foreign females must learn to read the rules and live by them. If a man speaks to you directly in a social context, he is dishonoring you. If someone speaks to you on the street, that is equally inappropriate. Pakhtoons avoid looking men in the eyes, and keep eyes lowered while walking down the street to maintain reputation.

Women must always dress properly to avoid unwanted attention. They should wear loose fitting pants under their skirts and be sure the definition of legs is undistinguishable. It is also strongly advisable to wear a headscarf in public. On the other hand foreign men should note that it is inappropriate to initiate social conversation with a woman, and one should not ask a male about his wife or female relatives. Men and women should never be alone in the same room. If this happens one should ensure a door is left open. Men and women should never touch one another under any circumstances (Ali, 1995).

The changes in the ideology have had more impacts on issues like this one as shown by the close investigation of the gender gap among Pakhtoons. As observed on occasions of marriage, fairs and festive gatherings, the young people seem to mix freely with guests irrespective of being from within or outside their ethnicity. Though there may be separate tents for males and females to celebrate the *mehandirat*, there are not as strict gender demarcations nowadays as they used to be even only thirty years ago.

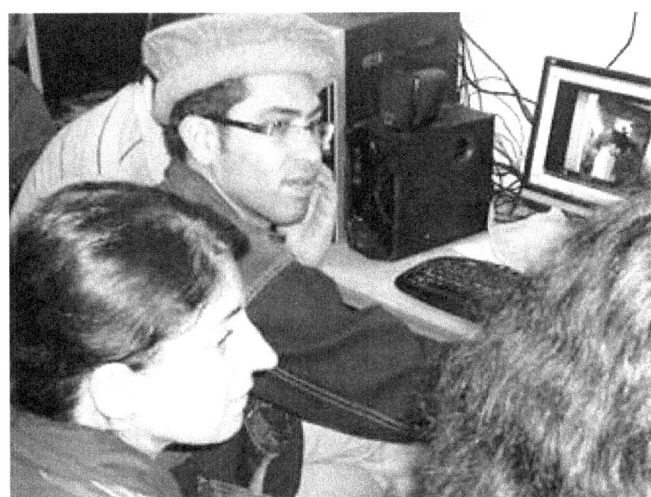

**The commensal relations have shifted from a traditional to a liberal outlook.**
**Source: pakhtoon.org**

Modernization and the contemporary education have changed not only the social but the psychological nature of the traditional restrictions of the Pakhtoon society in general and of Pakhtoons of Anantnag in general. The cultural restrictions are fading away or perhaps have already gone at least among the younger generations since last 30 years in Anantnag.

## Gift Giving Etiquette

First rule of gift giving is to never give alcohol. However, if you know from firsthand experience that the receiver drinks you may do so but covertly to avoid shame. The first time you go to someone's house for tea, it is appropriate to bring a small gift. If you are invited to lunch or dinner, bring fruit, sweets or pastries. Make sure the box is wrapped nicely. When bringing a gift be subtle in how it is given. Do not immediately give the present but rather discreetly place it near the door or where you sit down. When it comes to wrapping gifts there is no special protocol. Green is good for weddings. Gift giving is not restricted to marriage ceremonies. Appropriate gifts are given by Pakhtoons to relatives and friends on birth ceremonies, success in examination and job confirmation. The point to be noted here is that the gift ceremonies as well as the gifts which are given all have changed to modern versions of glamour and show. Traditionally among Pakhtoons it used to be land, ox or cow and a sword etc. but nowadays there are electronic, electrical and artificial aesthetic items used for that purpose.

## *Dining Etiquette*

Dining with Pakhtoons is a different experience and there are many differences in etiquette. Always remove your shoes at the door if visiting a home. If eating at someone's home, you will be seated on the floor, usually on cushions. Food is served on plastic or vinyl tablecloths spread on the floor. Wait to be shown where to sit. If you can, sit cross-legged. Otherwise sit as comfortably as you can. Do not sit with legs outstretched and your feet facing people. Food is generally served communally and everyone will share from the same dish. Do not eat with the left hand. Always pass and receive things using your right hand too. Food is eaten with the hands. It will be a case of watch and learn. Food is usually scooped up into a ball at the tip of the fingers, and then eaten. Leave food on your plate otherwise it will keep getting filled up again (Ahmad, 1980).

Today Pakhtoons take rice with vegetarian or non-vegetarian *saalan* the same way as Kashmiris do. *Roti* is also eaten but not as an option or substitute to rice but historically, there is the tradition of roti and not rice among them here. On festive occasions like marriages, the Indian or more precisely the Kashmiri *Wazwan* is followed not the Pakistani cuisine.

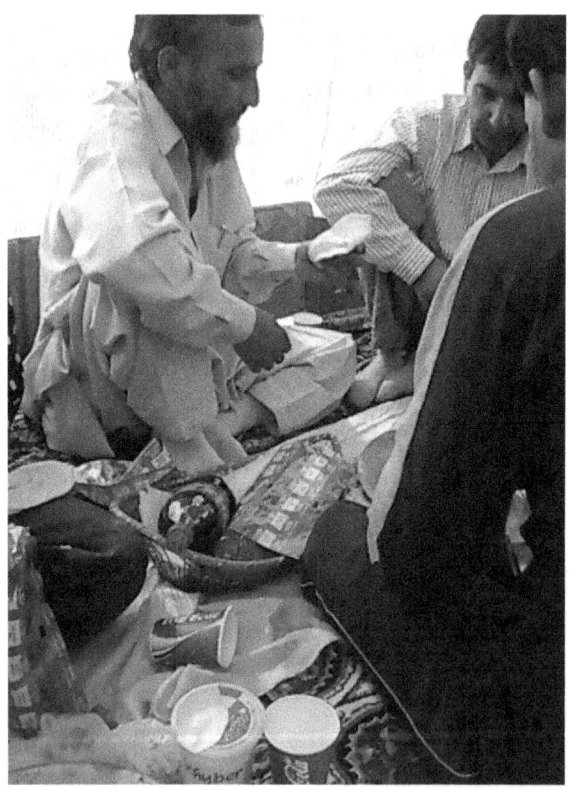

**Kashmiri tradition has been taken by Pakhtoons all along with its assimilations itself, like the new version of *Wazwan*.**
**Courtesy: Wantrag Anantnag**

## Assimilation in Social Institutions
### *Family*

An attractive feature of the Pakhtoon way of life is the joint family system which signifies their deep love for the family's solidarity and welfare. The desire of communal life emanates from a consideration of economic security and integrity. All the family members, even the married sons, live jointly in a house large enough to separately accommodate each married couple under the authority of the father who, as head of the family, manages the family affairs and exercises an immense influence in his own domain. All the earning hands of the family, married as well as un-married sons, contribute their share of income to the common pool of resources. All expenses on food, clothing, education, health, birth, marriages and deaths are defrayed from this common fund. The mantle of authority falls on the eldest son's shoulders after the death of the father or when old age renders him unable to discharge his functions efficiently (Ahmad, 1980).

The system of *Nikat* (ancestral line) which regulates the shares of losses and gains, debts and liabilities of each family, is the mainstay of Pakhtoon society. The internal management of the household rests with the mother who exercises her authority within her own sphere of influence. The joint family system, (where all the married children live with their parents in a combined household) however, is gradually giving way to individualistic trends under the impact of modern influences. It is losing its hold, particularly on educated classes and well off sections (ibid).

The present research shows that there is persistence of the joint family system among the Pakhtoons but as soon as the sons are married, nuclear settings are created for the new family. A few cases of extended families were also found. Table 1.3 illustrates the status of family typology in the three main villages.

**Table: 1.3: The main family types of Pakhtoon society.**

| Name of village | Type of family % | | | Average no. of family members | |
|---|---|---|---|---|---|
| | *Joint* | *Nuclear* | *Extended* | *Joint* | *Nuclear* |
| Wantrag | 70% | 25% | 5% | 12 | 7 |
| Satranj Maidan | 90% | 9% | 1% | 12 | 7 |

| Dadu | 95% | 5% | 0% | 14 | 7 |
|------|-----|-----|-----|-----|-----|

**Source: Field based data.**

## Division of Labor in Family

Previously the strict observance of purdah resulted in a marked division of labor between the sexes. Today Pakhtoon women not only participate actively in agriculture but also are doing jobs. However, mainly the division of labor operates on the same lines as among Kashmiris where women are preferred for doing domestic work and looking after the family.

## Marriage

Although polygamy with up to four wives is permitted under Muslim law, monogamy is prevalent. Marriages are overwhelmingly endogamous within the clan and to a large degree within the subsection. Parallel-cousin marriage with father's brother's daughter is preferred among some tribes. Marriages are arranged by the couple's parents and their plans are generally fulfilled. The union is commonly contracted on the basis of bride-price. Frequently the bride's parents spend the money received in bride-price as dowry to meet the future domestic needs of the couple.

A common practice is exchange marriage between close agnatic kin in which a sister or daughter is given and one simultaneously taken. Residence after marriage is virilocal, the bride coming to live in a single compound with the son, who receives separate quarters within it. The death of the patriarch of a family is frequently the time when such joint or compound families divide themselves into separate compounds. Despite the ease of obtaining a divorce under Muslim law, it is very rare among Pathans. The bride-price and the man's honor are lost if the woman remarries (Caroe, 1958).

**Marrying at a young age is still regarded as a social value among Pakhtoons of Kashmir. Courtesy: Satranj Maidan.**

**Arranged marriages** are usually the only choice for the rural people but also very common among those living in urban areas, although few select their own spouses. Weddings are often three days events, starting with the 'henna party' on the first day, followed by the main wedding day, and ending with a gifts party on the third day. A day before the wedding, dinner is prepared for the ceremony, and the women often dye their hands with henna. Wealthy Pakhtoons often rent a wedding hall inside well known hotel for three days, whilst less wealthy families usually host their weddings inside the house or build a large tent outside; in most weddings, males and females sit separately. In most cases the couples getting married are young, the groom usually in the early 20s and the bride in her teens (Vogelsang, 2002).

In Anantnag Pakhtoons follow the Kashmiri rules of marriage and residence with a few of their own like showering money during special dance (a faint form of traditional Attan) by family members of the groom or bride on *Mehandiraat*. Normally the married son who earns, builds a separate house to live with his bride and in certain cases, the parents also make such arrangement for their son but the father still remains the head of household. Table 1.4 indicates the nature of marriage among the Pakhtoons of Kashmir where it is clear that the percentage of arranged marriages varies inversely with respect to modernization in the particular village setting. Marriages with Kashmiris occur more often in the villages with equal or more population of the Kashmiri cultural group.

In villages with more or equal population of any other group like that of Gujjars in Rinhi Akingam, percentage of marriages with that group is again greater revealing clearly that assimilation is sometimes a necessity for Pakhtoons of Kashmir in order to get into the social realm of the setting where they are living. Moreover contrary to the arguments made by Caroe (1958) above there is no stigma of shame and dishonor associated with the marital breakup or divorce nowadays. Bride price or *mehar* is in most of the cases paid by the groom or his family at the time of *nikah* and in some cases on precautionary grounds an amount is mutually fixed which is payable if the groom breaks the marriage by divorce. On the other hand if the woman demands divorce the said amount or the balance from the actual bride price (as there is provision of half payment of bride price on the day of *nikah*) are generally not paid.

| Village | Association of marriage % | | | Nature of marriage % | |
|---|---|---|---|---|---|
| | Within Pakhtoons | With Kashmiris | With Gujjars | Arranged | Love |
| Wantrag | 85 | 15 | X | 97 | 3 |
| Satranj Maidan | 90 | 10 | X | 95 | 5 |
| Daddu | 90 | 5 | 5 | 97 | 3 |
| Rinhi | 49 | 1 | 50 | 98 | 2 |

Table 1.4: Marriage with other ethnic groups in Anantnag.
Source: Field based data.

In spite of the medical opinion that marriages among close relatives have the risk of congenital defects in the off spring, the practice of consanguineous marriages, particularly with first cousins is a common phenomenon. An exchange of betrothals, particularly cousins is also generally affected. The Pakhtoons feel reluctant to marry their daughters outside the family or tribe and they, therefore, prefer marriages among blood relations. Preference is given to girls of one's own tribe or sub-tribe, in case no girl is available within the family. There is no fixed age for betrothals and they usually take place a year or two before the marriage. In some cases engagements are contracted in childhood.

## Marital Customs and Change

*Wadah* (marriage negotiation); As a general rule, marriage is arranged by parents in Pakhtoon society and the boy and the girl themselves do not play any role in the negotiations. The Pakhtoon society frowns upon any one, who expresses his likeness for any particular girl. But now this trend is gradually undergoing a change (Afridi, 2005).

*Walwar* (head-money); which forms part of the negotiations, is also determined at the time of engagement. In accordance with the Jirga's decision the suitor's parents agree to pay in cash the stipulated amount to the girl's parents on the day of marriage. A part of the payment is made on the spot. The rest of the money is paid on the marriage day. The dowry is usually meager.

The practice of head-money or bride's price has sometimes been criticized as a sort of business transaction or selling out of the girl. This criticism is based on ignorance of problems of the tribesmen. The head-money does not mean that the girl is sold out like a marketable commodity or she is an "economic asset". The idea underlying is to provide some financial relief to the girl's parents while purchasing gold or silver ornaments, clothes, house-hold utensils etc for their daughters. If viewed from the Pakhtoon point of view, the head-money is a matter of honor for them. The more the bride's price the more she commands respect in her husband's family. Even wealthy and prosperous parents, who otherwise do not stand in need of the head money, reluctantly have to accept this for preservation of honor of their daughters in her in-law's circles (ibid).

*Kwezhdan* (Bethrotal); Customary overtures for betrothal commence with a visit by the mother or sisters of the boy, to the girl's parents. Negotiations for matrimony are undertaken either by the parents themselves or by friends and relatives. As a precautionary measure the girl's parents make searching enquiries about the character, education, occupation and other attributes of the prospective son-in-law. After an informal agreement has been reached, the boy's parents approach the girl's parents in a formal way i.e. a Jirga consisting of relatives and village elders call on the father or elder member of the girl's family. Similarly a female party calls on her mother on the day of public proposal. The Jirga settles terms and conditions regarding ornaments, clothes, *Mehr* (dowry) and *Sar* (bride's price or head money). The ceremony is rounded off with distribution of sweets among the people in the *Hujra* (Lindholm, 1982).

*Pakha Azada* or *Pkhay Artha*; means free visits between the fiancee and fiance's families. These calls upon each other begin a few days after the betrothal. The bridegroom's parents pay a visit to the girl's house and present her with a gold ring or a pair of silken clothes. They also send her presents on Eid and other auspicious occasions. This is called *Barkha* or the girl's share. Once the girl is engaged, she starts observing purdah from her would be in-laws, both men and women.

*Wadah* (Marriage); Marriage ceremonies usually take place on Thursday and Fridays. Marriage festivities commence three days before the scheduled date of the actual marriage. At night village maidens assemble in the bridegroom's house and sing epithalamia called *Sandaras* to the beat of drums and tambourine. Three or four respectable but elderly women visit the house of the bride a night before the marriage for dying her hands and feet with henna and for braiding her hair into three or more plaits. The braiding of hair is generally entrusted to a woman with several male children. The bride's *Jorra* or special bridal dress and ornaments etc are normally sent a day before the marriage. The bridegroom serves two meals to his own guests as well as the bride's villagers. Usually the feast is given on the wedding day.

*Janj* (Marriage Party); The bridal procession is called *Janj*. On the day of a marriage, the village of the bridegroom wears a happy look. Old and young alike, wear their best clothes. The marriage party or *Janj* generally starts for the bride's village at noon time with musicians leading the procession. The *Wra* or female marriage party starts from the village to the sound of drums and the male participants let off their guns (ibid).

*Nikah* (Wedlock); The friends and relatives of the bridegroom assemble in the village mosque for Nikah, by the Pesh-Imam or the religious leader. On this occasion the bride proposes the name of bridegroom's brother, uncle or any other near relative as her Nikah Father (Attorney). It becomes the moral duty of Nikah Father to give paternal love and affection to the bride and treat her at par with his own children. The Pesh-Imam repeats the names of the bride and bridegroom three times and seeks the approval of the bridegroom in the presence of two witnesses and some village elders. After this he recites a few verses from the Holy Quran and declares the couple wedded to each other. The Imam is given some money for this religious service (Ghani, 1947).

*Naindra;* At the time of Nikah, friends and relatives of the bridegroom contribute money to lighten his financial burden. This is called *Naindra.* It can be likened to a debt of honor or some sort of financial help repayable to the donors on a similar occasion. A proper record of the subscriptions is maintained and the names of the subscribers are entered into a note book for future reference.

*Rukhsati;* While men remain busy in target shooting, the female party gives a display of its skill in singing and folk dances. Divided into two groups they sing in the form of a duet. Sometimes they form a circle and dance and sing in a chorus. This is called *Balbala.* After this the parents bid farewell to the bride. The bride is handed over to the bridegroom's relatives in a solemn ceremony. One of her younger brothers conducts her to a *Doli* or a palanquin and a handful of money is showered over the Doli. The bride accompanied by the marriage party is led to a car or bus. The doli is carried on the shoulders if the distance is less than a mile. On the way back home one can witness scenes of merry making. The female party sings happy songs and men fire crackers and volleys of shots in the air.

On arrival at the village, the village youths carry the doli to the bridegroom's house. They do not place the *doli* on the ground till they are rewarded. After this the bride is made to sit on a decorated cot. All the women hasten to see her face. The mother-in-law or sister-in-law take the lead in un-veiling her face and other female relatives follow suit. This is called *Makh Katal.* The bride is presented with some money on this occasion. The record of such donations is also kept for re-payment on a similar occasion. Thus the marriage ceremony comes to an end with the transfer of the bride from her natal to marital house and distribution of sweets both in the Hujra and the house.

Wealthy people make a display of pomp and show at the time of marriage. The services of dancing girls and musicians are acquired to entertain the guests. The Pakhtoons in general feel reluctant to give their daughters in marriage to non-Pakhtoons but they are not averse to marrying girls of respectable non-Pakhtoon families. It is not usual for a Pakhtoon to take spouse from another tribe.

Pakhtoons also disapprove of overtures for the hand of a younger daughter in the presence of an un-betrothed elder daughter. Marriages with widowed sisters-in-law are common and a brother considers it his bounden duty to marry the widow of his deceased brother. The widow, however, is not compelled to marry her brother-in-law or anyone else for that matter against her wishes. In most cases widowed Pakhtoon women prefer not to marry after the death of their husbands. If she has children, it is thought most becoming to remain single.

Child marriages are un-common. Polygamy is practiced on a limited scale. A Pakhtoon takes a second wife only when the first one is issueless or differences between the husband and wife assume proportions beyond compromise. Divorces are not common as the Pakhtoons abhor the very idea of a *Talaq* or divorce. The word *Zantalaq* (one who has divorced his wife) is considered an abuse and against the Pakhtoon's sense of honor [53] (ibid).

Today marriage among Pakhtoons in Anantnag is all glamour, decorations and lights, music and feast with a few traditions as mentioned earlier in order to be worth at least for being called a Pathan. The ceremony starts a couple of days before the actual bridal ceremony to make arrangements for the big marriage feast in the coming days. Now there are firecrackers in place of guns; DJ has replaced the *dhol* and traditional *shehnai;* there is the modern version of Wazwan. Besides, there are a lot of customs which are exclusively new and have become a fashion at marriages among Pakhtoons including cake ceremony, grooming of the bridegroom and bride, singing and dancing in a non-traditional way.

During the present study no case of child marriage or polygamy as is prevalent in Afghanistan was found. There are, however, several cases of the latter in Gutlibagh, the largest Pakhtoon settlement in Jammu and Kashmir. The belief regarding these two social challenges in the present day society as found among Pakhtoons is shown in the pie diagram below;

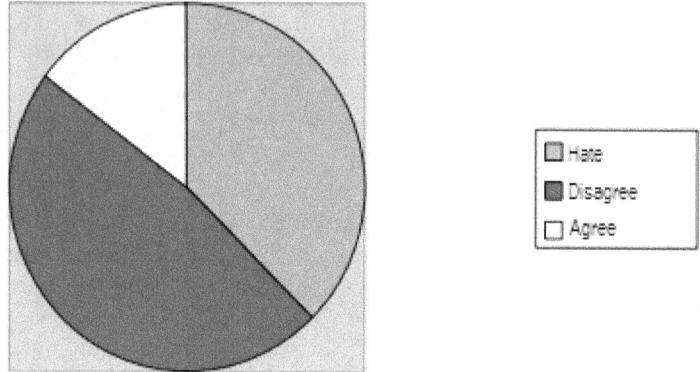

General view of Pakhtoons regarding polygamy and child marriage

**Source: Field based data.**

## Kin Groups and Descent

Segmentary tribal structure and unilineal descent define Pathan kin groups. Genealogical and geographic divisions generally coincide. The most pertinent division within the tribal structure is the clan subsection, that is, the children of one man, generally encompassing four or five generations. It is within this sphere that one marries, makes alliances, and is in conflict. The smallest unit is the *kor*, or household, and it implies cohabitation with a living grandfather. This is the major economic and social unit; its members may cohabit in a village, a single compound, or a nomadic group. Descent is patrilineal (Lindholm 1982).

## Kinship Terminology

Aspects of the Eskimo system, in which avuncular and cousin terms are uniform, is present, though certain collaterals are distinguished. For example, while all other female cousins carry the same term as *do* all other male ones, the father's brother's daughter and father's brother's son are given distinct terms (ibid).

## Inheritance

Land is divided as inheritance only among the males and on the basis of equality. The eldest brother is generally given an extra share to be used for the upkeep of the family guest house (hujra). It is over the inheritance of land that rivalry develops between brothers and, in the next generation, cousins. Though despite Islamic injunctions, neither wives nor daughters inherit property, some faithful Pakhtoons like same Kashmiri families do follow the Islamic rules of inheritance of both movable and immovable property.

## Changes in Socialization

With the separation of the sexes inherent in Islam, children are raised primarily by their mother and elder sisters. In the segregated atmosphere that prevails there is a great deal of competition for attention and affection, though men tend to be indulgent toward children. Boys are circumcised by their seventh year (Lindholm 1982).

As the whole social scenario has changed, there are now avenues for the socialization of children. The political situation is not the same as it used to be or still is among Pakhtoons in Afghanistan and Pakistan. Now these people are educating their children in order to make them better socialized, economically secure and personally successful than their parents or grandparents used to be.

**As compared to their counter parts in Afghanistan (Above) change in ideology, tradition and culture has changed the game to a better future for Pakhtoon children in Anantnag (Below).**

## Respect for Elders

The Pakhtoon children are taught to show a great degree of respect to their parents and elders. Senior members of the family, particularly elders, command great respect. Parents are properly and reverently looked after in old age and every effort is made to provide them with all possible comforts. There is a famous Pashto maxim that "Paradise lies under the feet of the parents" and Pakhtoons true to their faith leave no stone un-turned in obtaining their blessings. It is generally believed that parents' curses bring sorrows, miseries and hardships. Sons and daughters, therefore, refrain from incurring the displeasure and curses of their fathers and mothers.

## Manners

The Pakhtoons have several ways of greeting and salutation. Strangers passing on a road or thoroughfare exchange courtesies such as *"Starrey ma shey"* (May you not be tired) and *"Pa khair raghley"* (welcome). This is answered by *"Khudai de mal sha"* (May God be with you), *"Pa khair ossey"* (May you live in peace) and *"Ma khwaraigey"* (May you not be poor). The Pakhtoons usually embrace their friends and relatives when they meet them after a long absence and warmly receive each other by a hearty handshake. This is followed by a train of questions about each others' welfare like *"Jorr yey"* (Are you alright?), *"Khushal yey"* (Are you happy?), *"Takkrra yey"* (Are you hale and hearty?) *"Warra Zagga Jorr di"* (Are your family members hale and hearty?) and *"Pa Kor key Khairyat de"* (Is everybody well at home?).[55] A visitor entering a village Hujra is greeted with the traditional slogan of *"Har Kala Rasha"* (May you always come) and he replies *"Har kala ossey"* (May you always abide). Friends while parting commit each other to the care of God by saying *"Pa makha de kha"* (May you reach your destination safely), and

*"Da khudai pa aman"* (To the protection of God). When meeting a pious or an elderly person, a Pakhtoon bows a little and keeps his hands on his chest as a mark of veneration. When talking about a deceased person, they often say *"Khudai de obakhi"* (May God forgive him). If a man suddenly appears at the time of conversation between some or more persons about him, they immediately exclaim *"Omar de ziyat de, Oss mo yadawalay"* (You have a long life, we were just talking about you). The Pakhtoons very often use the word *"Inshaallah"* (God Willing) *"Ka Khudai ta manzura wee"* *"Ka Khair Wee"* (if all goes well) when they promise to accomplish a task at a particular time (Khattak, 1960).

Nowadays not only the traditional ways of greeting have reduced to a considerable extent due to the fading away of Pashtu language but in fact the symbolism for example kissing the hands of elders is almost gone. The most common form of greeting and salutation as exactly the same as among the Kashmiris composing of *salaam* with right handshake. A new form of male kissing was noticed at ceremonial occasions like marriages during the present study.

## Change in Rituals; Birth and Death
### Rites of passage

Pakhtoons are automatically considered Muslims (followers of Islam) at birth. When a baby is born, Pakhtoons whisper the call for prayer in the baby's ear. The male circumcision ceremony is held at the same time as the birth celebration at about the age of one week or up to seven years. Children officially join in the rituals of prayers and fasting when they reach sexual maturity, but in practice they begin much earlier.

The expected advent of the child is kept secret as far as possible. The expectant mother is kept secluded and only an old woman proficient in midwifery or one or two female relatives are allowed to attend to her (Spain, 1972).

The news of a new birth spreads like wild fire in the neighborhood and messengers hasten to distant places to break the happy tidings to paternal and maternal uncles etc. This is called *Zairay*. The person who breaks the good news first to a near relative receives a handsome reward in cash. Relatives and friends felicitate the proud parents and let off their guns as a mark of jubilation. The father warmly receives the guests, slaughters a ram or goat and serves a sumptuous lunch to the visiting guests. Sweetmeats are also distributed among the young and old alike.

Female relatives also hurry to the house to offer congratulations to the child's parents. They bring presents, including clothes for the infant and also offer some money. A record of the money, so proffered, is kept for repayment on a similar occasion. All women who offer money are given *loopatas* (Scarf's) in addition to sweetmeats.

The village Mullah or priest or an old pious man performs the first important ceremony in the child's life. The Mullah whispers *Azaan* (call to prayers or profession of faith) in his or her ears. The village Mullah receives some money for this religious service. The child is also given a dose of indigenous medicine called *Ghotti*. A pious woman, preferably mother of several sons, administers this liquid compound to the child. Within seven days of the birth, the child is named (*noom shovana*) as Ayub, Ali, Ishaq, Yaqoob, Aisha, Fatima etc as the custom of naming children after the Prophets, particularly Mohammad (Peace Be Upon Him) and his companions, is very common. Pashto names are also popular.

The infant is wrapped in swaddling clothes with his hands tied to his body. This binding practice continues for over six months. The idea behind the binding of infants from shoulders to toes seems to be to prevent him from exhaustion or causing an injury to himself. For most of the time during the day, the child is kept in a swinging cradle, which is in common use all over the sub-continent. At night the child is laid beside its mother. The child entirely belongs to the mother; she feeds it at least for two years and makes every possible endeavor to protect it from the malignant eye or the glance of evil spirits.

Those women who have no male issue pay visits to the holy shrines on Thursday nights and beseech the favors of the holy saints for a male child. They offer alms and sometimes bind a stone to one of the flags hanging beside a wall or tree near the saint's *mazar*. They add one more flag to the existing numbers when their cherished desire is realized. Those women, who give birth to females in succession without any male issue, curse their misfortune and shed tears of remorse on the birth of a female child.

After the child's birth, precautionary measures are taken to protect the mother from evil spirits and genii. She does not take a bath, at least, for a fortnight after the birth of the child. The mother is never left alone in the house at least for forty days in succession for fear of evil spirits. It is generally believed that both mother and child are susceptible to the influence of genii etc during the first forty days. The mother refrains from doing any work for a week and she resumes her usual occupations after a lapse of 40 days (Smith, 2003).

The belief in evil eye, ghosts called *Jinns* and shrine worship are still there but that should not be misunderstood as a mark of Pakhtoon tradition because these things were and still are strongly held among Kashmiris. Thus the fact is that such belief and rituals as found among the Pakhtoons have again been taken and adopted in a Kashmiri way. A couple of cases of tying up of the new born were reported in Anantnag. The baby is massaged thoroughly and then wrapped up in cloth. Moreover as it is among almost all the cultures of Jammu and Kashmir today, there is no disparity between the male and female child. In fact Pakhtoons are now more conscious about their girl child which has been seriously neglected historically.

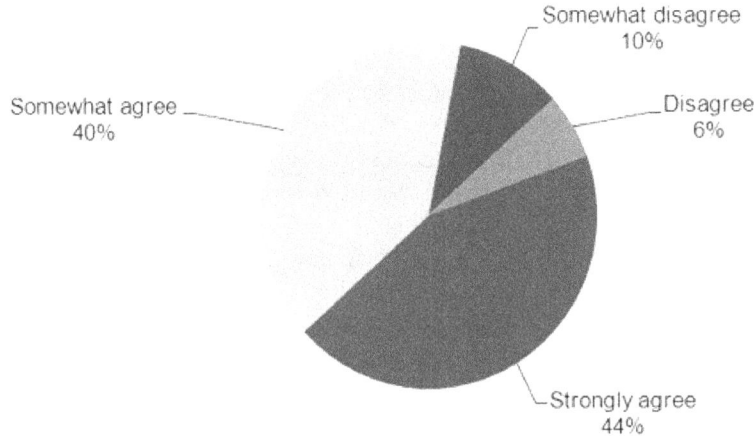

**Belief in ghosts, evil eye and fortune among Pakhtoons. [Total 200 households].**
**Source: Field based data.**

*Sar kalai* (Head-Shaving); The second important ceremony in a child's life is *Sar Kalai* or hair cutting. When the child is about 40 days old, a village barber shaves his or her hair. The barber is given some money for this service. This event is also celebrated with the slaughter of a goat or sheep for guests.

*Soonat* (Circumcision); The third important ceremony is known as *Soonat* i.e. Circumcision of a male child. The village barber again performs the circumcision ceremony when the boy is over one year old. On this occasion the boy is made to sit on an earthen platter called *Khanak* in the compound of the house duly attended by his relatives. They also offer some money to the child. Well-to-do persons with pomp and sumptuous feast observe this ceremony (ibid).

Today the upper as well as the middle class Pakhtoons perform this ritual preferably through artificial techniques in private clinics and the ceremony of feast attached to it is provided at home later.

## Schooling

In the fourth stage the child, generally is sent to a Mullah in the village mosque for religious education, including learning by heart of *Namaz* and reading of the Holy Quran. He is first taught *Kalma Tayyaba* and later other tenets of Islam. He also starts going to school at the age of five to six years. Along with spiritual and temporal education he makes a debut in sports of masculine nature, including wrestling called *Parzawal*. Later he adopts shooting as his hobby. After school hours he goes on shooting excursions and shoots down birds. He uses a catapult like weapon called *Ghulail* for hunting. In this stage of life he develops an aptitude for sporting excursions such as target shooting and finally starts going round with a rifle slung over his shoulder for self protection. At that time he begins helping his father in his work. The young girl on the other hand assists her mother in household work and shares the domestic duties with her. Pakhtoons are fond of rifles and young boys can be seen carrying rifles under their arms. Seldom will they be seen un-armed. Their fondness for arms is evident from a Pashto proverb that though they might not have good food they must be in possession of fire arms (Spain, 1972).

The schooling today is as formal as among other ethnic groups of the Valley of Kashmir. The tradition of sending children to the *Madrassas* was found in a single village Wantrag. Depending on the availability, the private run educational institutions are preferred for sending their children to by the Pakhtoons. As shown by the fieldwork in Anantnag the rate of sending children to receive only the religious education is 4 % among the Pakhtoons and 3 % among Kashmiris.

The findings of J. Spain in the 1970s will be a mis-comparison not only to the Pakhtoons of Jammu and Kashmir today but more precisely even to those living in the areas of his actual research. The possession of arms has not only dropped but as a fact not a single household was found to have weapons, in spite that some of them like Pakhtoons of Manzmuh in Qazigund have large herds of cattle. Swords and other such armory like *Drath* (sickle shaped swords as found among Gujjars of Rajasthan) were found in households dwelling near the forest belt for self defense against wild beasts as told by the respondents.

## The rituals of death

The Pakhtoons give more importance to participation in funeral processions than festive occasions like marriages etc. At the time of someone's death, the elders of the surrounding villages come to the village *Hujra* to express their sense of grief and sympathy with the bereaved family and the youngsters hasten to the graveyard for digging a grave and making necessary funeral arrangements. The women of the neighborhood also go to the house of the bereaved family carrying articles of daily use such as sugar, *gur*, wheat, rice etc and to offer condolences.[54]

The moment any one expires, his eyes are closed, toes tied, face turned towards Kaaba and placed on a cot (*charpaee*) in the courtyard. Women sit around the dead body in a circle and weep over it in unison. The females of the neighborhood generally join the lamentation. Embracing the wife, mother and sisters of the deceased and wailing over the passing away of their dear ones, is the traditional way of lamentation and expression of sorrow. The wailing also includes words in praise of the deceased. Such praise assumes the form of the chanting of short rhythmical phrases of rhymed prose or verse. Some women, in a state of deep anguish, resort to *Weer* i.e. beating of face and chest with both hands and with loud sobs.

The burial takes place on the day of death, if the death occurs in the morning, otherwise on the following day. Weeping in the house continues for at least three days but it sometimes continues intermittently for a fortnight or even forty days. No marriages take place among the deceased's near relatives till the first anniversary of the deceased is observed. Only in rare cases marriages take place within a year of the occurrence of death and that, too, with the consent of the members of the bereaved family. Music and jolly activities are avoided for at least forty days. Relatives and friends feed the deceased's family for three or seven days (Ghani, 1947).

It was found during the present study that likewise Kashmiris, religion is the least assimilated cultural institution of Pakhtoons. The reason for that is evident that religious belief is regarded above culture and tradition among them. The beliefs which were taken from Kashmiri religious belief system had no negative impacts on the one Pakhtoons came with. That is why the absorption of the new religious traits was not regarded to confront with those of Pakhtoons particularly those regarding death rituals which were to some extent same among both the cultural groups. It is so because the religious beliefs of both the cultures are predominantly based on Islamic rather than on Pakhtoon or Kashmiri tradition.

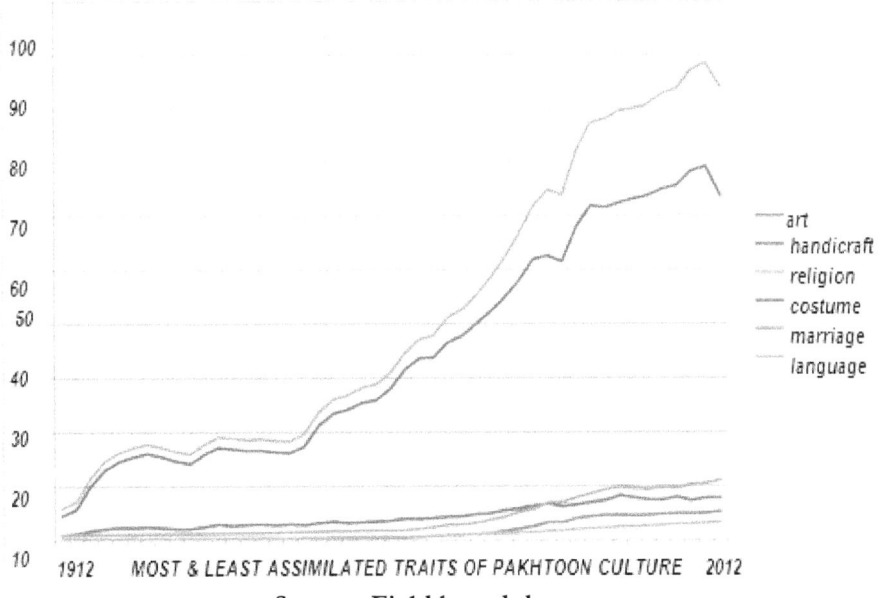

**Source: Field based data.**

*Funeral;* Before burial, the village Mullah or some other old man bathes the corpse. The dead body is usually washed in the veranda or in a corner of the house. A few candles or a lamp is lighted at this place in the evening for at least three nights to scare away the evil spirits, and people avoid passing over the spot. After the bath the dead body is wrapped in a shroud, placed on a bier, a sheet thrown over it and then taken to the village graveyard in a funeral procession. A Mullah and three or four persons, carrying the Holy Quran on their heads, precede the funeral procession. Friends and relatives join the funeral procession and carry the bier turn by turn. Even passers-by become the pal-bearers and accompany the procession for some distance for the attainment of *Sawab* (virtue).

The *Janaza* prayers (recitation of the burial service by an Imam) joined by mourners from all over the area, are offered in the community graveyard and then the body is lowered into the grave which is always dug north to south with its face turned towards the Kaaba. Later special prayers are offered for the eternal peace of the departed soul. After the burial, alms are distributed among the poor and indigent at the graveyard. This is called *Iskat*. The Pakhtoons consider the payment of *Iskat* as an essential part of the religious service and a question of their prestige. Even the poor, who can hardly afford two square meals, borrow money for this purpose to vindicate their honor. It is also one of the customs to present on this occasion a few copies of the Holy Quran to the Mullahs of the area for *Quran Khwani* (recitation) on the following four Thursdays (ibid).

**Khairat;** The burial ceremony over, some food is served in charity to the poor. This is called *Khairat*. Rice is cooked in a few cauldrons and the participants in the funeral procession are invited to partake of it. The *ulema* (Islamic scholars) have preached against this custom, time and again but with little positive effect (Smith, 2003).

**Draima;** The third day of the death is called *Draima* in Pashto or *Qul* in Urdu. The day is observed with due solemnity. The women of the vicinity assemble in the deceased's house on that day. They pay a visit to the graveyard in the morning, lay a floral wreath on the grave and offer *Fateha*. Meanwhile, friends and relatives continue pouring into the village *Hujra* for offering condolences. This practice continues at least for seven days.

**Salwekhti;** The 40th day of the death is called *Salwekhti* in Pashto. The day is rounded off with *Khatm-e-Quran* (recitation of whole Quran), Khairat and distribution of alms. It is observed on a Thursday, five or seven weeks after the day of death (ibid).

An interesting fact about the death rituals of Pakhtoons in Anantnag is that as compared to all other traditional rituals, they have remained comparably unchanged. As found during the literature review also there is a general observation in anthropological research that death rituals seldom change under assimilation of cultures. The reasons for that is the relatively more social importance and an emotional attachment associated with such rituals which consequently reduce the chances of compromise and intentional changes which are associated with the assimilation of culture.

## An ancient tradition of Pakhtoons

When spalanaey seeds (more commonly known to Westerners by their Persian name *espand*) are dropped on red-hot charcoal they make a popping noise and give off a great deal of fragrant smoke. This is done to ward off the "evil-eye". The evil eye belief is that a person, otherwise not evil in any way, can harm you, your children, your house, your health and so on by looking at you with envy and/or praising you. The evil eye or *nazar* can be done out of love and unintentionally so it does not always have "evil" intentions attached to it. Spanaley burning has a tradition attached to it but in Anantnag Pakhtoons use another variant called *izband* in copper vase, simply a Kashmiri tradition.

This ancient tradition has its origins from Zorostrianism and is still widely practiced today. In Iran, Afghanistan, and Tajikistan when a child returns home after being among strangers, some parents will light a charcoal disk and burn the spalanaey seeds while reciting a poem, actually an ancient Zoroastrian prayer, against the evil eye and directing the smoke around the child. This is done as a protective measure, whether or not it is suspected that the child has been given the eye. The rite dates back to the invocation prayer to the historical king of Persia known as Naqshband, while burning espand/ spalanaey seeds. In some homes today verses from the Quran are recited instead of that ancient prayer (Adams 2006).

### Culture and Assimilation

Pakhtoon culture has been formed over the course of many centuries. Pakhtoon culture is mostly based on *Pashtunwali* and the usage of the Pashto language. Pre-Islamic traditions, dating back to Alexander's defeat of the Persian Empire in 330 BC, possibly survived in the form of traditional dances, while literary styles and music reflect influence from the Persian tradition and regional musical instruments fused with localized variants and interpretation. Pakhtoon culture is a unique blend of native customs with some influences from South and Western Asia. Like other Muslims, Pakhtoons celebrate *Ramadan* and *Eid ul-Fitr*. Some also celebrate *Nouruz*, which is the Persian new year dating to pre-Islamic period (Tony, H 1998). Research has revealed that Pakhtoons, particularly women love modernization which assures a liberal way of life.

The culture of Kashmiri Pakhtoons is an assimilated blend of the traditional Pushtoon culture they brought with them and that of the Kashmiri traditions as they posses since the last about a century. For Kashmiris they are not a people among their culture and for the Pakhtoons of Afghanistan, they are a *kashmirized* community of their people who have lost their language and encyclopedic traditions all together.

## Food in Daily Life

Everyday food consists of flat bread cooked on an iron plate in the fire or on the inner wall of a clay oven. Bread often is dipped in a light meat stock. Yogurt and other dairy products (butter, cream, and dried buttermilk) are an important element of the diet, as are onions, peas and beans, dried fruits, and nuts. Rice is eaten in some areas and in urban settlements. Scrambled eggs prepared with tomatoes and onions are a common meal.

Food is cooked with various types of oils, including the fat of a sheep's tail. Tea is drunk all day. Sugar is used in the first cup of the day, and then sweets are eaten and kept in the mouth while sipping tea. Other common beverages are water and buttermilk. Pakhtoons use the right hand to eat from a common bowl on the floor. At home, when there are no guests, men and women share meals.

The common Islamic food prohibitions are respected among Pakhtoons. For example, meat is only eaten from animals that are slaughtered according to Islamic law; alcohol, pork, and wild boar are not consumed, although some people secretly make wine for consumption at home. The Shiites avoid rabbit and hare.

As shown by the present research, the food etiquette of the Pakhtoons of Kashmir today is nothing but a replica of the Kashmiri food habits. The morning starts with the *noon chai* (traditional salted tea of Kashmir) with some of the traditional bakings like *lawas* in the areas where they are available or with hand doughed *roti*. Before noon they have the tradition of sipping the common lipton tea sometimes with ghee and fried *roti*.

Rice is taken in the afternoon with veg or non-veg cuisine versions. Before evening another break for the salted tea is taken followed finally by rice again for dinner. The traditional hearth was found in a single household in Anantnag at Satranj Maidan which as per the family head is kept for use on some special occasions and not for daily use at all. Following the Kashmiri cuisine in such an undifferentiable manner clears the status of assimilation of the eating habits of Pakhtoons in the valley in general and Anantnag in particular. The traditional roti (*khan chot*) and way of preparing it are gone among Pakhtoons of Anantnag.

**Shifting to Kashmiri cuisine has consequently leaded to the death of such traditions in Anantnag.**
**Courtesy: Satranj Maidan Anantnag.**

## Food Customs at Ceremonial Occasions

On special occasions, *pulau rice* is served with meat, carrots, raisin, pistachios, or peas. The preferred meat is mutton, but chicken, beef, and camel also are consumed. Kebabs, fried crepes filled with leeks, ravioli, and noodle soup also are prepared. Vegetables include spinach, zucchini, turnip, eggplant, peas and beans, cucumber, and tomatoes. Fresh fruits are eaten during the day or as a dessert. In formal gatherings, men and women are separated. Dinners start by drinking tea and nibbling on pistachios or chickpeas; food is served late in the evening on dishes that are placed on a cloth on the floor. Eating abundantly demonstrates one's enjoyment (Tony, H 1998).

Pakhtoons have been historically known for their cuisine and even today in Afghanistan and Pakistan, one of the best Asian cuisines are served on ceremonial occasions. During participant observation in Anantnag, lot of dry fruit use was found among Pakhtoons here particularly almond, pistachios and cashew nut. Ghee is also used in plenty with tea and in the roti whenever it is served. Traditional food for which Pakhtoons are known globally were, however, not found in use like for example *tandoori kebab*. On ceremonial occasions simply the *Wazwan* is served as Kashmiris do and the point of interest is that it is regarded as a matter of pride for the host to serve as far as possible the modernized version of *Wazwan*. With the death of the elderly people, recipe of traditional food like *Kabuli Pulaw* died of their own.

**Assimilation in food; mixing tradition with McDonald's.**
**Courtesy: Satranj Maidan.**

The Kashmiri Pakhtoons do eat in plenty and the guests are expected the same. "Eating is strength and mental power" told Ashiq Hussain Khan one respondent at Daddu village. Upon refusing to take all the ghee the respondent said "this much of ghee is taken by our children daily". On his marriage feast one respondent Mehraj Khan of Satranj Maidan exclaimed *"abhi aap ne khaya hi kya hai.. nahi ye to ap ko khatam karna hi hoga..."* (You have eaten but only little and you have to finish it). Eating rich and nutritious food seems to be a value among them and it goes all along their tradition and may be one of the reasons for their sound physique and fairness. Though the values may have been retained but the point is that food is not at least the same as it used to be.

**Linguistic Assimilation**

The Pakhtoons speak Pashto, an Indo-European language, belonging to the Iranian sub-group of the Indo-Iranian branch, within Eastern Iranian and Southeastern Iranian. Pashto writing uses the Perso-Arabic script, dividing into two main dialects, the northern "Pukhtu" and the southern "Pashto" (Nicholas and Sarwan, 2002).

*Pashto*

Pashto is a member of the southeastern Iranian branch of Indo-Iranian languages spoken in Afghanistan, Pakistan and Iran. There are three main varieties of Pashto: Northern Pashto, spoken mainly in Pakistan; Southern Pashto, spoken mainly in Afghanistan; and Central Pashto, spoken mainly in Pakistan. The Pashto spoken in Anantnag belongs to the Southern branch.

The exact number of Pashto speakers is not known for sure, but most estimates range from 45 million to 55 million. Pashto is the first language of between 40% and 55% (11 to 15.4 million) of the people of Afghanistan, and 10% to 28% (2.8 to 7.8 million) speak it as a second language, and the total is around 18 or 19 million (ibid).

Pashto has about 25 million speakers in Pakistan (15% of the population) in the North-West Frontier Province (NWFP) the Federally Administered Tribal Areas (FATA), and the provinces of Balochistan, Mianwali, Attock, Sindh, and Punjab. There are also communities of Pashto speakers in the northeast of Iran, as well as in the UAE, Saudi Arabia, London, USA and a number of other countries where Pakhtoons have migrated.

## Pashto at a glance

- Native name: پښتو [paʂˈto]
- Alternative names: Pushtu, Pushto, Pukhto, Afghani.
- Linguistic affiliation: Indo-European, Indo-Iranian, Iranian, Southeastern
- Number of speakers: 45-55 million
- Spoken in: Afghanistan, Pakistan, Iran, India and Tajikistan.
- First written: 16th century.
- Writing system: Arabic script
- Status: one of the official languages of Afghanistan

The name Pashto is thought to derive from the reconstructed proto-Iranian form, *parsawā* Persian language. In northern Afghanistan speakers of Pashto are called *Pakhtūn*; in sourthen Afghanistan they are known as *Pashtūn*, and as *Pathān* or *Afghan* in India and Pakistan.

Pashto has ancient origins and bears similarities to extinct languages such as Avestan and Bactrian. Its closest modern relatives include Pamir languages, such as *Shughni* and *Wakhi,* and *Ossetic,* and have an ancient legacy of borrowing vocabulary from neighboring languages including Persian and Vedic Sanskrit. Invaders have left vestiges as well as Pashto has borrowed words from **Ancient Greek**, Arabic and Turkic, while modern borrowings come primarily from English (ibid).

**Table 1.5: Languages spoken by Pakhtoons in Anantnag; taken over 200 families/ District.**

| Age group | Only Pashtu % | Pashtu and Kashmiri % | Pashtu and Urdu% | Pashtu, Dogri, Pahadi and Punjabi % |
|-----------|---------------|------------------------|-------------------|--------------------------------------|
| 10-20 | 10 | 40 | 45 | 5 |
| 20-30 | 15 | 35 | 40 | 10 |

| | | | | |
|---|---|---|---|---|
| **30-40** | 20 | 30 | 40 | 10 |
| **40-50** | 40 | 30 | 24 | 6 |
| **50-60** | 51 | 20 | 24 | 5 |
| **60 & above** | 65 | 10 | 20 | 5 |
| **Total** | **33%** | **27.5%** | **32.16%** | **6.8%** |

**Source: Field based data.**

As clear from the data above, the young generations are not as good Pashtu speakers as the elderly population. Instead majority among former can speak Kashmiri due to the linguistic assimilation which has been sharp since the last two decades. Urdu is spoken well by all the age groups due to its prevalence in the regions from where they migrated as well as in the Valley. As the age group 20-40 is most exposed to other cultures for reasons of job and education etc., they were found capable of speaking multiple languages during the present study. It was further found that the oldest people are weak at speaking Kashmiri and they would naturally switch to Urdu while speaking to non-Pashtu people or to Kashmiris.

## Bearing of culture on language

85 percent of the respondents irrespective of their level of education agree with the fact that their language is an essential component of their culture. As per the views of the educated and employed people, the very first impact of modernization on Pakhtoon culture comes on to language itself. The older women who have lowest contact with other cultures can hardly speak Kashmiri. Haralambos (2006) wrote, that the experiments done by William Lobov on cultural deprivation clearly reveals that one of the first cause as well as consequences of this is linguistic deprivation. In yet another experiment Lobov draws the results that cultural exposure leads to effective communication and interaction.

Under the intense impact of modern English education in today's schools, Pashtu language has also met a setback like other local languages in Jammu and Kashmir did. This effect was, however, a big challenge particularly since the last two decades for the traditional dialect of Pakhtoons. Since 1991, there has been about 20 percent decrease in the Pashtu language use among Pakhtoons of Anantnag. The biggest reason for that is the present education system where the new generations of Pakhtoons not only lose their language to their peer groups but also to the Urdu and English mediums running in most of the present day schools. Secondly while living with a dominant language group, the new generations find the use of their language in daily life meager as compared to the linguistic utility of

Kashmiri and Urdu. The graphic table below shows the abrupt decrease in Pashtu language use since the last two decades.

Assimilation of Pashtu language of Pakhtoons in Anantnag District

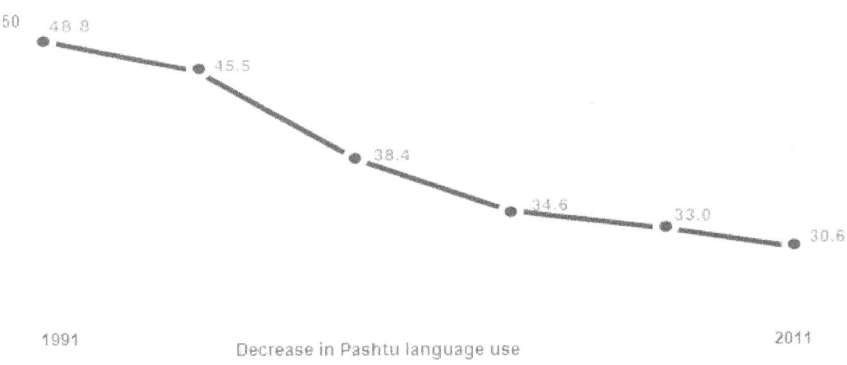

Decrease in Pashtu language use

**Source: Field based data.**

The present status of the traditional ethnic language of Pakhtoons, therefore, remains of a language which is mainly spoken by the elderly population or that having a restricted use at ceremonial occasions or home use. Pashtu surely is not the language which is taken to the work place or market by the Pakhtoons today. The present status of Pashtu in Anantnag is shown by the pie chart below.

**Present status of Pashtu language in Anantnag**

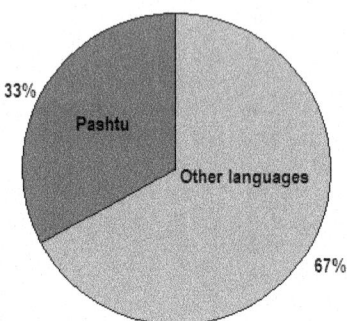

**Source: Field based data**

## Pashtu alphabet

| Letter name | Translit. | IPA |
|---|---|---|
| alif | aa | [ ʔ, Ø, ə, ɑ(:), i, u ] |
| be | b | [ b ] |
| pe | p | [ p ] |
| te | t | [ t ] |
| tte | tt | [ t ] |
| se | θ | [ s ] |
| gim | j | [ dʒ ] |
| ce/che | č | [ tʃ ] |
| dze/ze | dz/z | [ dz ] |
| ce/sche | c/sch | [ ts ] |

| Letter name | Translit. | IPA |
|---|---|---|
| he | h | [ h, Ø ] |
| xe/khe | x/kh | [ x ] |
| dal | d | [ d ] |
| dal/ddal | d/dd | [ ɖ ] |
| zal | z | [ z ] |
| re | r | [ r ] |
| re/rre | r/rr | [ ɽ ] |
| ze | z | [ z ] |
| ze/zhe | z/zh | [ ʒ ] |
| ge | g | [ ʐ ] |

| Letter name | Translit. | IPA |
|---|---|---|
| sin | s | [ s ] |
| sin/shin | s/sh | [ ʃ ] |
| xe/shin | x/sh | [ ʂ ] |
| sad | s | [ s ] |
| zad | z | [ z ] |
| ta | t | [ t ] |
| za | z | [ z ] |
| ayn | r | [ ʔ, Ø, ɑ ] |
| gayn/ghayn | g/gh | [ ɣ ] |
| fe | f | [ f ] |

| Letter name | Translit. | IPA |
|---|---|---|
| qaf | g | [ q ] |
| kaf | k | [ k ] |
| gaf | g | [ g ] |
| lam | l | [ l ] |
| mim | m | [ m ] |
| num | n | [ n ] |
| nun/nnun | n/nn | [ ɳ ] |
| he | h | [ h, ɑ, ə, Ø ] |
| waw | w | [ w, o, u(:) ] |
| ye | ay | [ j, e, aj, i(:) ] |

| Letter name | Translit. | IPA |
|---|---|---|
| saxta ye | i | [ i ] |
| pasta ye | e | [ e ] |
| xadzeena ye | əy | [ əy ] |
| feliya ye | ə | [ ə ] |

## Dying Pashto literature

Throughout Pakhtoon history, poets, prophets, kings and warriors have been amongst the most revered members of society. For much of Pakhtoon history, literature has played a minor role as Persian served the literary *lingua*

127

*franca* used for communication purposes by neighboring peoples and generally relied upon for writing purposes. By the sixteenth century early written records of Pashto began to appear, the earliest of which describes Sheikh Mali's conquest of Swat. The advent of Pashto poetry and the revered works of Khushal Khan Khattak and Rahman Baba in the seventeenth century helped transition of Pashto towards the modern period. In the twentieth century, Pashto literature gained significant prominence with the poetic works of Ameer Hamza Shinwari, noted for his development of *Pashto Ghazals*. In recent times, Pashto literature has received increased patronage, but due to relatively high illiteracy rates, many Pakhtoons continue to rely upon the oral tradition. Pakhtoon males continue to meet at *chai khaana*s or tea cafés to listen and relate various oral tales of valor and history (Khattak, 1960).

**Noted Pashtu poets Khushal Khan Khattak and Rahman Baba.
Source: wikipedia.org**

Despite the general male dominance of Pashto oral story-telling, Pakhtoon society has some **matriarchal** tendencies. Folktales involving reverence for Pakhtoon mothers and matriarchs abound, passed down from parent to child, as with most Pakhtoon heritage, through a rich oral tradition that has survived the ravages of time (Aisha and Boase, 2003).

The single record of collection of Pashtu literature is preserved by Amanullah Khan of Wantrag. He served the Indian Army and during his services, he volunteered to establish a Pashtu Literary Society in which gradually he could not succeed. He continued his efforts and with the help of his senior officials departmentally got three of his works published including *Pashtu Baazgasht, Aaw Pashtu seekhe* and *Pashtu Qaida*. All these works have their Urdu and Hindi translation versions also. Besides through his constant individual efforts, he collected Pashtu dictionaries, religious scriptures including Pashtu version of the Holy Quran and Pashtu text books up to the 10th standard which are being taught in the frontier areas.

Amanullah Khan told the researcher that he could not succeed due to non-cooperation by his community fellows. The shift in ideology under the need and will to assimilate may be the main cause that Pakhtoons are not taking a serious note of such efforts which may help to revive their culture. Among all the respondents who were interviewed, only 2 % were found who can write in Pashtu with the Urdu script.

## SOME PAKHTOON PROVERBS

HAR CHATA KHPAL WATAN KASHMIR DE
(for everyone his country is like Kashmir)
Everyone sees his country or area the most beautiful in the world.

KOAG BAR TAR MANZELA NA RASAGEI
(A tilted load won't reach its destination)
Honesty is the best policy.

KHAR CHA HAR CHAIRE HUM LAR SHE, BIA HUM HAGHA KHAR WE
(The donkey will remain donkey, no matter where ever it goes)
Nature cannot be changed.

DA KHALI DAIG GHAG LOR DE
(The empty vessel noise is more)
An empty vessel makes much noise.

KHORI SAAG AW PASKAY DA PULAO ACHAWI
(He eats very simple food, but boasts as he is eating very rich food)
 Be contented with what you have.

DA CHA? PAKHPALA, GILA MA KAWA DA BALA
(This is by whom? by myself, So do not blame anyone else)
These are self-inflicted wounds, not by others.

CHINDAKHA PA LOOTA WAKHATA, WAYAL CHE KASHMIR MAY WALAIDO
(a frog climbed a stone, and said that I saw Kashmir)
It is said about somebody who is claiming to have done something which he does not have the power to do.

STA DA KHAIRA MAY TOBAH DA, KHO DA SPIE DE RANA KURRAY KA.
(Don't give me your alms, just save me from your dogs)
Do not do anything good to me, but it will be a great favor to me if you do not do any harm to me.

DA MAAR BACHAI MAAR WEE.
(The snake's baby is also a snake)
Nature can't be changed.

KA YAW WAR MAY KHATABASAY TA DA KHUDAI WOWAHI, AW KA DWA WAR MAY KHATABASAY MA DE KHUDAI WOWAHI.
(If you fool me once a curse on you, if you fool me twice a curse on me.) One must learn from his past experiences.

CHE ADE, HAGHASE YE LMASAY.
How the grand mother is, same is her grand-daughter.

CHI NA KAR, PA HAGHA THE SA KAR
When it is not any of your business, then stay away.

MOLA BAL TA MASALI KAVI PA KHAPLA PRI HAMLI KAWI
(Moulvi preaches to others, but sins himself)

CHI DA KAMAKAL LA DANG OUE UKHYAR LA ISHARA
(For foolish a kick, and for wise, only pointing out)

DA KAMAKAL MALGARI NA KHO UKHYAR DUSHMAN KHA DAE!
(A wise enemy is better than a foolish friend)

WRORI BA KAWU HESAB TAR MENZA
(The brotherhood at one side, and the business matters at the other)
We will behave like brothers, but we shall know what is yours and what is mine.

KHAR CHE MAKKAY TA LAR SHE, NO HAJI NE SHI
(If a donkey goes to Mecca, that doesn't make him a pilgrim of Hajj.)
Surrounding yourself with something you like won't turn you into it.

MUCH PA TOPA MA WALA
(Don't hit mosquito with tank.)
Don't waste your energy and resources on minor things.

WROR A GORRA KHORR A GHWARA
(It means from the brother you can predict the beauty of the girl.)

TOORR DA TORRAY DAE, SPIN DA INJUNO DAE
(Means that a man of dark complexion is for wars and the one with
white complexion is only for girls.)

## Religion

Pakhtoons are predominantly Sunni Muslims who follow the Hanafite
branch of Sunni Islam. A small minority of *Shia* Pakhtoons are largely
concentrated in Afghanistan. Studies conducted among the *Ghilzai* reveal
strong linkages between tribal affiliation and membership in the larger
*Ummah* (Islamic community), as most Pakhtoons believe themselves
descendants of Qais Abdur Rashid who purportedly had been an early
convert to Islam, thus bequeathing the faith to the entire Pakhtoon
population. A legacy of **Sufi** activity remains common in Pashtun regions as
evident in song and dance. Many Pashtuns have gained prominence as
Ulema (Islamic scholars), such as Dr. Muhammad Muhsin Khan who
translated the Noble Quran and Sahih Al-Bukhari and many other books
into English (S. Akbar, 1980).

| Muslim | | | | | Others | |
|---|---|---|---|---|---|---|
| Hanafite | | Shaafi | Jamat-e-Islami | Shiite | Hindu | Sikh |
| Barelvi | Deobandi | | | | | |
| 71% | 22% | 2% | 5% | 0% | 0% | 0% |

**Religious belief and schools of thought found among Pakhtoons in
Anantnag.**
**Source: Field based data.**

Little information is available on non-Muslim Pakhtoons as there is limited
data regarding irreligious groups and minorities, especially since many of the
Hindu and Sikh Pakhtoons migrated from Pakhtunkhwa after the partition
of India and later, after the rise of the Taliban. There is an affirmed
community of Sikh Pakhtoons residing in Peshawar, Parachinar, and
Orakzai Agency Pakistan. The origins of the Sikh Pakhtoons are unclear[3]
(ibid).

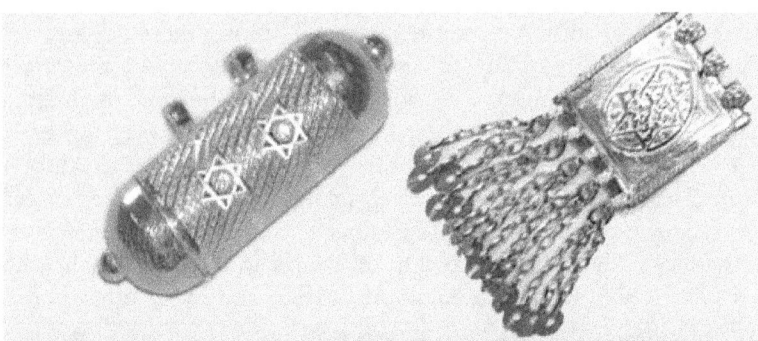

Afghan (Pashtun/Pukhtun) Taaweez. These are lockets worn around the neck. Notice the Star of David.

**One reason for least religious assimilation of Pakhtoons is the strict adherence to the ritualistic part of religion by these people.**
**Pic. Source: Pakhtoon.org**

The whole population of Pakhtoons of Anantnag like almost all Pakhtoons of the valley is Muslim with 93 % of them belonging to the Hanafite School. *Deobandi* sub sect of the Hanafite School are the people associated with the *Tabligue* movement (known as *Allah Wale* throughout India); *Barelwi(s)* are the followers of Ahmad Raza Khan and are known for their belief in shrines. Religion again is not in its traditional form or as it is among Pakhtoons of that side of border because fundamentalism has faded away with the ideological modernization of Pakhtoons particularly since the expansion and privatization of education in the valley which helped the cultural mixing and interchange of the tribal peoples of the valley as it did so with the Kashmiris.

## Women and Change

The lives of Pakhtoon women vary from those who reside in conservative rural areas, such as the tribal belt, to those found in relatively freer urban centers. Though many Pakhtoon women remain tribal and illiterate, others have become educated and gainfully employed. In Afghanistan the ravages of the Soviet occupation and the Afghan wars, leading to the rise and fall of the Taliban, caused considerable hardship amongst Pakhtoon women as many of their rights had been curtailed, in favor of a rigid interpretation of Islamic law.

The difficult lives of Pakhtoon female refugees gained considerable notoriety with the iconic image of the so-called "Afghan Girl" (Sharbat Gula) depicted on the June 1985 cover of *National Geographic magazine*. In addition in the rest of Asia, particularly in the rural settings, the male-dominated code of *Pashtunwali* often constrains women and forces them into designated traditional roles that separate the genders. The pace of change and reform for women previously has been slow as a result of the conservative social set up of Pakhtoon societies but modernization and education has to a considerable extent lead to the empowerment of Pakhtoon women (Benedicte, 1992).

**The world famous *Sharbat Gula*.**
**Source: nationalgeographic.com**

Modern social reform for Pakhtoon women began in the 20th century. During the early 20th century, Queen Soraya Tarzi of Afghanistan had been an early feminist leader whose advocacy of social reforms for women proved so radical that it led to the fall of her and her husband King Amanullah's dynasty. Even during the tumultuous Soviet occupation of Afghanistan, **civil rights** remained an important issue as feminist leader Meena Keshwar Kamal campaigned for women's rights and founded the Revolutionary Women of Afghanistan (RAWA) in the 1980s.

**The tendencies to modern outlook are evident among Pakhtoon
women globally today.**
**Source: Pakhtoon.org**

Today, Pakhtoon women vary from the traditional housewives who live in
seclusion to urban workers, some of whom seek or have attained parity
with men. Due to numerous social hurdles, the literacy rate for Pakhtoon
women remains considerably lower than that of males. Abuse of women
has been widespread, yet women's rights organizations, which find
themselves struggling with conservative religious groups as well as
government officials, have been actively challenging the practices. Benedicte
writes "a powerful ethic of forbearance severely limits traditional Pashtun
women's ability to mitigate the suffering they acknowledge in their lives"
(ibid).

As one can see among Pakhtoon women in Anantnag today, there are two
main divisions or sections of them, the age group of up to 30 which
includes the girl population in their teens and young ladies and the second
comprises the age group of 40 and above. There is a marked difference in
the ideology of these two groups due to the impact of assimilation viz-a-viz
modernization on the former group and of the traditionality and an
ideological attachment with the tradition on the latter one. The

responses/views of these two groups regarding some developmental issues related to assimilation are indicated in table 1.7 below;

**Table 1.7: There is a clear impact of the assimilation on the ideology of the Pakhtoon women as it is on the men folk since the last two decades in particular. Source: Field based data.**

| Women Group | Social Issue | View/Response |
|---|---|---|
| **Up to 30** | Women education | Strongly agree |
| | Jobs by women | Agree |
| | Age at marriage. | 20-25 |
| | Women as head of family | Agree |
| | Cultural expression of women | Agree |
| | Women in singing & other such areas | Agree |
| **40 & above** | Women education | Agree |
| | Jobs by women | Partially agree |
| | Age at marriage | 18-20 |
| | Women as head of family | Don't agree |
| | Cultural expression of women | Don't agree |
| | Women in singing & other such areas | Don't agree |

Today Pakhtoon women are not only on singing, sports and fashion but in military and politics throughout Asia. In Anantnag there is a new trend which is taken as a matter of pride that is to send girls for professional courses like Computer Science and Management. *Noreen*, a BCA student from Wantrag wants to do masters in Computer Science and go for an academic job. The main obstacles to women empowerment, the ideological and traditional restrictions are gone and now socio-economic development is the variable on which the development of Pakhtoon women folk in Anantnag depends. It is a general observation that Pakhtoons nowadays do not wait to invest on the education and all round development of their girls when they have the resources for it.

As found during the present study about 80 percent Pakhtoon women favor the present trend of their development and empowerment particularly receiving good education, doing jobs and giving away of the strict traditions like women should remain in the four wall, women can not do any job and the like. There may be a little or more disfavor to these modern values regarding the women status by the dominant male population in their patriarchal society but the fact is that Pakhtoon women surely want to come out of the veil, receive sound education and skill, work as their males do and want to express themselves, their talent and skill to the people of the valley and to the people of the world.

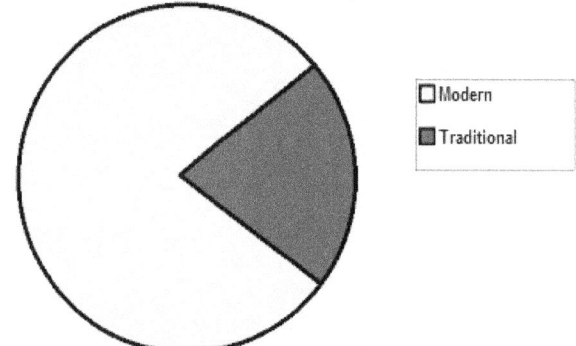

VIEW OF PAKHTOON WOMEN REGARDING WHAT THEIR STATUS SHOULD BE?

**Source: Field based data.**

Summarizing this chapter, it could be maintained that Pakhtoons of Anantnag in spite of having lost much of their culture to assimilation are at least distinct in their physique, color and mentality, features common to these people globally. The existence of a number of tribes and sub-tribes has not negated the fact that these people belong, as established by most of the theories on their ethnology to the Jewish race.

The social organization of Pakhtoons has been assimilated to the extent that almost every cultural component today is un-differentiable from their host culture. Ideology of these people has considerably changed to a status of modernism from traditionalism. Family, marriage and kinship have transformed to modern versions of their kind, where there is still a trend of further blending towards more global than local perspectives. The ethnic identity of Pakhtoons, their language and the status of women have been compromised to about 80 percent of it under the impacts of cultural assimilation.

# CHAPTER IV

# ASSIMILATION OF MACRO SOCIAL INSTITUTIONS AMONG PAKHTOONS

## CHAPTER IV

## ASSIMILATION OF MACRO SOCIAL INSTITUTIONS AMONG PAKHTOONS

As mentioned in the earlier chapter on ethnicity, Barth (1969) introduced a broad framework of macro-social formulations, meso-institutional and micro-individual levels of society. At each of these levels ethnicity is conceptualized in different ways. Viewing ethnicity within these layers is one way to make sense of ethnicity's many sides whilst demonstrating the inter relationships, the strong links that exist between layers of social structures. At the macro level are the broad frameworks which underpin the economic and political composition of society. Macro-structures are intertwined with the distribution of power, wealth and authority. Once entrenched, these may have significant influence on outcomes for ethnic minorities and majorities, often with oppressive consequences as attested by the treatment of mixed-race people.

This chapter also based largely on the fieldwork conducted during the present study discusses the impacts of assimilation on the macro social institutions like political and economic systems of the Pakhtoon society in Kashmir through a comparative analysis with the Pathans of India and Pakistan. It also deals with the changes and new cultural adoptions in crafts and sports among the Kashmiri Pakhtoons. Assimilation has also been analyzed in relation to the education and economic institutions like the occupational structure of the Pakhtoon society in Anantnag.

Meso-structures are the institutions which connect the state to the individual. These may be independent or regulated by the state. It is through this level of institution that ethnic identities are preserved or distinguished.

### The Jirga

The *Jhirga* is a tribal assembly of elders which takes decisions by consensus, particularly among the Pakhtoon people but also with other ethnic groups near them; they are most common in Afghanistan and among the Pakhtoons in Pakistan near its border with Afghanistan. It is similar to that of a town meeting in the United States or a regional assembly in England, where important regional matters are addressed among the people of the area.

The basis for Jirga is the Holy Quran which commands Muslims to *Shura* (consultation). *Loya* Jirga is held when there is an issue of special importance concerning the community's vital national and international interests. Jirga is a process of decision-making within the Pakhtoon societies in which serious discussions and decisions are made by involving all layers of the society. It is an unprejudiced and impartial body that takes decisions based on facts and logic. Indeed, evolution of political systems in different countries demonstrates that governments and institutions are built as a result of local gatherings and councils. Therefore, it is proclaimed that Jirga is an important political pillar of the civil system practiced and evolved in Pakhtoon societies for many years (Caroe, 1958).

In Jirga, comprehensive collective discussion and examination of the issues enable in-depth understanding, development and formulation of a common view or consensus that leads to a cohesive approach dealing with the concerning issue. This traditional process of mutual consultation also assists in developing a commitment shared by the community to implement the resolution that has been resolved. In the presence of a proper mechanism and the way Jirgas are held, the consequent broad-based understanding and the consensus reached facilitate to surmount fundamental issues threatening the Pakhtoon Society (Lindholm, 1982). The Jirga mainly comprises of the senior and elderly community members, more often politically influential and retired officials. The local *Auqaf* (a Jirga like body meant for similar functions in the Kashmiri society) also has members in the Jirga sometimes. Some recent issues that came to limelight as settled by the jirga in Wantrag and Pingwan Villages in Anantnag were those concerning inter-ethnic marriages and the efforts to avail the Scheduled Tribe status for the Pakhtoon community.

**Jirga which is still an important institution among Pakhtoons of Afghanistan exists only as a weak social fact in Anantnag.**
**Source: Pakhtoon.org**

In Anantnag, The All J & K Pakhtoon Jirga Forum looks after the issues of Pakhtoon welfare and development issues like those concerning reservation, cultural expression through media, rural development and the like. It also concerns the social issues related to the tradition and the normative structure of the Pakhtoon community within and in relation to other communities as well. The general secretary of the Forum Master Bashir Ahmad Khan told the researcher that banning of the cultural programmes staged by Pakhtoon women of Kashmir valley through T.V was a reaction to the exposure of the Pakhtoon women which is always regarded as a matter of dishonor by the Jirga. Since the last about two decades, however, the Jirga is losing its hold as the apex social body due to the shift in the ideology of Pakhtoons from conservative to the modernized. The main reason behind that is that the Jirga follows the basic traditional principles of the Pakhtunwali and thus sometimes leads to ideological clashes with the broad minded approaches of the new generations.

## Pashtunwali Code of Honor

The term *"Pakhto"* or *"Pashto,"* from which the Pashtuns derive their name, denotes a pre-Islamic honor, a religious code formally known as Pashtunwali (or *Pakhtunwali*) as well as the name of their language. Religious anthropologists believe Pashtunwali originated millennia ago during pagan times and has, in many ways, fused with Islamic tradition. Pashtunwali governs and regulates nearly all aspects of Pashtun life ranging from tribal affairs to individual "honor" *(nang)* and behavior (Bourdieu, 1966).

Numerous intricate tenets of Pashtunwali influence Pashtun social behavior. *Melmastia,* or the notion of hospitality and asylum to all guests seeking help, represents one of the better known tenets. Perceived wrongs or injustice calls for *Badal* or swift revenge. The British borrowed and popularized in the West a popular Pashtun saying, "Revenge is a dish best served cold". The code demands that men protect *Zan, Zar, Zameen,* which translates to women, treasure, and land. Some aspects promote peaceful co-existence such as *Nanawati* or the humble admission of guilt for a wrong committed, which should result in automatic forgiveness from the wronged party. Many Pashtuns continue to follow those and other basic precepts of Pashtunwali, especially in rural areas (Akbar, 1976).

As a matter of fact the historically strict traditional system of Pakhtoons has its roots in the very existence of the Pakhtunwali code. This system leaving no space for any process or action which results in the breaking or fading away of the Pakhtoon tradition and culture, was in itself an important social institution for the Pakhtoon culture. As today no such institution is operating and governing the social and cultural matters of the Pakhtoon society. In the households running under the joint system paradigm or have a patriarchal dominance, there are set rules for governing the overall social behavior of the family members but that operate at the micro level within the familial arena. It is clear that the death of or non existence of such institutions among the Pakhtoons of Anantnag is an acute sign of institutional assimilation among them because once they leave such institutions, their social setup has naturally to operate under the moral institutions of the dominant cultural groups. This may be one of the reasons that there is more influence of the local *Auqaf* system among them as compared to the Jirga.

## Primary Concepts of Pakhtunwali

*Melmastia* (hospitality) - To show hospitality to all visitors, regardless of whom they are, their ethnic, religious, or national background, without hope of remuneration or favor. Pakhtoons are widely considered to be the most hospitable people in the world; a Pakhtoon will go to great extents to show his hospitality, so much so, that in very many recorded cases it has been observed that a Pakhtoon has even provided his deadly enemy with sanctuary when he was asked for sanctuary by his rival. But in return, those guests who are accorded this are expected to do the same for their host (Akbar 1976).

*Badal* (justice/revenge) - This applies to injustices committed yesterday or 1000 years ago if the wrongdoer still exists. Justice in Pashtun lore needs elaborating: even a mere taunt (or "*Paighor*") is regarded as an insult - which can only usually be redressed by shedding of the taunter's blood (and if he isn't available, then his next closest male relation). This in turn leads to a blood feud that can last generations and involve whole tribes with the loss of hundreds of lives. Normally blood feuds in this all male dominated setup are then settled in a number of ways. Functionally, revenge protects the Pakhtoon social order (Girard, 1972).

*Nanawateh* (asylum) - Derived from the verb meaning to go in, this is used for protection given to a person who requests protection against his/her enemies. The person is protected at all costs. It can also be used when the vanquished party is prepared to go in to the house of the victors and ask for their forgiveness. It is a peculiar form of 'chivalrous' surrender in which an enemy seeks "sanctuary" at his enemy's house.

*Zmeka* (land) - A Pakhtoon must defend his land/property from incursions wherever he or she might reside.

*Nang* (honour) - The preservation of honor entails the defense of one's family and one's independence, while upholding cultural and religious requirements. The norm is that family relationships are the highest priority for an act of Nang, but when a situation of national or Pakhtoon honor arises, the priority changes. Khushal Khan Khattak has written that,

جهان شرم نام و ننگ دے........كهٔ دا نهٔ وي جهان رنگ دے

"The world is all but shame, good name and honor; if there is no honor the world is but naught" (Khushal, 1960).

*Namus* (Honor of women) - A Pakhtoon must defend the honor of

Pakhtoon women at all costs and must protect them from vocal and physical harm.

*Hewad* (nation) - Love for one's nation in Pakhtoon culture isn't just important, it's essential. A Pakhtoon is always indebted to their nation and must strive to perfect and improve it. A Pakhtoon considers it his obligation to defend his country Pakhtara ("Pakhtunkhwa" in modern colloquial Pashto) against any type of foreign incursion. Defense of nation means defense of honor, values, culture, tradition, countrymen and self (ibid).

*Dod-pasbani* (Protecting Pakhtoon culture) - It is obligatory for a Pakhtoon to protect Pakhtoon culture from dilution and disintegration. Pashtunwali advises that in order to successfully accomplish this, a Pakhtoon must retain the Pashto language since Pashto is the prime source of Pakhtoon culture and its understanding is therefore essential. Not being able to speak Pashto to Pakhtoon society often leads to the inability to understand the Pakhtoon culture, values, history and community.

*Tokhm-pasbani* (Protecting the Pashtun race) - Pakhtoons with their distinct Aryanic features are often immediately recognizable. Pakhtoons must take another Pakhtoon as a marriage partner. This stems from the general belief that 'half-Pashtuns' do not retain Pashtun language, culture, and physical features.

*De Pashtunwali Perawano* (Adhering to Pashtunwali) - In order to keep one's descendants from becoming *"durvand"* (Non-Pashtuns), a Pashtun must adhere to the Pashtunwali principles of culture, kin and pedigree. Those who do not will ultimately face revulsion and expulsion from Pakhtoon society (ibid).

## Secondary Concepts of Pakhtunwali

*Lashkar* - The tribal army. It implements the decisions of the *Jirga*.

*Loya Jurga* - An assembly of tribal elders called for various purposes whether waging war or composing peace, tribal or inter-tribal.

*Tsalweshti* - Derived from the word for forty, this refers to the tribal force that would implement the decision of a jirga. Every fortieth man of the tribe would be a member. A *shalgoon* is a force derived from the number twenty.

*Badragga* - Tribal escort composed of members of that tribe through which the travelers are passing. If a badragga is violated a tribal feud will follow.

*Hamsaya* - A non-Pashtun dependent group who attaches themselves to a Pashtun group, usually for protection. The Pashtun protector group is called a *naik*. Any attack on a *hamsaya* is considered an attack on the protector.

*Mlatar* - Literally, tying the back or "support". This refers to those members of the tribe who will actually fight on behalf of their leaders.

*Nagha* - Tribal fine decided by the council of elders and imposed upon the wrongdoer.

*Rogha* - Settlement of a dispute between warring factions.

*Hujra* - Common sitting or sleeping place for males in the village. Visitors and unmarried young men sleep in the *hujra*.

*Lokhay Warkawal* - Literally means 'giving of pot'. The idea that the tribe will do everything to protect an individual from an enemy (Nicholas and Sarwan, 2002).

## *Loosing of face*

Loss of face is irreconcilable with Pakhtunwali. According to Goffman (1955) and others, a person may experience embarrassment or blushing when the person perceives his/her face has been discredited in a particular encounter. Embarrassment felt by a person could disrupt the interaction, and thus, the person and the other participants have vested interest in protecting the person's face to keep the social encounter smooth. Goffman called this effort to maintain or to save face work (Kim & Nam, 1998).

Face is lost when the individual, either through his action or that of people closely related to him, fails to meet essential requirements placed upon him by virtue of the social position he occupies. Face may be lost when conduct or performance falls below the minimum level considered acceptable or when certain vital or essential requirements, as functions of one's social position are not satisfactorily met (Yau-fai Ho, 1976).

Today the Pakhtoons have such an ideological and mental makeup that there is no scope for that stoning to death, hanging, revenge or loosing of face. The present study brought to limelight lot of psychological facts and stigmatic attributes about these people which have all together gone but are still associated with their culture. Such things may exist among Pakhtoons depending upon the type of social organization but among the Pakhtoons of Anantnag, these are forgotten legends. One of the elderly respondents of Satranj Maidan (name withheld) told the researcher "our ancestors were insane, blood was cheaper than water for them; but now our girls go to school; we left that side because… what is there? No security, no jobs, no education".

### Education and Change

As mentioned earlier in the chapter on introduction, Pakhtoons migrated into the valley of Kashmir about 100 years back i.e. in 1912. Their population migrated with an estimated literacy of below 10 % for males and below 1 % for females. The enrollment in Afghanistan in 1926 was 21 % with the literacy rate gradually increasing up to 18.7 % for males and 2.8 % for females by 1973-74 as per the United States Agency for International Development and Government of Afghanistan, *National Demographic and*

*Family Guidance Survey of the Settled Population of Afghanistan* I, Kabul, 1975.

As Pakhtoons initially were not provided with the permanent citizen status of the J & K state, their education and literacy remained in the dark till the regime of Gulam Mohammad Bakshi the then Prime Minister of the state. Since then their literacy level has been improving gradually touching an average of 56.33 % with 32.16 % for males and 24.16 % for females in 2011 (As per the research data). There is an evident proof of assimilation in all the educational developments going on ever since their migration. It reveals considerable modernizing changes in the Pakhtoon ideology and way of life.

| Sex | Literacy at various levels of Education % | | | | | | Average |
|---|---|---|---|---|---|---|---|
| | Middle | 10th | 10+2 | Grad. | P.G | M. Phil /Ph. D | All levels |
| ♂ | 70 | 65 | 30 | 20 | 7 | 1 | 32.16% |
| ♀ | 65 | 60 | 10 | 7 | 3 | 0 | 24.16% |
| Average whole literacy | | | | | | | 56.33% |

Table 1.8 : Literacy of Pakhtoons at various educational levels.

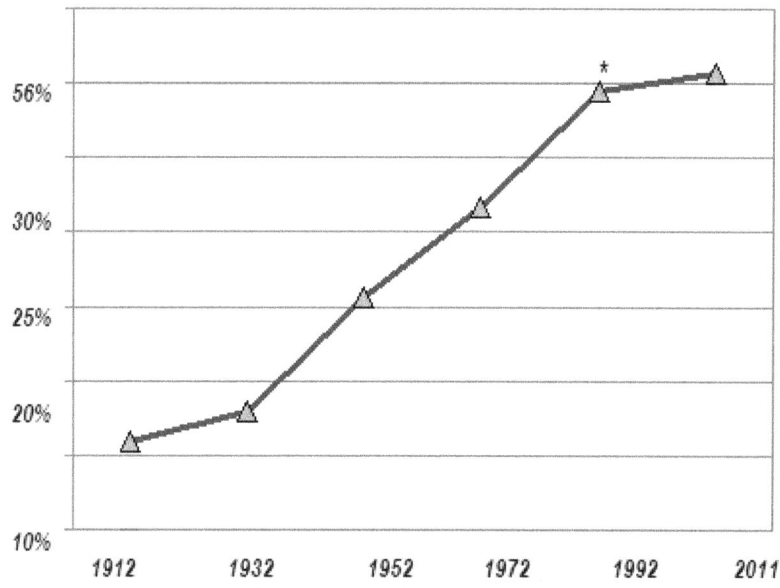

ESTIMATED LITERACY PATTERN OF PAKHTOONS SINCE THEIR MIGRATION

**\*Due to the political turmoil in the Valley in 1990s, the literacy remained at a halt for about a decade.**
**[Source: Field based data.]**

## Occupational Structure: The Trends

Many industrial activities such as carpentry, bricklaying, and shoemaking are done by part-time Pakhtoon specialists who also farm. However, in many areas non-Pathan occupational groups carry out these activities, as well as others such as weaving, black smithing, and gold smithing. An exception is the manufacture of guns; in certain areas, notably Derra Adam Khel south of Peshawar, Pathans produce guns in small factories.

In spite of the fact that a considerable number of Pakhtoons in Anantnag have government jobs, the main occupation is fruit business which exists as a major business enterprise among 65 percent of the Pakhtoons of the district. The difference in the fruit trade is topographical. Pakhtoons of the main town like Wantrag and Satranj Maidan produce about 200 boxes on an average while as there is prevalence of trading of cherry in Daddu, of walnut in *Cherpura* and among the Pakhtoon dwellings in Pahalgam, of maize in *Vailoo* zone and Manzmu in Qazigund. Pakhtoons, however, possess less land as compared to Kashmiris of the respective areas. Armed forces and Police are among the most favored government sectors for jobs among Pakhtoon youth of Anantnag.

The occupational structure of Pakhtoons of Afghanistan and Pakistan as listed above is quite different when compared with that existing here. During the fieldwork mere 2 % of the male population was found engaged in industrial arts like carpentry, smithing work, craftsmanship and 9 % with shop keeping as a side business other than agriculture. As a lot of ideological similarity was found between Pakhtoons and Kashmiris, the former likewise the latter, will only say they are employed when they have a government job and those vast orchids and rice fields are not counted for that matter.

Education sector has the most number of Pakhtoons working in mainly as teachers; however, Armed Forces and Police are the most favored in all the village settings. The least number goes to the Medical profession like doctor and Civil services, though there is of course a trend towards the latter among Pakhtoon youth. A considerable proportion is doing Engineering, preferably in the Electronics branch. The graphic representation of the mostly found job profiles among Pakhtoons in Anantnag is shown below:

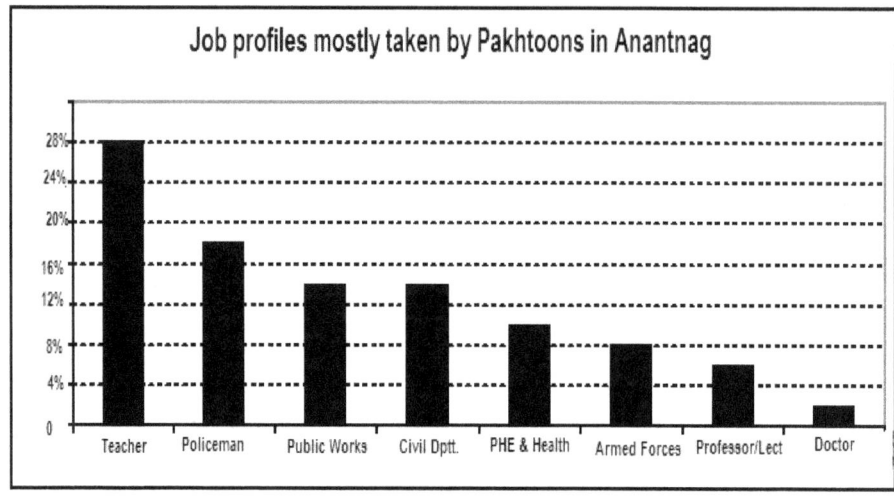

Table 1.9: Occupational structure of Pakhtoons for different age groups.

| S. No. | Age group | Sex | Occupation % | | | |
|---|---|---|---|---|---|---|
| | | | Government employee | Student | Peasant | Laborer |
| 1. | 10-20 | | 4 | 80 | 3 | 13 |
| 2. | 20-30 | | 20 | 40 | 30 | 10 |
| 3. | 30-40 | ♂ | 27 | 3 | 50 | 20 |
| 4. | 40-50 | | 10 | 0 | 70 | 20 |
| 5. | 50 & above | | 5 | 0 | 70 | 25 |
| 6. | 10-20 | | 1 | 80 | 3* | 0 |
| 7. | 20-30 | | 3 | 20 | 5 | 0 |
| 8. | 30-40 | ♀ | 4 | 2 | 7 | 0 |
| 9. | 40-50 | | 0 | 0 | 10 | 0 |
| 10. | 50 & above | | 0 | 0 | 3 | 0 |
| 11. | ALL | ♂ & ♀ | 7.4 % | 22.5 % | 25.6 % | 8.8 % |
| GRAND TOTAL | | #63.3 % | | | | |

*For females, being peasant is not an occupation but as a mark of division of labor.

# The remaining 36.2 % includes the dependent and children below 10.

[Source: Field based data.]

*Handicraft which is gone*

*Khamak* an intricate form of embroidery is worked in silk thread and is a trademark of Kandahar. Girls learn this ancient art form at an early age and continue to do it throughout their lives. Inspired by complex Islamic geometric patterns, Khamak is unique to Kandahar and is considered by art experts to be one of the world's finest embroidery techniques. It is traditionally used to decorate the striking, floor-length shawls worn by Southern Afghan men, as well as table linen, women's head-coverings, and girls' wedding trousseaus.

The practice of Khamak involves counting the threads of the fabric weave (hence cotton and linen are the best raw materials for this embroidery) in order to stitch geometric shapes with silk-thread. The work is done in a sitting position with the embroidery positioned on the top of a bended knee.

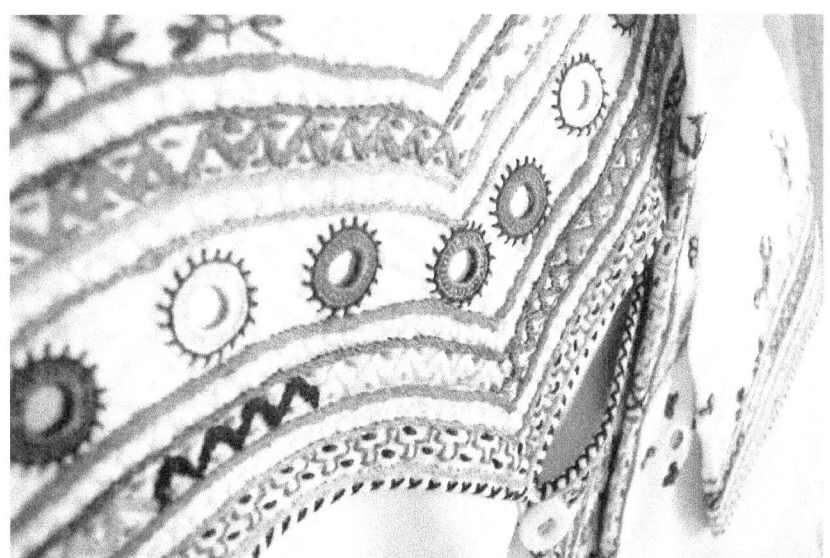

**Khammak is not today a part of Pakhtoon handicraft in Anantnag. Source:Pakhtoon.org**

Traditional Khamak includes natural themes, such as flowers, leaves and trees, in addition to the geometric shapes of Islamic art. The Pakhtoon women creatively combine natural and geometric shapes to create patterns much like their ancestors did. But they are also continuously creating new designs, many of which will be showcased for the first time to the public on their most beloved man (a brother, husband, or son). In Southern Afghanistan, women rely on their men to be the exhibitors of their fine art, and men have naturally learned to "show-off" publicly with the best embroidered work on their attire. There are various groups of Pakhtoon, each with their own style of embroidery. There is also a difference between

Pakhtoon urban embroidery and Pakhtoon nomadic embroidery (Bahl and Syed, 2003).

Pakhtoon women of Anantnag unlike doing their traditional handicraft were found doing the traditional *tilla* (needlework with silver threads) and *gabba* (a form of carpetry with woolen threads woven through woolen cloth and blankets).

## Business Shift

Fruit is the main asset of marketization among Pakhtoons where again they have followed the business tradition of Kashmiri local people of the respective areas. Apple trade is quite flourished in Satranj Maidan and Wantrag while as cherry is commercialized in Daddu on large scale besides apple. There are also dry fruit variants for export from these Pakhtoon dwellings like walnut from the former two villages and almond from the latter.

**Apple orchid in Satranj Maidan Anantnag.**

Doing such business is yet another area of the assimilation of Pakhtoons because there is no history of fruit business among them except for dry fruit and opium among the Pakhtoons of Afghanistan and Pakistan. They took such business only after their migration into the valley and gradually learned the dealings after succeeding in getting and cultivating enough land which could be utilized for commercial purposes. Table 1.10 shows the amount of land and orchid possessed by an average household in the three major Pakhtoon dwellings of Anantnag. The dry fruit is either sold to merchants outside or processed for local business.

| Name of the | Average land (in | Average orchid (in |
|---|---|---|

| Village | kanals) | kanals) |
|---|---|---|
| Satranj Maidan | 4 | 10 |
| Wantrag | 4 | 8 |
| Daddu | 3 | 7 |

**Table 1.10: Average orchid and land possessed in three large Pakhtoon dwellings in Anantnag.**

Pakhtoon communication style in the commercial field is rather indirect. It is therefore sometimes necessary to read between the lines for an answer rather than expect it to be explicitly stated. For example, if someone is asked if he can complete a job on time, it rarely gets "no" as the answer. It is, therefore, also important to phrase questions intelligently. Honor and shame should always be considered (ibid).

## Changes in Performing arts

Pakhtoon performers remain avid participants in dance, sword fighting, and other physical feats, Pakhtoon dances standing out as the most common form of artistic expression. The *Attan,* a dance with ancient pagan roots later modified by Islamic mysticism in some regions, has become the national dance of Afghanistan. A rigorous exercise, dancers perform Attan as musicians play native instruments including the *dhol* (drums), *tablas* (percussions), *rubab* (a bowed string instrument), and *toola* (wooden flute). Involving a rapid circular motion, dancers perform until all stop dancing in a fashion similar to Sufi whirling dervishes. Numerous other dances, affiliated with several tribes, include the *Khattak Wal Atanrh* (named after the Khattak tribe), *Mahsood Wal Atanrh* (which, in modern times, involves the juggling of loaded rifles), and *Waziro Atanrh* among others. A sub-type of the *Khattak Wal Atanrh* known as the *Braghoni* involves the use of up to three swords and requires great skill to successfully execute. Though males dominate most dances, some dance performances such as the *Spin Takray* feature female dancers. Additionally, young women and girls often entertain at weddings with the *Tumbal* (tambourine) (Spain, 1972).

**The traditional dances like *Khattak* are now only stage glamour and
in Anantnag no performer could be traced.
Source: Pakhtoon.org**

Traditional Pakhtoon music has ties to *Klasik* (traditional Afghan music
heavily inspired by Indian classical music), Iranian musical traditions, and
other various forms found in South Asia. Popular forms include the ghazal
(sung poetry) and Sufi qawwali music. General themes tend to revolve
around love and religious introspection. Modern Pashto music currently
centers around the city of Peshawar due to the various wars in Afghanistan,
and tends to combine indigenous techniques and instruments with Iranian-
inspired Persian music and Indian filmy music prominent in Bollywood.

Other modern Pakhtoon media include an established Pashto-language film
and television industry based in Pakistan. Producers based in Lahore have
created Pashto-language films since the 1970s. Pashto films, once popular,
have declined both commercially and critically in recent years. Past films
such as *Yusuf Khan Sherbano* dealt with serious subject matter, traditional
stories, and legends, but the Pashto film industry has, since the 1980s, been
accused of churning out increasingly lewd exploitation-style films. Pakhtoon
lifestyle and issues have been raised by Western and Pakhtoon expatriate
film-makers in recent years. Notable films about the Pashtun experience
include British film-maker Michael Winterbottom's *In This World* which
chronicles the struggles of two Afghan youths who leave their refugee
camps in Pakistan and attempt to move to the United Kingdom in search
of a better life, and the British mini-series *Traffik* (re-made as the American
film *Traffic*) which featured a Pashtun man (played by Jamal Shah) struggling

to survive in a world with few opportunities outside the drug trade. In addition, numerous actors of Pashtun descent also work in India's Bollywood film industry including Shah Rukh Khan, Kader Khan and Feroz Khan.[4] As discussed at length in the chapter on assimilation, the process is about giving away one's own culture only to adopt the dominant culture and it is not necessary that assimilation should always mean a trend towards modernity. Assimilation takes the migrated cultures away from their tradition and that may be towards modernization in some matters and otherwise in others. Same happened with the performing arts among the Pakhtoons of Anantnag because giving up the culture of theatre and stage performance seems a shift back to traditional culture. There are two different angles to look at it and Pakhtoons of Anantnag are through both the dimensions fallen prey to assimilation. Firstly, after settling in the valley, they left the tradition of performing arts because they have to surrender their culture to Kashmiri tradition where such performing was not prevalent. Secondly, once they left such tradition of theirs, they lost the chances of their cultural expression and thus again were left with no option than to adopt the Kashmiri art and cultural performing which is today quite evident in Pakhtoon marriages and festive,occasions.

## Sports: From *Buzkashi* to Cricket

*Naiza bazi,* a game involving riding horses and throwing spears, is a sport enjoyed among the Pashtun. Some Pashtun also have rock-throwing competitions. Pakhtoons in the northern regions of Afghanistan enjoy *buzkashi,* or "goat pulling," a game in which men on horseback compete for possession of a dead goat or sheep. 'Buz' means 'goat' and 'Kashi' means 'dragging' or "pulling" in Pashto language. The sport dates back to Genghis Khan's reign and continues with very little alteration today. The basic objective is to carry the headless carcass of a calf or goat around a flag and back to the starting point while on horseback with other riders trying to do the same thing by taking the carcass away from you. It's not a team sport, it's every man for him and that becomes apparent as soon as the game starts. It is played on a large open dusty field which does not appear to have many boundaries. Although *buzkashi* is primarily an individual sport, alliances are built up between various players. And then, between the alliances, the strongest players finally take control (or in this case the remnants of a headless calf) and ride off to victory (Nicholas and Sarwan, 2002).

**Traditional sport like *buzkashi* is indeed an extinct tradition among Anantnag Pakhtoons.**

**Source:Pakhtoon.com**

Polo, an ancient traditional sport in the region, has been popular among many tribesmen such as the Yusufzai. Like other Afghans, many Pakhtoons engage in wrestling *(Pehlwani),* often as part of larger sporting events. Cricket, largely a legacy of British rule in the North-West Frontier Province, has become popular, many Pakhtoons having become prominent participants (such as Shahid Afridi and Imran Khan). Football appeared more recently, the sport attracting that increasing numbers of Pakhtoons. Children engage in various games including a form of marbles called *buzul-bazi,* played with the knuckle bones of sheep. Although traditionally less involved in sports than boys, young Pakhtoon girls often play volleyball and basketball, especially in urban areas (Adams, 2006).

If we talk about the status of traditional sports of Pakhtoons in Anantnag, *buzkashi* and *naiza bazi* are the forgotten recreations. In a couple of households, the traditional sword was found but no sport associated with it was noticed. One of the respondents having one such sword in a rusted condition at Daddu told the researcher that *talwar bazi* (fighting with the swords) is played on ceremonial occasions in Gutlibagh. During the preliminary field visits there were affirmations about the existence of *talwar bazi* but it was not noticed on the marital ceremonies visited during the present study. There is, however, an overwhelming fashion of cricket among the new generations and a deep love for the game among the elderly population due to the attachment with the game as there are some world famous Pakhtoons in it like Shahid Afridi, Imran Khan, Irfan Pathan and the like.

**Cricket not *Buzkashi* is the most favored Sport among Pakhtoon youth today.**
**Courtesy: Gutlibagh.**

## *Use of Drugs: The Tradition That Must Go Here*

Pakhtoons of Afghanistan have been previously or still notorious for opium and other such drugs but those who migrated to the valley knew that they would not be accepted with such traditions in the Kashmiri society. So far during the present research no use of such drug variants has been found in vogue. The tobacco known as *Naswar* is associated with Pakhtoons. Naswar is primarily used in Central Asia, Iran, Afghanistan, Pakistan, Tajikistan, Sweden and India. In Pakistan it is predominantly used by members of the Pakhtoon ethnic group. Some of the many varieties of *Naswar* are produced in different parts of the Khyber-Pakhtunkhwa Province of Pakistan and the city of Bannu is especially famous for producing the best *Naswar* in Asia.

Naswar is held in the mouth for 10 to 15 minutes. If it is chewed it produces a bad taste in the mouth. Usually, the consumption varies but mostly people take it on an hourly basis as it is highly addictive. Nowadays most of the educated Pakhtoons are against the use of this product because of its detrimental health effects.

Though the tradition is still alive among the population group of above 50, it has abruptly dropped among the young generations counting to about 70 percent drop rate. The new versions of such drugs which are used include cigarette and the traditional Kashmiri *huqqa* called *Jajeer*. Unlike among their counterparts in Afghanistan and Pakistan addictive versions like opium and *gaanja* are not used among the Pakhtoons here. Naswar tradition belongs to Pakhtoon as well as Kashmiri culture and is fading away in both.

## Housing Pattern Transformations

The household (*kor*) is the primary unit of consumption and cooperation and is conceived of as those who share a hearth or as a man and/or his sons. Three main types of domestic unit are found: (1) the nuclear family; (2) the compound family, in which a patriarch and/or his sons and their wives live together and share expenses; and (3) the joint family, in which the nuclear families in a compound, frequently brothers, keep independent budgets. The fashion today is that soon after marriage a son starts his own nuclear family in 75 % cases in a newly built house or in extensions in the existing houses as shown below in the picture below;

**Compound structures are rare in the Pakhtoon dwellings in Anantnag.**
**Courtesy: Wantrag Anantnag.**

The analysis as illustrated by field observation of housing settlements of the Pakhtoon villages reveal certain transformations which exist along the lines of assimilation. It focuses on housing transformation in terms of pattern, process, and housing typology. These three transformation attributes reflect housing characters physically, socially and psychologically. The choice of housing pattern in villages like *Wantrag* is influenced by its neighborhood divisions particularly the Kashmiri housing patterns. The housing transformation pattern involves external additions, internal alterations, the choice of housing consumption, and threshold stress (Tipple 1991; 2000). Two categories of transformation, namely add-in type and add-on type, were retained. The former consists of changes within the existing building and the latter means the additional construction done on the building or within the premises to increase its floor area. Tipple's (1999) two categories of transformation are conceptually add-on (external adjustment) and add-in (external addition). Emergent features/concepts include rental housing typology, bungalow housing type, residential-cum-shop housing type, sharing of a kitchen, en-suite water closet, the popularity of toilets and a reduction in open spaces/courtyards; and the loss of reception to economic functions. The rural housing values such as kitchen gardens, animal rearing, and keeping chickens dropped by nearly one-quarter. From respondents' respective oral compound histories, the fencing of compounds increased, while the application of vegetable building materials dropped significantly. "Space specialization" with high-density furnishing is another feature of the Pakhtoon spatial setting of this era.

The retention of core ethnic housing values and the loss of peripheral spatial quality suggest a cultural transition of the social group. This suggests that ethnic sustainability is challenged by the urbanization process. The traditional mud houses are no longer in vogue, however a few of such houses were found as being used to keep grass and cattle fodder in Satranj Maidan and in Wantrag they are used as stores and cowsheds.

**The new housing structures reveal a complete transformation of housing pattern.**
**Courtesy: Satranj Maidan Anantnag.**

## Modernization and Pakhtoon Tradition

The operational definition of modernization is a change from traditional customs to ones that are forcibly or voluntarily borrowed from a dominant society that results in changes in behavior or customs. As a result of using principal component analysis, we interpret the modernization process as a series of four separate stages that societies go through (Divale and Seda 2001). The first stage (changes in government, trade, and education); the second stage (changes in health, technology and transportation); the third stage (changes in family structure, religion and personal toilet), and last stage (changes in behavior). Modernization occurs when a more dominant and complex society comes into sustained contact with a less complex society and the more dominant and complex society exerts an influence for change in the less complex society. Some of the change is involuntary, such as the influence of technology and more complex social organization imposed by the dominant culture, and some of the changes are voluntary, such as changes in role expectations and material culture desired by the members of the less complex society. When the differences in complexity between the two cultures are great the results can be psychologically traumatic (Wallace 1966; 1969). Much of the literature on modernization has focused on changes in the mental outlook of members of cultures that are adopting "Western" values and behavior as a result of colonial heritage. However, this process has occurred whenever a more complex culture conquered or had sustained contact with less complex cultures. One can imagine that these same processes happened when imperial Romans conquered Spain and Gaul, when the Harappa civilization spread in the Indus valley, and when the Assyrians conquered Mesopotamia. The birth of Christianity is probably the result of a revitalization of Israeli culture caused by Roman conquest and influence. The process of changes in worldview that occurs among members of the conquered culture is what we call "modernization." In general, social scientists measure these changes in worldview through changes in the material and social reality of the conquered culture (Divale and Seda 2001).

Smith and Inkeles (1966) state that modern generally means a national state characterized by a complex of traits including urbanization, high level of education, industrialization, high rates of social mobility, and the like. Many of the items used in instruments of individual measures of modernization suggest they are measuring psychological change in the individual as he or she goes from a traditional to a modern worldview.

Neo-liberal scholars and development gurus who perceive existing marginalization of non-western cultures, traditional western and non-mainstream cultures as desirable and the postmodernists and critical theorists who conclude that it is undesirable to agree on the sources and facilitators of cultural homogenization in the globalizing world. The consensus is that cultural homogenization is the result of a powerful globalizing force. Various perspectives highlight aspects of the globalizing force - migration/immigration, capitalist industrialization, western patriarchy, tourism, international trade, colonization, the media and the new communication/ information technology such as the Internet (ibid).

The evolutionary process of globalization is beyond human control, according to functionalists. The dynamics of human demographics and the social structure initiate migration processes that gradually facilitate and widen the circle of culture contact to a global scale. Once the contact is made an evolutionary, progressive, irreversible cultural process is set into motion moving through competition, accommodation, and eventual assimilation into a core culture (Park, 1950; Gordon, 1964). From the perspective of Gordon (1964) and according to Feagin and Feagin (1999), accompanying cultural assimilation are structural assimilation (gaining entry into associations and primary groups of the core society), marital assimilation (increased intermarriages), identification assimilation (developing identity and image linked to the core society), attitude assimilation (acceptance of physically diverse members of society), behavior assimilation (absence of intentional discrimination against physically diverse people), and civic assimilation (disappearance of value and power conflict from society). As is evident from the theoretical discussion above, modernization which is almost the another name of development in the developing countries like India, has always provided a considerable boost to the assimilation process for the Pakhtoon society in Anantnag more sharply for the last two decades. 95 % of the respondents irrespective of age, sex and literacy agree with the fact that any sort of modernization will always be benefited from at the cost of local language in the areas like English Education; at the cost of traditional costume in areas like media and communication; at the cost of moral values in the areas of women liberalization and at the cost of the Pakhtoon culture in the modern globalised world.

Modernization brings more choices, assets, luxury and comfort as most of the Pakhtoons believe. But for an ethnic group based on fundamentals of tradition and religion, it will consequently mean a lot of compromise with the value system as *Purdah* and working women can not go comfortably together under such system. Most of the Indian traditionalists like Yogendra Singh (1996) have maintained that tradition and modernity can't go together without negating each other. Thus Pakhtoons had to choose and they opted for modernization and development and thus have to bear assimilation.

**Pakhtoons of India: A Comparison**

India has been attracting invaders, travelers and traders since the time of Alexander the Great. Every invader had left its marks on the geography, history and culture of the country. The impact of some like the Moguls is very prominent in the monuments like the Taj Mahal. The others such as Iran had left its legacy in the language and literature. One set of invaders whose marks are either not visible or little attention has been paid to them were by the Afghans or the Pathans as they are popularly known in India (Haleem, 2005).

The word Afghan and Pathan is synonymous when we deal with the history of the sub-continent. Pathans came as invaders, traders and they served in the armies of the rulers, whoever was on the Throne. They were hired as soldiers, officers and diplomats by different rulers throughout the history of the last few centuries. Moreover, all the clans would follow from the tribal areas of Afghanistan and settle in the green pastures of India.

Very little is known of the legacy of these Pathans, except that they still live as close community in, Punjab, Uttar Pradesh, Central India and Bihar on the North Eastern borders. The Indian film industry has always thrived on the actors with the family name of *Khan* and it was always assumed that their ancestors were Pathans.

**Khan Abdul Gaffar Khan.**

*Pathans of Punjab*

The Pathans of Punjab are originally Pakhtoon people (Pathans) who have settled in the Punjab region of Pakistan and India. These Pakhtoon communities are scattered throughout Punjab. These non-frontier Pathans are usually known by the town or locality in which they are settled, e.g., Kasuri Pathans or Multani Pathans. They should not be confused with the Hindkowan people, who have a distinct identity from the Punjabi Pathans and are geographically viewed as a transitional ethnic group between Punjabis and Pashtuns (Haleem, 2005).

These colonies of Pathans (Pashtun people or ethnic Afghans) are accounted for by Sir Densil Ibbetson in the following manner "during the Lodi and Suri dynasties many Pathans migrated to India especially during the reign of Bahlol Lodhi and Sher Shah Suri. These naturally belonged to the Ghilzai section from which those kings sprung" (ibid).

Large number of Pathans accompanied the armies of Mahmud of Ghazni, Muhammad of Ghor and Babur, and many of them obtained grants of land in the Punjab plains and founded Pathan colonies which still exist. Many Pathans have also been driven out of Afghanistan due to devastated invading forces such as Genghis Khan and his Mongol armies, including internal feuds or famine, and have taken refuge in the plains east of the Indus River where the Mongols marked the line of their aggression.

The tribes most commonly to be found in the Punjab region are the Yusufzai, Mandanr, Lodhi, Kakar, Sherwani, Orakzai, Tanoli, Karlanri and the Zamand Pathans. Of these the most widely distributed are the Yusufzai, of whom a body of 12,000 accompanied the Mughal Emperor Babur in the final invasion of India, and settled in the plains of India and the Punjab. But as a rule the Pathans who have settled away from the frontier have lost all memory of their tribal divisions, and indeed almost all their traditional characteristics.

## *Bhopal*

This Pathan state was founded by an Orakzai tribesman from the Tirah area in 1710-11. Dost Mohammad Khan was a soldier in the Mughal King Aurangzeb's army. It was the time when the Mughal Empire was crumbling and the small states and their rulers were employing fighters to keep their fiefdoms. Dost Mohammad Khan became one of such Warriors with a group of 100 Pashtoons who earned their living by using their skill of swordsman ship and horse riding. He started capturing the areas around Bhopal in the middle of 18th Century and built strong forts to establish himself as the Ruler. Ever since he took over the area, the other tribesmen followed and the practice stopped only after the Partition of India in 1947.

Traditional foods of Pakhtoons in Bhopal are no different from the rest of India, however the Pathans eat a lot of meat and they do not serve lentils to the guests especially in the villages. They prepare fried sweet pastry pieces called *Ghonzakhi* which is given to the bride when she goes to her in laws or someone who is travelling far. They also prepare pancakes on rainy days or for the guests which are called *Waishallay* (called *Cheelay* in Bhopal Language) (ibid).

## Bihar

The Pathan lands and villages are scattered all over Bihar. There is a famous place called *Sher Ghati* and villages in that area are reputed for having wild Pathans. In Patna there are many Mohallas inhabited by the Pathans and they are named after the clans such as "Lodhi Kadrra", *"Khattak Toli"* and *"Afridi Tola"*. There are also two gardens named Kalo Khan and Mallo Khan. These were the two of the commanders who came with Taimur when he attacked India in 8th Century.

Some of the family traditions still followed strictly in Bihar include:

1. When a child is born, they shoot in the air. Three shots for a boy and two for a girl.
2. The family has kept some of the swords and shields safe although they were in a bad condition.
3. The men shout outside the door when they enter their own house, so that if there are any women guests, they could cover themselves.
4. The family is strictly religious and they kept the men and the women quarters separate from each other.
5. At the time of the wedding, no demand is made for the Dowry and the boy's family will always present two gold coins in a plate at the time of the Rukhsati (bride leaving her parent's house) to the bride's family. It is usually given to the bride now a days.
6. A lot of meat is cooked at the wedding feast. Special meat with no spices is cooked in earthenware and is eaten with leavened bread baked on the Charcoal (ibid).

## Maleer Kotla

Situated at a distance of 28 miles to the south of Ludhiana and 36 miles from Patiala. It has a population of 100,000 and the total area of the state is 164 square miles. It is comprised of 213 villages and has rich fertile land plain broken by sand drifts here and there. The Muslims are 65% of the population and 20% of them are of Pathan origin (ibid).

The level of education amongst the Muslim population is low, but those Pathans who do get education, usually join the government service. Their preferred field is Police and it happened that they are successful Police officers. Some of the Pathans are renting out their properties and a few of them are still keeping the old family business of rearing horses and selling them in the annual fairs of Punjab.

Most of them are religious, and they send their children to several of the Madrassas in the city where the boys and girls study. Children from the nearby villages also come to such Madrassas and Quranic education is considered compulsory. There are schools and one college for girls. For

Post Graduation, they go to either nearby Patiala or Ludhiana.

- The Kamees Shalwar is called "The Pathan dress".
- The traditional embroidered shoes are also called *Pathani* shoes by the local population and they are worn on special occasions.
- Pathan women observe Purdah strictly when they go out. They used to wear *Burqas*, but now they are using Shawls and big sheets of material to cover themselves.
- The Pathan married women will always spend the weekend (Sundays) with her parents along with her husband and children. Her parents make sure that she is well entertained and there are plenty of meat especially Kabab and Tandoori Naan are cooked for her. This tradition continues until her death. In the absence of her parents, the brothers and their wives will keep this tradition.

Up until 1903, the Pathans of Maleer Kotla did speak Pashto amongst themselves. However it gradually died down and now Punjabi is the common language with Urdu spoken by the Muslims. There are 29 shrines of all sizes in Maleer Kotla and most of the saints buried there came from Afghanistan. The Pathans respect and believe in the power of these saints (ibid).

## Uttar Pradesh

It is the biggest state of India which had the largest number of Pathans living in many big cities. Rohilla State (Rohail Khand) is the area in U.P Province, in which Pakhtoons were either given land by the emperors or they settled for trade purposes. *Roh* was the name of the area around Peshawar city, in Pakistan. Yousafzai Pathans especially Mandarr sub clan, living in this valley were also known as Rohillas when they settled down the area was known as *Katehr*, which literally means soft well aerated loam which is extremely suitable for cultivation. It later became known as Rohil Khand (the land of the Rohillas). The great majority of Rohillas migrated between 17th and 18th Century (ibid).

Although the Pathans are poor in this area they are still living off their wits and courage, sometimes taking law into their own hands. Taking revenge is still common and on a few occasions, there were murders which even the police could not handle.

Farrukhabad has a mixed population of Pathans dominated by the Bangash and Yousafzais. In Qaim Ganj there are many Pathan landlords who do not do much and give their land to be cultivated by other communities. They keep guns and shoot at the time of the weddings or at childbirth.

## Pathan Traditions in U.P

- *Orbal*: The tiny plaits of hair at the time of the weddings for the bride. It is dying now in the educated families.
- Boiled meat eaten with Nan bread. It is called *Tar Tanoori*.

- Rampur knife industry was the pride of the town. Some knives are still being made and the young men carry them to show off. These days the same professional ironmongers are making good copies of the guns at a small level. These guns are used for hunting which is a pastime of the Pathans.
- The Jirga system is intact and for small disputes people do call a Jirga.
- Snuff is used and special, elaborate boxes were in fashion but not now.
- The youngsters kiss the hands of their elders.
- They do not smoke or chew *Paan* (beetle leave) in front of their parents.
- Until 1940s the white *Burqa* (shuttle cock like shroud which women of Afghanistan wear when they go out) was abandoned by many women of Uttar Pradesh 20 years ago but it is in fashion now in an Arab style, due to the identity crises.
- The first Thursday of the Lunar month is considered auspicious and sweet dishes are prepared to send to the local shrine for the poor to eat.
- A married woman should spend the first day of the new moon in her Parents' house and she has to sight the moon there.
- A pregnant woman should drink milk in the light of the full moon if she wants her baby to be fair skinned. On the sixth day after the Childbirth, the woman is taken out at night in the courtyard and she looks at the stars. If it is a cloudy night she must do it the next day.
- At weddings, most of the traditions are common with the other U.P Muslims but when bride and the groom are brought together for the Ceremonies of the Mirror and Quran (*Arsy Mashaf*) an elderly lady of the bride's family must pull her plaited hair before the groom looks at her face in the mirror for the first time.
- *Shalwar Qamees* and Turban is a must for the men on special occasions.
- If you don't eat enough meat, it is considered a lack of proper diet. *Handay Ka Gosht* (meat cooked in a clay pot) *Tikka* (small pieces of meat which is barbecued).
- Some of the Pashto words are still use e.g. *Patka* (turban) *Peshawari Chappal* (Sandles from Peshawar) *Loopatta.* (Long scarf) *Saaloo* ( shawl ).
- Parda is strictly observed by women in the countryside (ibid).

The Indian Pathans residing in these states have lot of traditional differences as compared to Pakhtoons of the valley of Kashmir. In their case it again becomes clear that though they are holding a few of their traditions to retain their *Pakhtunness* like observing purdah and using the Pathan dress yet their language is gone or is dying, the traditional rituals are now being abandoned by the young generations, they are shifting from their traditional occupations and the like. However, as far as the studies done on the Pathans in these states are concerned there seems to be a low impact of the local cultures on them as compared to the scenario in the valley. This may be because of the demographic majority of Pakhtoons in these areas or due to the their frequent and constant cultural contacts with their counterparts unlike the Pakhtoons of Anantnag as it was noticed that only a 10 % of the Pakhtoons here have contacts with their relatives on the other side of the border and 20 % have contacts with Pakhtoons in other states of the country.

One generalization, however, could be established based upon the studies on Pakhtoons outside Jammu and Kashmir and the present one on the Pakhtoons of Anantnag in Jammu and Kashmir that their culture was brought through migration of these people into India due to economic, political and social causes and was initially retained. But gradually it started assimilating and is today moving on the same fashion throughout India. Though some people or organizations of this community are trying to retain or save their culture and tradition with the help of media, education and information technology. As the findings and data reveal Pakhtoon culture has been and is assimilating throughout India towards the cultures they contacted and are living with.

The only social institution which comparably has been least compromised is religion of Pakhtoons of Anantnag which is predominantly Islam. It is globally known by studies on assimilation that religion always is the least assimilated. The reason to that for Pakhtoons is that the social organization of these people is itself based on the fundamental sub structure of Islamic law. The *Pakhtunness* is nothing but a local interpretation and social implication of Islamic doctrines adopted and traditionally held by Pakhtoons not only throughout India but globally too. Thus loosing religion is almost a taboo for these people implying social execution.

The macro-social institutions of the Pakhtoon society were in fact the first to assimilate because they are socially external unlike the institutions based on psychology, ideology and belief system like cultural values, marriage and kinship. The political systems like Jirga have been left with less scope under the impacts of modernization which is based on rationality and global perspectives. Education as revealed by the data on literacy is always positively associated as in this case with development and modernization. Business and entrepreneurship have got a boost with the growth in transport and communication technology in the valley and particularly for the last twenty years so for the Pakhtoons of Anantnag. Traditional sport is almost gone with the youth taking contemporary global games like cricket to be mentioned here for which Pathans are globally known. Housing transformations from old traditional to the modern cement and iron structures was an immediate consequence of the likeness towards a modern image by Pakhtoons as evident in villages like Satranj Maidan.

## REFERENCES [For Chapter IV & V]

Adams, Tim. (2006). The Path of Khan. *The Observer.* London.

Ahmad, Aisha and Roger Boase. (2003). *Pashtun Tales from the Pakistan-Afghan Frontier.* New Delhi: Saqi Books.

Ahmed, Akbar S. (1976). *Millennium and Charisma among Pathans: A Critical Essay in Social Anthropology.* London: Routledge & Kegan Paul.

Ahmed, Akbar S. (1980). *Pukhtun economy and society.* London: Routledge and Kegan Paul.

Ahmed, Akbar, S. (1982). Order and Conflict in Muslim Society: A Case Study from Pakistan. *Middle East Journal,* Vol. 36, No. 2 (Spring, 1982), pp. 184-204.

Aisha, Ahmad and Roger, Boase. (2003). *Pashtun tales from the Pakistan-Afghan frontier.* Saqi Books.

Ali, Sharifah Enayat. (1995). *Cultures of the World: Afghanistan.* New York: Marshall Cavendish.

Alice, Albinia. (2010). *Empires of the Indus: The Story of a River.* W.W. Norton & Company.

Allen, Charles. (2000). *Soldier Sahibs: The Men Who Made the North-West Frontier.* London, UK: Abacus.

Bahl, Taru and M. H. Syed. (2003). *Encyclopedia of the Muslim World.* New Delhi: Anmol Publications.

Barth F. (1969). *Pathan Identity and its Maintenance.* In, *Ethnic groups and Boundaries. The social Organization of Culture Difference.* Boston: Little, Brown.

Barth, Fredrik .(1972). *Political Leadership among Swat Pathans.* London: Athlone Press.

Barbara, Robson; Juliene, Lipson; Farid, Younos; Mariam, Mehdi. (2002). *The Afghans – Their History and Culture.* United States.

Benedicte, Grima. (1992). *Performance of Emotion Among Paxtun Women,* University of Texas Press.

Bonilla, E. S. (2005). *Ethnogenesis: Foundations of thought and action.* Canada: Trafford.

Bourdieu, P. (1966). *The Sentiment of Honour in Kabyle Society.* In J. G. Peristiany (Ed.), *Honour and Shame: The Values of Mediterranean Society.* Chicago: University of Chicago Press.

Bowles, Gordon. (1977). Peoples of Asia. Oxford University Press.

Burnes, Alex. (1835). *Travels intoBokhara.* London: Eland Books.

Caroe, Olaf. (1958). *The Pathans 550 B.C. - A.D. 1957.* Oxford University Press.

Clifford, Mary Louise. (1989). *The Land and People of Afghanistan.* New York: Lippincott.

Divale, William ; Seda, Albert (2001) Cross Cultural Codes of Modernization. *2000 World Cultures,* 11 (2): 152- 170.

Elster, J. (July, 1990). Norms of Revenge. *Ethics,* 100 (4), 862-885.

Dupree, Louis. (1980) *Afghanistan.* London: Oxford.

Edwards, David B. (1996). *Heroes of the Age: Moral Fault Lines on the Afghan Frontier.* Berkeley: University of California Press.

Feagin, J. and Feagin, C. (1999). *Racial and Ethnic Relations.* Upper Saddle River, NJ.: Prentice Hall.

Fenton, S. (1999). *Ethnicity: Racism, class and culture.* Hong Kong: Macmillan.

Fenton, S. (2003). *Ethnicity.* Cambridge: Polity Press in association with Blackwell.

Firasat, S. Khaliq; S, Mohyuddin A. et al. (2007). Y-chromosomal evidence for a limited Greek contribution to the Pathan population of Pakistan. *European Journal of Human Genetics.*

Girard, R. (1972). *Violence and the Sacred.* (Patrick Gregory, Trans.) Baltimore: The Johns Hopkins University Press. (Originally published 1972) as *La Violence et le sacré.* Paris: Editions Bernard Grasset.

Goffman, E. (1955). On face work: an analysis of ritual elements in social interaction. *Psychiatry,* 18. 213-31.

Goffman, Erving. (1959). *Presentation of Self in Everyday Life.* Garden city: N. X. Doubleday.

Gordon, M. N. (1964). *Assimilation in American Life: The Role of Race, Religion and National Origin.* New York: Oxford University Press.

Gould, R. V. (2000). Revenge as Sanction and Solidarity Display: An Analysis of Vendettas in Nineteenth-Century. *American Sociological Review,* 65 (5), 682-704.

Haleem, Safia. (2005). *Study of Pathan Communities in Four States of India.*

Halliday, Tony. (Ed.) 1998. *Insight Guide Pakistan.* South Carolina: Langenscheidt Publishing Group.

Haralambos, M and Heald, R.M. (2006) *Sociology: themes and perspectives.* New Delhi: Oxford University Press.

Inglehart, R. (1990). *Culture Shift in Advanced Industrial Society.* Princeton University Press.

J. B. Frazer. (1843). *An Historical and Descriptive Account of Persia and Afghanistan.* Oxford University Press.

Kakakhel, Syyed Bahadur Shah Zafar. (1981) *Pashtoon Taareekh Kay Aienay Main* (Pashtoons in the light of history). Gujrat: Abdur Rasheed Press.

Khan, Ghani. (1947). *The Pathans.* Peshawar.

Khattak, Khushal. (1960). (Ed.) *Divan-e-Khushal Khan Khattak.* Peshawar:

Idara-e-Ishaat-e-Sarhad.

Kim, J. Y. & Nam, S. H. (1998). The Concept and Dynamics of Face: Implications for Organizational Behaviour in Asia. *Organization Science*, 9 (4), 522-534.

Leach, Edmund R. (1960). *Aspects of Caste in South India, Ceylon, and Northwest Pakistan*. Oxford University Press.

Lewis, Paul M. (2009). *Pashto - Northern*. Dallas, Texas: SIL International.

Lindholm, C. (1982). *Generosity and Jealousy, The Swat Pukhtun of Northern Pakistan*. New York: Columbia University Press.

McCarthy, Rory. (2010). Pashtun clue to lost tribes of Israel. *The Guardian*. London.

Moore, James (1861). *The Lost Tribes*. Oxford University Press.

Nath, Samir (2002). *Dictionary of Vedanta*. New Delhi: Sarup & Sons.

Niamatullah. *History of the Afghans*. Indus Publications.

Nicholas Awde and Asmatullah Sarwan. (2002). *Pashto: Dictionary & Phrasebook*. New York: Hippocrene Books.

Nyrop, Richard F., and Donald M. Seekins, (Eds.) (1986). *Afghanistan: A Country Study*. Washington.

Park, R. (1950). *Race and Culture*. Glencoe, Illinois: Free Press.

Pennell, T. L. (1975). *Among the Wild Tribes of the Afghan Frontier*. (2$^{nd}$ ed.). Karachi: Oxford University Press.

Raverty, H. G. (1878). Notes on Afghanistan and Balochistan, Vol I & II, Quetta: Nisa Traders.

Shackle, C. (1980). Bulletin of the School of Oriental and African Studies. (3$^{rd}$ ed.). Cambridge University Press. 43, pp. 482–510.

Singh, Yogendra. (1996). *Modernization of Indian Tradition: A Systemic study of Social Change*. India: Rawat.

Smith, A. D. (1986). *The Ethnic Origin of nation*. New York: Basil Blackwell.

Smith, D. H; and Inkeles A. (1966) The OM Scale: A Comparative Socio-psychological Measure of Individual Modernity. *Sociometry*, 29:353-77.

Smith, Huston. (2003). *The New Encyclopædia of Islam*. Rowman Altamira.

Smith, L. (2002). *The Marriage Model with Search Frictions*. Working Paper.

Spain, James W. 1972. *The Way of the Pathan*. Oxford University Press.

Vidya Prakash Tyagi. (2009). *Martial Races of Undivided India*. New Delhi: Gyan Publishing House.

Vogelsang, Willem. (2002). *The Afghans*. Wiley-Blackwell.

Wallace, A. (1969) *The Death and Rebirth of the Seneca*. New York: Vintage Books.

Wallace, A. F. C. (1966). *Religion: An anthropological view*. New York: Random House.

Wallace, Anthony, F. C and Raymond, D. Fogelson. (1965) *The Identity Struggle*. In, I. Boszormenyi and J. L. Framo (Eds.), *Intensive Family Therapy, Theoretical and Practical Aspects*. New York: Harper & Row.

Wallerstein, I. (1974). *The Modern World-System: Capitalist Agriculture and the Origins of European World-Economy in the Sixteenth Century.* New York: Academic Press.

Waters, M. (1995). *Globalization.* New York: Routledge.

Wimmer, A. (2008a). Elementary strategies of ethnic boundary making. *Ethnic and Racial* Studies, 31(6): 1025-1055.

Wimmer, A. (2008b). The making and unmaking of ethnic boundaries: A multilevel process theory. *American Journal of Sociology*, 113(4): 970-1022.

Yossi, Klein, Halevi. (1991). In Search of the Ten Lost Tribes. *The Jerusalem Report*, Jun 13, 1991.

Yusufzai, Rahimullah. (1989). The Frontier Connection. *Newline*, October 1989 (pp.26-27).

## Other Sources [Unpublished/Thesis/Organizational Data]

1. Afridi, Azim. (2005). *Pashtun Customs Related to Weddings.* [www.khyber.org]
2. Encyclopædia Britannica Online Edition. Retrieved 18 January 2007.
3. "*Afghanistan: Glossary*". British Library. Retrieved 15 March 2008.
4. "*Pathan*". Houghton Mifflin Company. Retrieved 7 November 2007.
5. Ghani, K. G. *The Pathan-* Retrieved August 13, 2008, from: http://khyberwatch.com
6. Inam-ul haq. *Pukhtunwali.* Unpublished article.
7. Mohammad Sher. *The Pathan Customs.* Self published.
8. *Encyclopædia of Muslim Biography.* A.P.H. Publishing Corporation.
9. Alfred Edersheim. *The Life and Times of Jesus, the Messiah.*
10. Sir Thomas Holditch. *The Gates of India.*
11. "*Ethnic groups*". The World Fact Book. Central Intelligence Agency (CIA).

## Webliography

51. http://www.guardian.co.uk/world/2010/jan/17/israel-lost-tribes-pashtun
52. http://www.khyber.org/culture/customs/birth.shtml
53. http://www.khyber.org/culture/customs/wedding.shtml
54. http://www.khyber.org/culture/customs/death.shtml
55. http://www.khyber.org/culture/customs/sociallife.shtml
56. *Pashtun.* Britannica On-Line. retrieved 18 January 2007.
57. M. Kieffer. Encyclopedia Iranica Online Edition.
58. Pashto language and identity formation. *Contemporary South Asia*, (1995, July), Vol 4, Issue 2, p.p 151, 20.
59. *The Pashtun Code* The New Yorker. Retrieved 18 January 2007.

## SUMMARY

There is a dire need to preserve the ethnicity of Pakhtoons mostly the *Pashtu* language among the new and coming generations if this community wants to survive their culture and tradition. Pashtu language is surely dying away with time among the new generations. In Akingam and Kokernag areas, there are Pakhtoons who do not speak *pashtu* language at all. Thus the question of such peoples' Pakhtoon ethnic identity remains unjustified.

The local custom, particularly the traditions of marriage is to be recovered and retained as well. Ethnic endogamy as it always does have been found effective in the passage of tradition from generation to generation. Marriage with Kashmiris as in Pingwan Achabal was found to foster assimilation and even decay of Pakhtoon culture.

Pakhtoons have not learned maintaining a balance between preserving their ethnicity and working for the socio-economic development of the community because on one hand they are losing their culture and language for example but on the other hand they are still far away from what may be called a developed or self sustained community.

Pakhtoons have to inculcate and encourage the use of traditional costume among the new generations. There is still lot more to be done for women education particularly in the rural settings. Socialization needs a shift given the trend of nuclearity of family where the fashion of English education, internet and cable network leaves less scope for traditional language use and ethnicity.

Focus on enhancing the literacy and research on Pakhtoon culture will be quite helpful in highlighting the challenges like the cultural loss which the community is facing today.

The people mainly those engaged with poetry and writing can think about the present decaying condition of Pashtu literature. The unpublished scriptures of local writers can be identified and work initiated or possibly enhanced towards developing a platform which serves for the betterment of Pashtu literature, folklore and oral tradition. The un-successful efforts of one Amanullah Khan from Wantrag towards establishing a Pashtu literary Forum was one of the efforts which may be considered for that matter.

Modernization has been found to have negative implications on the Pakhtoon ethnicity as shown by the fading away of Pashtu language with the coming of English education. The traditional dress pattern is going away with the impacts of western values of living on it. The change in ideology, the main outcome of modernization has not only fostered the assimilation process but also is consistently fading away the traditional ethnic identity of Pakhtoons in Anantnag.

Due to modernization, people of different cultural groups are coming closer and becoming similar. Globalization loosens the traditional nature of indigenous cultures. In certain cases as with Pakhtoons under the impact of contact between two different cultures, assimilation often occurs.

Where the distinction continues between two cultural groups in spite of several efforts by the cultural group which is assimilating, such a group loses its cultural identity to the dominant cultural group like the Kashmiri community here. The processes of modernization and urbanization further accelerates the situation.

The community measures like establishment of the All J & K Pakhtoon Jirga Forum initially proved out to be an effective measure for highlighting and creative awareness about Pakhtoon tradition and ethnicity, thus paving the way for the prediction that such attempts can prove fruitful from the perspective of Pakhtoon cultural preservation.

In the areas like Satranj Maidan in Anantnag like Gujjar Nagar in Jammu where the impacts of urbanization are more intense, ethnicity was found weaker and it is a generalized fact that urbanization is directly related with the cultural assimilation among Pakhtoons. The villages located in close proximity to the town clearly have more assimilation rate as compared to the villages at periphery like Manzmu in Qazigund or Cherwad in Akingam.

Villages like Wantrag with large population of the local Kashmiri cultural group have assimilated faster and still follow the same trend. This is justified by the facts and data collected from the field that population of the local cultural group is also directly related to the assimilation rate of Pakhtoon culture.

## REFERENCES

Afridi, Azim. (2005). *Pashtun Customs Related to Weddings*. [Retrieved from: www.khyber.org]

Alba, R. & Nee, Victor. (2000). Rethinking assimilation theory for a new era of immigration. *International Migration Review*, 31, 826-874.

Alba, Richard. (2005). Bright vs. blurred boundaries: Second generation assimilation and exclusion in France, Germany, and the United States. *Ethnic and Racial Studies*, 28:1, 20-49.

Bacal, Azril. (1991). *Ethnicity in the Social Sciences: A view and a review of the literature on ethnicity*. University of Warwick.

Back, Les. (1995). *New Ethnicities*. London: UCL Press.

Barth, Frederick. (1969). *Ethnic Groups and Boundaries*. London: George Allen and Unwin.

Byman, Daniel. (2002). *Keeping the Peace: Lasting Solutions to Ethnic Conflicts*. London: John Hopkins University Press.

Caroline, R. Nagel. (2009): Rethinking Geographies of Assimilation. *The Professional Geographer*, 61:3, 400-407.

Emberling, Geoff. (1997). Ethnicity in Complex Societies: Archaeological Perspectives. *Journal of Archaeological Research*, (Vol. 5), 295-99. New York.

Evara, Van Stephen. (2001). *Causes of War: Power and the Roots of Conflict.* London: Cornell University Press.

Goldscheider, G. (2002). *Ethnic categorizations in censuses: Comparative observations from Israel, Canada, and the United States.* In Kertzer, D. and Arel, D. (Eds.), *Census and Identity: The Politics of race, Ethnicity and Language in the National Census.* Cambridge: University press.

Glazer, N. (1993). "Is Assimilation Dead?" *The Annals of the American Academy of Social and Political Sciences,* 530:122-136.

Glazer, N; Moynihan. (1963) *Beyond the melting pot: the Negroes, Puerto Ricans, Jews, Italians and Irish of New York City.* Cambridge: MIT.

Hasnain, Nadeem. (1994). *Tribal India,* Delhi: Palaka Prakashan.

Jacobsen, J. (1997). Religion and ethnicity: dual and alternative sources of identity among young British Pakistanis. *Ethnic and Racial* Studies, 20 (20): 238-256.

Momin A.R. (2009). *Diversity, Ethnicity and Identity in South Asia.* Jaipur: Rawat.

Portes, Alejandro and Min Zhou. (1993). The New Second Generation: Segmented Assimilation and Its Variants. *The Annals of the American Academy of Political and Social Science,* 530: 74-80.

Sam, L. David. (2006). *Acculturation: conceptual background and core components.* U.K: Sam & Berry.

Senior, Clarence and Reuben, Hill. (1957). Research on the Puerto Rican Family in the United States. *Marriage and Family Living,* Vol. 19, No. 1.

Smith, Huston. (2003). *The New Encyclopedia of Islam.* Rowman Altamira.

Song, Miri. (2001). *Comparing minorities' ethnic options: Do Asian Americans possess 'more' ethnic options than African Americans?* London: Sage.

Ward, C; Bochner, S; & Furnham, A. (2001). *The psychology of culture shock* (2nd Ed.). Boston: Routledge Kegan Paul.

Weinreich, Peter. (1998). Social exclusion and multiple identities. *Soundings,* issue 9, summer 1998.

Wimmer, A. (2008a). Elementary strategies of ethnic boundary making. *Ethnic and Racial* Studies, 31(6): 1025-1055.

Wimmer, A. (2008b). The making and unmaking of ethnic boundaries: A multilevel process theory. *American Journal of Sociology,* 113(4): 970-1022.

**Dr. Mudasir Ahmad Lone** is a research scholar affiliated with the University of Jammu in the Indian state of Jammu and Kashmir. He did his Schooling as a student of Medical and Seed Technology eventually shifted to the Social Sciences with Sociology as the main Subject. He did his B.A and M.A in Sociology from the University of Kashmir. He has qualified the NET exam in June 2008. He has got PhD in Sociology on Ethnicity and Cultural Assimilation. He has presented research papers in five National and one International Seminar and NWISA conference on the thrust areas: Ethnicity, Gender issues, Family and Marriage, Power Politics, Higher Education and Himalayan Tribal people. He has got 28 international publications besides research experience in the areas of Anthropology, Culture and Language. He is presently working as Reviewer and Advisory Board Member for International Journal of Multidisciplinary Educational Research [IJMER]. He is actively engaged in research and is continuously contributing to International research.

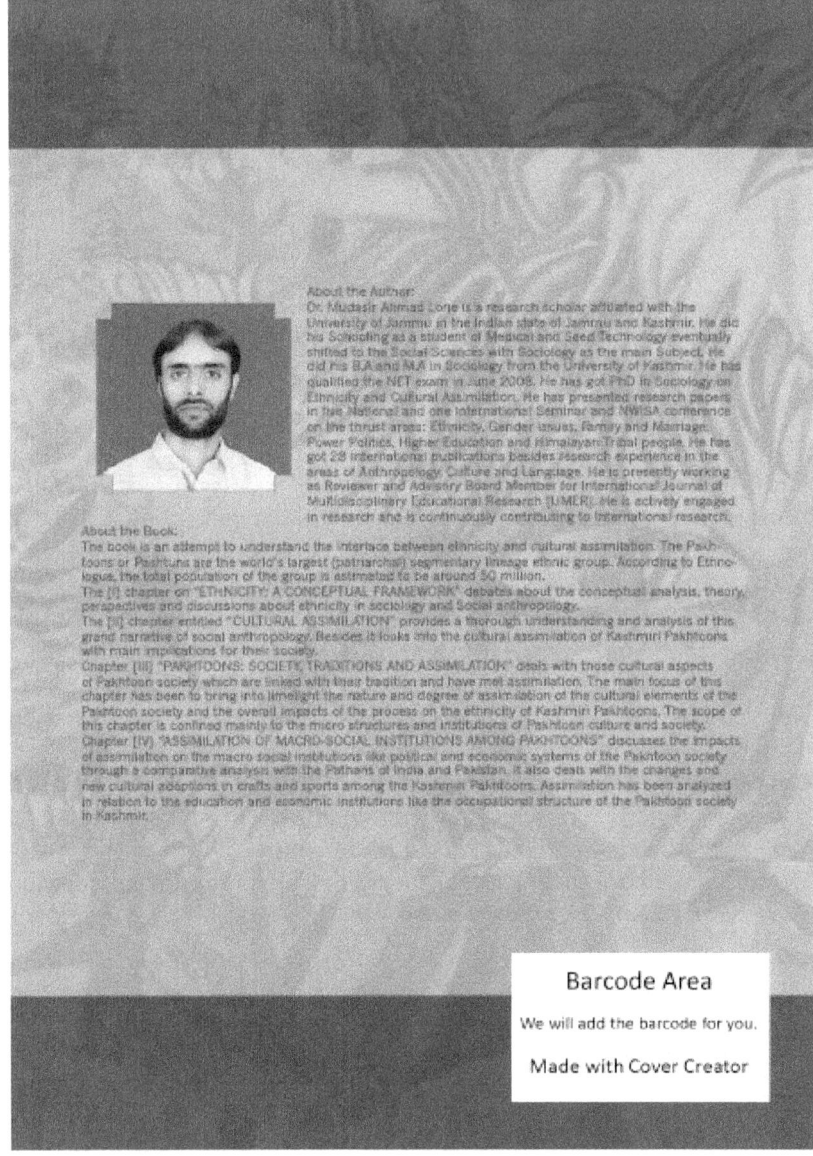

www.ingramcontent.com/pod-product-compliance
Lightning Source LLC
Chambersburg PA
CBHW060506290526
45791CB00001B/294